A History of South Carolina, 1865-1960

A History of
South Carolina, 1865-1960

E 70 ᴀ

By

Ernest McPherson Lander, Jr.

SECOND EDITION

UNIVERSITY OF SOUTH CAROLINA PRESS
Columbia, S.C.

To Elizabeth and Caroline

Preface

In 1934, Dr. David Duncan Wallace published a four-volume *History of South Carolina* which has remained the most valuable study ever made of South Carolina, its people, and their institutions. During the 26 years that have elapsed since the appearance of Dr. Wallace's volumes, however, significant changes have taken place in South Carolina society, and scholars have uncovered much additional information about the state's past. I therefore propose to give the general reader a brief, up-to-date survey of South Carolina's political, economic, educational, and religious development from 1865 to 1960. It is my hope that public-school and college students will also find this monograph useful.

As my chief emphasis is on political history, the first three chapters in the book deal primarily with the political story from 1865 to 1941. Next, there are three chapters devoted to industry and transportation, agriculture, and education and religion, tracing each of these topics chronologically within the 1865-1941 period. The following two chapters cover events from 1941 to 1960, and the final chapter contains a brief summary.

Except for the end of Reconstruction (1877), there was little significant break or change in South Carolina history from the end of the Civil War until the outbreak of World War II. Neither the advent of Benjamin R. Tillman nor the Spanish-American War, the coming of Coleman L.

Blease nor World War I, produced any permanent or deep-seated change in South Carolina's one-party politics and cotton economy. Nor did South Carolina's educational and religious institutions, white or black, undergo any drastic innovations. Since 1941, however, the usual patterns of agriculture, industry, education, race relations, and even one-party politics have been greatly, and sometimes severely, altered. For this reason I have dealt with the 1941-60 years separately. Although my organization may be considered arbitrary, it has merit, I hope, in that any single chapter may be read as a separate essay.

In my footnotes I have acknowledged indebtedness to numerous persons who have written in the post-Civil-War period of South Carolina history. I am further indebted to many others. My fellow historians, Daniel W. Hollis of the University of South Carolina, and Carl L. Epting, Robert S. Lambert and Jack K. Williams of Clemson, read parts of the manuscript and offered valuable suggestions. My wife, Sarah Shirley Lander, aided me greatly on matters of style and spent endless hours proofreading. Thomas C. Witherspoon of the English Department at Clemson rendered editorial assistance, and Mrs. Vivian H. Lewis of Clemson typed the manuscript. I have learned much about South Carolina's past from my parents, Ernest McPherson and Kizzie Jones Lander. My father grew up in the piedmont, my mother in the lowcountry, and their lives have covered most of the years about which I have written. I also wish to express my appreciation to the Kress Foundation of Clemson College by whose financial assistance publication of this volume was made possible.

Preface
to Second Edition

It has been almost ten years since the publication of *A History of South Carolina, 1865–1960.* It now needs to be revised to bring it up to date in time and in reference to new scholarship. I shall not, however, attempt a comprehensive review of books published in the 1960s dealing with South Carolina since the Civil War. Instead, I propose to mention only what seem to be the more important findings that modify or add to my story. And I will summarize trends and events of the 1960s. In my approach I will deal with each chapter separately. Some deserve much attention, others little or none.

Chapter I, "Reconstruction and Restitution of Home Rule, 1865–1877," is in need of considerable revision of emphasis and some of fact. Within the past ten years a large number of new books have been written on Reconstruction. Two important studies deal exclusively with South Carolina. One is Martin Abbott, *The Freedmen's Bureau in South Carolina, 1865–1872* (Chapel Hill, 1967). Though limited in scope, Abbott's monograph thoroughly investigates the Bureau, its work, and its officials. Fewer Bureau officials were charged with corruption (about 10 per cent), fewer became involved in party politics, and they were more impartial in racial disputes than I have indicated.

The second book, and more important, is Joel Williamson, *After Slavery: The Negro in South Carolina During Reconstruction, 1861–1877* (Chapel Hill, 1965). It is an excellent study that supplements and revises the long standard work *Reconstruction in South Carolina* by F. B.

Simkins and R. H. Woody (Chapel Hill, 1932). Williamson had access to much primary source material not seen
by Simkins and Woody.

Williamson (and Abbott) covers well the Negroes'
efforts to obtain land, aided by Freedmen's Bureau, General Rufus Saxton, and General Sherman. But neither
state nor federal government gave much help. Thus, the
blacks' hopes died hard and "often violently." In attempting to regulate black-white economic relations,
federal authorities sometimes found it necessary to use
force against both sides. Williamson points out that at
first white South Carolinians were reluctant to face up
to the new situation and misunderstood Northern opinion. A few South Carolina diehards even hoped to re-
enslave the Negroes. They felt that the "Black Codes"
were too lenient. After 1868 federal intervention yielded
to state control of race relations.

As for the Radical Republican program, recent scholars have placed more emphasis on the idealism behind it
than I did. The ideals of the pre-war abolitionists did not
disappear overnight. In fact, there is evidence today that
the Republican Party leadership committed this nation
to equal suffrage for Negroes not for political gain but for
idealistic reasons and at considerable risk to the party
in the North. [See LaWanda and John H. Cox in *Journal
of Southern History,* XXXIII (August, 1967) 303–330.]

On politics Williamson modifies my account of the
Radical politicians' role. He notes that the average
Negro legislator lived a drab, frugal, and largely segregated life in Columbia, and, if dishonest, "found the
wages of sin were pitifully small." He paints a favorable
picture of Governors Orr and Chamberlain and Negro
leader Francis L. Cardozo. Orr, who later joined the
Radicals, realized, as few South Carolinians did, that
Northern opinion had to be placated. Williamson also
has praise for carpetbaggers Reuben Tomlinson and

Justus K. Jillson, both of whom contributed substantially from their own pockets to aid South Carolina education. Most carpetbaggers were not "bootless adventurers" when they came South, and many of the Northern Negroes were zealots.

Segregation of the races became fairly well established by custom before Radical Reconstruction began, and in few instances did the Radicals breach the wall. Wherever in public places the Negroes demanded racial equality, they usually acted with restraint. Privately, the Negro community separated itself from the white, and to a considerable extent Negro politicians gradually separated themselves from their white Republican colleagues.

As for violence, Williamson notes three waves: (1) 1865–1866—three race riots, (2) 1868—when the blacks gained the suffrage, and (3) the election of 1876. But there was no statewide Ku Klux Klan conspiracy; it did not exist above the local level. Most violence came spontaneously, not as a result of widespread conspiracies.

One of Williamson's most significant contributions (which I missed) is his exposure of the Democrats' post-Reconstruction propaganda to taint all Republicans with fraud and incompetence. The anti-carpetbagger and anti-scalawag snobbery so prevalent in later years was largely created by Democrats after 1877. Williamson does not excuse Republican incompetence and corruption (any more than I). But he and others show that Democratic newspapers of the time were out to give the Republicans a bad image, while ignoring their accomplishments. A question raised by several recent historians, but unanswered, is this: Did the conservative South Carolina whites object to Republican rule largely because of corruption and extravagance or because Negroes had a hand in it?

Finally, recent writers have emphasized, more than I, the federal government's failure to stand by the freedmen.

They were neither furnished land to realize their economic independence nor given continued protection of their civil rights. The South Carolina blacks found themselves gradually pushed into peonage with no means by which to extricate themselves. Before long they were once more completely at the mercy of their former masters.

On Chapter II, "South Carolina under Democratic Party Rule, 1877–1917," my brief section dealing with the Conservative Democrats (Bourbons) can now be upgraded. A monograph by William J. Cooper, Jr., entitled *The Conservative Regime: South Carolina, 1877–1890* (Baltimore, 1968), gives us for the first time a clear and accurate account of the post-Reconstruction Conservative Democrats who ruled South Carolina.

The Conservative leaders were primarily elderly Civil War veterans who wished to re-create the world as they had known it before 1860. They held their positions largely out of public respect for their services to the Confederacy. They also wished to resurrect South Carolina College as an institution to educate the youth of the state in proper antebellum values. The Conservatives were primarily agrarians, but they welcomed railroads and manufacturing. They envisioned no conflict between industry and agriculture.

One of Cooper's most significant points, revising my story, is that there was no class conflict in South Carolina under the Conservatives. The nearest class opposition that appeared came from the weak Greenback-Labor Party in 1882. Even with Republican support the Greenback-Labor candidate for governor could poll only 21 per cent of the vote. And Martin W. Gary was no "poor man's friend." Gary was merely an ambitious politician who felt he had not received his proper reward for his part in Hampton's victory in 1876. Hampton distrusted him, disagreed with his extreme racist views, and thwarted his ambitions for high office. The chief disturbance among the Conservatives was an upcountry rumbling in 1885 and 1886 because the state Senate blocked a scheduled legislative re-apportionment.

Cooper writes that Hampton remained the strong party leader until 1882. By then there was unity among the Conservatives, and there was little likelihood of Republican resurgence. Also, Hampton and Washington authorities had mutually agreed to drop state prosecutions of South Carolina Republicans accused of corruption and federal prosecutions of South Carolina Democrats involved in the bloody Ellenton Riot. Thereafter, Hampton's role in politics became less active, and the Conservatives lacked a forceful commander to replace him. Cooper reveals that Francis W. Dawson, editor of *The News and Courier,* was highly capable and influential among the Conservatives. He might have succeeded to the leadership, but he was foreign-born and a Catholic.

Cooper gives a clearer picture of Hampton's moderate racial policy than I have, and he carefully shows how it was slowly but surely undermined. In political affairs the Democratic Party was autonomous on the county level. Here, beginning with Edgefield in 1878, blacks were gradually excluded from most Democratic clubs, conventions, and primaries. (By 1888 all but two counties used primaries for Democratic Party nominations.) In 1882 the "eight box" election law eliminated many illiterates. The law, however, had a provision which required the polls manager to read the boxes upon the request of a voter. This gave the manager an opportunity to misinform illiterates whenever he wished. The Democrats also gerrymandered the state's seven congressional districts so that the Negroes could control only one.

Although Hampton knew of the fraud and violence to eliminate the Negro vote and deplored it, apparently he was unwilling to admit publicly that it existed. In 1884 he told a Negro audience in Anderson: "As I stand here in the sight of people and of God, I say we have carried out every pledge made to you as a part of the people of South Carolina."

At one time Hampton and Senator M. C. Butler became so alarmed over the prospects of racial violence that they seriously proposed emigration of blacks from America. Yet, the Conservatives, though firmly committed to white man's rule, were tolerant of Negroes' rights outside the realm of politics. They enacted no Jim Crow legislation, and they generally accorded the Negroes a fair share of the meager public school funds. In other words, the Conservative leaders were tolerant white supremacists.

The Conservatives' undoing was due to their poor leadership, their reverence for the past while failing to understand the economic problems of the 1880s, and the generation gap. Tillman represented a new generation and a different class in South Carolina politics. He proclaimed himself the farmers' advocate, but he welcomed nonfarmers into his organization. His program was modest—establishment of an agricultural college, an experiment station, and farmers' institutes, reorganization of the state agricultural agencies, and economy in government. He made no class appeal. He did not even support the Farmers' Alliance, which had a national economic program. Nor did he ride into power on the race issue. Tillman remained a faithful Democrat. He capitalized on economic discontent, and he and his supporters simply took control of the Democratic Party machinery by effectively denouncing those backward-looking ex-Confederates then in control.

Little has appeared in print since 1960 to call for significant revisions in the remainder of Chapter II. In Chapter III, "From World War I to World War II," new information is now supplied by W. D. Workman, Jr., *The Bishop from Barnwell: The Political Life and Times of Senator Edgar A. Brown* (Columbia, 1963). Workman, a career journalist who has closely followed South Carolina politics for many years, writes from first-hand knowledge. His book is further enhanced by inclusion of state Senator Brown's own recollections of various political episodes. Brown, not without prejudice, presents some interesting views on the state's leading politicians, including Olin D. Johnston, "Cotton Ed" Smith, Burnet R. Maybank, James F. Byrnes, Donald Russell, and Strom Thurmond. At times Brown is quite caustic. Although Workman adds much that I have omitted, he makes no significant modification of my brief judgments.

On Chapter IV, "The Industrial Revolution Comes to South Carolina, 1865–1941," and Chapter V, "South Carolina Agriculture, 1865–1941," I am again indebted to Cooper's *The Conservative Regime* for new information on the 1877–1890 years. With regard to the encouragement of industry, Cooper notes the editorial pleas of Francis W. Dawson in *The News and Courier* and the state government's propaganda efforts to publicize South Carolina resources. Additionally, from 1873 to 1885 the legislature granted 10-year tax exemptions to new manufacturing companies; in 1878 it enacted a comprehensive law giving phosphate companies exclusive rights to mine within specific areas; and in 1885 it enacted a general incorporation law.

The legislature cut its aid to railroads, aid so generously bestowed in antebellum and Reconstruction years. Instead it encouraged local governments to aid the rail lines—117 acts authorizing local aid between 1865 and 1900. Towns and cities vied with each other to get railroads. Tillman's advent to power did not change this policy. Nevertheless, the Conservatives, despite their laissez-faire reputation, made serious efforts to regulate the railroads. Charlestonians in particular felt the pinch of railroad discrimination. In 1878 the legislature created a one-man railroad commission, under Milledge L. Bonham, a wartime governor. Bonham became a dedicated railroad commissioner. He, with the help of Charleston interests, soon pressed for rate control. Their efforts bore fruit, for in December 1882 the legislature established a three-man commission with power to set railroad rates. Bonham now got some tangible results—but only briefly. Railroad lobbying, pressure, and money won a reversal of the commission's rate-setting power in 1883. In any event, the South Carolina government was one of the front runners in the nation in its efforts to regulate railroad rates. For his information on railroad regulation Cooper relied chiefly on Albert N. Sanders, "The South Carolina Railroad Commission, 1878–1895" and "State Regulation of Public Utilities by South Carolina, 1879–1935" (unpublished Master's thesis and Ph.D. dissertation, University of North Carolina, 1948 and 1956, respectively).

Generally, as Cooper says, the Conservatives welcomed industry, and no one feared its promotion would harm the well-being of agriculture. Nor is there evidence of collusion between industrialists and politicians to enrich each other at the public's expense. One of the chief controversies among farmers was the crop lien, but the farmers were divided in opinion on what should be done. So was everyone else. The average lien in 1885 and 1886 was about $100, indicating the small farmers seemed to be the chief employers of the system. Once in office, Tillman made no effort to change the lien law. The Conservatives' major effort on behalf of agriculture was the establishment of the state Agricultural Bureau. But Conservative leaders apparently did not understand the agricultural depression, and in their ignorance they publicly denied its existence.

On Chapter VII, "Political Developments and Problems, 1941–1960," Workman's *Bishop from Barnwell* covers the period and adds much in the way of Senator Brown's vivid personal recollections. Brown, a Democratic regular, recounts the great pressure that Governor Byrnes put on him and Senator Maybank to support

Eisenhower in the 1952 election. As for his own race for the United States Senate in 1954, Brown, with some bitterness, blames his defeat by Strom Thurmond on the "Republican Press" and Governor Byrnes. The Governor, according to Brown, "had reached the point that he hated everything in the Democratic party, including, I believe, the memory of Franklin D. Roosevelt, because he did not get the vice-presidential nomination in 1944." Brown believes he could have forestalled Thurmond's candidacy as a "write-in" if, when the executive committee nominated him, he had immediately offered to resign two years later and face a primary contest. Brown said he considered such but felt he was not able physically to have made a campaign.

In the governor's race of 1958, in which E. F. Hollings met Donald Russell in the runoff primary, Russell suddenly denounced the "Barnwell Ring." Brown's account is an interesting sidelight to the contest. "I was amazed at Don Russell's attack in 1958. I never had the slightest difference with Russell because of my association with Fritz Hollings." Brown said Russell's supporters expected him to lead in the first primary, perhaps win. He recalls: "Well, he didn't beat him [Hollings] in the first race, and they were bitterly disappointed. I always thought that Walter Brown from Spartanburg and his advisers (I'm not so sure that Jimmy Byrnes wasn't in on it, but he disavows it) thought they had to get him a quick issue, a flash issue, to let him bounce back in the race. And somebody suggested that he jump on the Barnwell Ring." However, after Russell's defeat, his relations with Brown became cordial once more.

Since the election of 1958, the last I recorded, a number of significant political developments have taken place in South Carolina. In 1960 most ex-Dixiecrats were at last willing to become Republicans in name as well as in fact. Therefore, in the presidential contest of that year the issue was not confused. Democratic candidate John F.

Kennedy barely defeated Republican Richard Nixon.

In spite of the large Republican vote for Nixon there were hardly any South Carolina Republicans running for state or local office. Since 1960, however, more and more Republicans have contested Democrats for positions in government at all levels. In addition, some conservative Democrats who were already in office have switched over to the Republicans. Two outstanding examples are Congressman Albert Watson and Senator J. Strom Thurmond. Thurmond's change just before the presidential election of 1964 helped Republican nominee Barry Goldwater carry South Carolina. Although Goldwater was decisively defeated in his race against Lyndon Johnson, his victory in South Carolina was the first for a Republican presidential candidate since Reconstruction. Goldwater was well-liked among South Carolina whites for his states' rights views and for having voted against a civil rights bill in the Senate.

Especially valuable for a detailed analysis of South Carolinians' voting habits in recent presidential elections is Donald L. Fowler, *Presidential Voting in South Carolina, 1948–1964* (Columbia, 1966). Fowler finds that "in the coastal, rural counties the presence of high percentages of Negro population seems to have forged substantial unity among white voters," who tend to vote against the national Democrats, either as Republicans or independents. On the other hand, "in the Piedmont counties the smaller concentrations of Negroes apparently permitted divisions among the white voters. These divisions seem to have occurred along economic lines," with the poorer whites generally voting Democratic. Geographically, the lowcountry tends to vote Republican or independent, with the exception of the Pee Dee counties bordering North Carolina. The Piedmont is usually the Democratic stronghold, with the significant exception of Greenville County.

In the 1966 congressional and state elections, Republican candidates for the legislature swept several counties, and in several congressional races they strongly contested the Democrats. Republican Marshall Parker came within 10,000 votes of upsetting Democrat Fritz Hollings for the United States Senate. At stake were two years remaining of the late Senator Olin D. Johnston's term. Johnston had died in early 1965, and Donald Russell served briefly in his seat; that is, until Hollings ousted him in the Democratic primary in 1966.

In the 1968 three-cornered presidential contest Republican Nixon won South Carolina on a plurality of less than 40 per cent of the vote. The remainder was about evenly divided between Democrat Hubert Humphrey and independent George Wallace. Senator Thurmond, who had been given much credit for holding Southern delegations loyal to Nixon at the national Republican Convention, saw his influence wane during the election. Generally, it is believed that his efforts kept South Carolina in the Nixon camp, but otherwise his old Dixiecrat region went to Wallace, and within South Carolina, Republican candidates for state, local, and congressional offices took a shellacking. The Republicans' lone congressman, Albert Watson, managed to hold his seat in a close contest. Elsewhere, Republican congressional candidates did poorly, and Hollings defeated Parker's second effort by a wide margin. The entire Charleston County Republican delegation was swept from office. There is evidence that the Wallaceites, disappointed that Thurmond did not join them, voted heavily Democratic in state and congressional elections.

The 1960's have brought a gradual desegregation of public education, which began peacefully in 1963 with Harvey Gantt's entry into Clemson. During the next five years most colleges and public schools opened their doors to black students. Oftentimes, however, it was token integration. The year 1970 promises to bring almost total integration of pupils and faculties in the public schools.

This undoubtedly will create numerous problems, and the Nixon administration indicated in mid-1969 that some postponements may be permitted.

At the same time the schools were being integrated, the Civil Rights Acts of 1964 and 1965 outlawed enforced racial segregation in public life, opened the door for Negro workers in many industrial plants, and eliminated the literacy test for voting. It is difficult to judge accurately white opinion of these sweeping changes. To date, South Carolina whites have generally accepted racial integration in good grace. In fact many whites who were silent for years now openly oppose racial discrimination. The issue of race, perhaps more than any other, led to the recent revival of the Republican Party in South Carolina. The Republicans seem less willing than Democrats to accept these changes. Consequently, most Negro voters in South Carolina are Democrats at this moment. This was seen when 170 black delegates attended the state Democratic Convention in Columbia in the spring of 1968. By contrast, only two Negro delegates attended the Republican Convention. It is not that the state Democratic Party is so liberal on racial matters; it is simply less conservative than the Republican. The fact of the matter is that both South Carolina parties are more conservative than their national counterparts. The state has a long tradition of supporting conservative principles. South Carolina whites are generally cautious, slow to change, suspicious of labor unions, oppose deficit spending, and fear big government.

Besides the gradual elimination of racial discrimination in South Carolina and the rise of the Republican Party, another change which may have great effect on Palmetto politics is the reapportionment of the state Senate. The Supreme Court's "one man, one vote" decision of 1964 meant that state senators had to be apportioned according to population. Instead of one senator per county, now Greenville and Richland counties each have four, while Bamberg, Barnwell, and Allendale together have only one. No longer can the small rural counties dominate the state Senate. For instance, it now appears that South Carolina will soon have a new state constitution, long blocked by the small county senators.

In Chapter VIII, "South Carolina Today: Some Economic and Cultural Aspects," most of the trends in the 1950s hold true for the 1960s, though in some cases at an accelerated rate. However, my statistical data need to be brought more up to date. Most of my information comes from the *Statistical Abstract of the United States.*

South Carolina's investment in equipment, new industrial plants, and expansion of old plants rose from $114 million in 1957 to a phenomenal $635 million in 1968, according to an announcement of the State Development Board in July, 1969. Industrial workers increased from 230,000 in 1957 to 319,000 in 1967, the majority still in textiles and apparel. Industrial wages increased from $62.02 per week in 1959 to $84.66 in 1967, but South Carolina remains fourth from the bottom of the American states. By contrast, wages rose in Michigan (second to Alaska) from $111.62 to $145.78 during the same years. In South Carolina only 6.7 per cent of non-agricultural workers were unionized, the lowest of any state in America. Also significant is the fact that the Civil Rights Act of 1964 opened the door of the textile industry to Negroes.

Meanwhile, the state's power resources and transportation facilities have kept pace. The outstanding example of electric power is the Duke Power Company's mammoth Keowee-Toxaway project centered in Oconee and Pickens counties and well under way in 1969. In transportation Highway Commissioner McMillan announced in 1958 that 678 miles of federally-sponsored Interstate highways would be built in South Carolina. By mid-1969, 461 miles had been opened to the public and 132 were under construction. When completed, the Interstate roads will reach within 30 miles of 93 per cent of the state's population. Air transport has improved with jet service at Greenville-Spartanburg, Columbia, and Charleston, and with the opening of a number of smaller airports elsewhere in the state. In rail transportation, the major change has been consolidation, with several smaller lines being bought out by the larger roads. The most important change, however, was the union of the Seaboard Air Line with the Atlantic Coast Line to form the Seaboard Coast Line, now the largest railroad in the state.

In agriculture the trends of the 1950's continue—less cotton, more trees, larger farms, less cropland, fewer tenants, more mechanization, and higher yields per acre. Between 1954 and 1964 (last agricultural census) the number of South Carolina farms declined from 124,200 to 56,200, while acreage rose from 89 to 172 per farm. During the same years farm values rose from an average of $7,769 per farm to $25,000. At the same time the United States average increased from $20,405 per farm to $51,000. Total farm acreage in South Carolina dropped from 11,069,000 in 1954 to 8,101,000 in 1964. Crop acreage declined from 3,825,000 in 1955 to 2,348,000 in 1967. That year the principal crops in South Carolina were tobacco, soybeans, cotton, and corn, in that order. As for livestock, there has been little change in cattle and swine population since 1958; broiler production which was 17 million in 1958 was more than 19 million in 1967. Mule population continues to decline, though statistics are unavailable; and sheep production has almost completely disappeared from the state.

Total farm income has remained fairly stable in South Carolina during the 1960's. For example, the total value of all South Carolina crops was $253.3 million in 1958 and $276.4 million in 1967 (including $57.4 million in government payments). But the farm income is uneven. Although tenancy dropped from 39.3 per cent in 1954 to

30.8 per cent in 1964, at least one-third of all fulltime South Carolina farms sold less than $5,000 worth of agricultural products in 1964. A study by Clemson University economists of 1,000 rural families in ten Pee Dee counties in 1966 shows that a majority of these people either live in poverty or on its edge.

In the field of education the most important change in South Carolina has been racial integration, now taking place at an accelerated pace. The 1960 census reveals that the median school years completed by South Carolina adults (above 25 years) was 8.7. This state is thus tied with Kentucky for 50th position. In 1950, 27.4 per cent of all adult South Carolinians were classed by the census as functionally illiterate. By 1960 this had dropped to 20.3 per cent.

School population increased in South Carolina from 584,283 in 1957–58 to 647,000 in 1967–68. During those same years school expenses rose from $90 million to an estimated $298 million. South Carolina teachers' salaries moved up from an average of $3,005 in 1956 to $5,630 in 1968. Nevertheless, the state could scarcely keep up with the rest of the nation, for only three states paid lower salaries than did South Carolina.

In higher education, a tremendous amount of money has been poured into South Carolina colleges and universities during the last ten years, and overall there has been much improvement. At the same time tuition costs have risen so much that South Carolina middle income families can hardly afford to send their children to college, unless they can get financial aid. However, enrollments are up, and some colleges which in the 1950s were eagerly searching for students are now booming. The University of South Carolina and Clemson University (name recently changed) have broadened their graduate schools so that they now offer good doctoral programs in a wide variety of curriculums. The Negro colleges still suffer from meager financial support, although South Carolina A & M, which is dependent on state support, has fared rather favorably in the past decade.

In Chapter IX, "Summary," I have little to add except some statistics. The Negro population in South Carolina dropped from 38.9 per cent in 1950 to 34.8 in 1960. Between 1950 and 1960 there was a net outmigration of 218,000 Negroes from South Carolina. And the state's per capita income increased from $1180 in 1957 to $2,339 in 1968. Despite this increase, only Mississippi, Arkansas, and Alabama rank lower.

ERNEST MCPHERSON LANDER, JR.
July, 1969

Contents

I. Reconstruction and Restitution of Home Rule, 1865-1877   3

II. South Carolina under Democratic Party Rule, 1877-1917   24

III. From World War I to World War II   56

IV. The Industrial Revolution Comes to South Carolina, 1865-1941   82

V. South Carolina Agriculture, 1865-1941   106

VI. Education and Religion, 1865-1941   122

VII. Political Developments and Problems, 1941-1960   169

VIII. South Carolina Today: Some Economic and Cultural Aspects   207

IX. Summary   240

Select Bibliography   246

Index   249

Maps

	Page
South Carolina Railroads, 1867	99
South Carolina Railroads, 1926	100
South Carolina Highways, 1929	105

Tables

Page

1. South Carolina Textiles   83

2. Other Industries, 1939   95

3. South Carolina Railroads   98

4. Educational Achievement Statistics   123

5. South Carolina Public School Statistics   127

6. South Carolina Colleges   146

7. South Carolina Church Statistics   162

8. South Carolina Industry   212

9. New Factories in 1955   214

10. South Carolina Farm Statistics   223

11. South Carolina Farm Equipment   223

12. South Carolina Crop Production   224

13. Livestock and Poultry on South Carolina Farms   228

A History of South Carolina, 1865-1960

Chapter One

Reconstruction and Restitution of Home Rule, 1865-1877

There was probably no more trying period in South Carolina's history than the years 1865-77. The people were exhausted by the war, stunned by defeat, and overwhelmed by the political confusion arising out of the Reconstruction. Actually, the social, economic, and political changes that followed the war shook South Carolina to her depths.

Reconstruction fell into two periods: (1) Presidential Reconstruction, 1865-68, and (2) Radical Reconstruction, 1868-77. All 11 ex-Confederate states went through some form of Reconstruction. But only in South Carolina, Louisiana, and Florida did Reconstruction last until 1877. By contrast, Reconstruction in Virginia, North Carolina, and Tennessee was brief and not nearly so violent and tragic.[1]

A. Presidential Reconstruction

1. Conditions in South Carolina at the End of the War

It is now impossible to grasp the magnitude of the terrible destruction inflicted on South Carolina by the war. Sherman's army was the major destroyer of property. The Union forces literally burned their way across the state.[2]

However, Sherman was not the only destroyer of proper-

1. The best accounts of Reconstruction in South Carolina are found in Francis B. Simkins and Robert H. Woody, *South Carolina during Reconstruction* (Chapel Hill, N.C.: University of North Carolina Press, 1932); David Duncan Wallace, *The History of South Carolina* (4 vols.; New York: American Historical Society, 1934), III, 222-321; David Duncan Wallace, *South Carolina: a Short History, 1520-1948* (Chapel Hill, N.C.: University of North Carolina Press, 1951), pp. 556-606. I have relied heavily on all three.

2. This story is ably told in John G. Barrett, *Sherman's March through the Carolinas* (Chapel Hill, N.C.: University of North Carolina Press, 1956).

ty in South Carolina. Disastrous fires befell Charleston in 1861 and 1865, and Union warships bombarded the city a number of times. Shortly after the war John T. Trowbridge, a newspaper correspondent, described the city in this manner:

It has still many fine residences, built in a variety of style; but since those recent days of pride and prosperity, it has been woefully battered and desolated. . . . [Its] ruins are the most picturesque of any I saw in the South. The gardens and broken walls of many of its fine residences remain to attest their former elegance. Broad semi-circular flights of marble steps, leading up once to proud doorways, now conduct you over cracked and calcined slabs to the level of high foundations swept of everything but the crushed fragments of superstructures, with here and there a broken pillar, a windowless wall.[3]

Trowbridge was also impressed with the numerous buzzards perched amid the ruins "wherever garbage abounds."

Besides the wartime destruction, much South Carolina property suffered from neglect. This was particularly true of the farms and plantations. With their menfolk at the battlefront, the women did their best to keep the farms in operation. Frequently, the job was too great. As a consequence, terraces and dikes fell into disrepair, and flooding of lowlands and erosion of uplands occurred. Many flooded rice fields were never reclaimed for cultivation.

The state's financial resources were exhausted. Nearly every patriotic Confederate had invested heavily in Confederate bonds. These bonds became worthless when General Lee surrendered. In addition to these financial losses, Union officials seized thousands of bales of cotton belonging to private citizens. The Union agents claimed that the cotton had been the property of the Confederate government, hence subject to lawful seizure.

These injuries were grievous, but South Carolina's great-

3. John T. Trowbridge, *The Desolate South, 1865-66* . . . , ed. Gordon Carroll (New York: Duell, Sloan and Pearce, 1956), pp. 274-75.

st loss was her men who died in the war. Altogether,
about 71,000 South Carolinians took part in the conflict.
Of these, 12,922 died in action or later from battle wounds.
No Northern state suffered a proportionately greater loss
of manpower (on the basis of the size of its white population).

Finally, South Carolina underwent a great social and
economic upheaval when its 400,000 slaves were set free.
The suddenness of this freedom dazed both whites and
blacks. The Negroes had little or no understanding of
what freedom meant. They believed the "Day of Jubilee"
had arrived. There would be no more work, no more
worry, only singing and dancing—so the majority thought.

Most Negroes, it is true, remained at their jobs on the
plantations, but thousands wandered off to the cities or
followed Union armies. Many Negroes caught contagious
diseases due to improper food and unsanitary living conditions, while thousands of both races were in danger of
starvation in the months immediately following the war.

The Freedmen's Bureau gave a helping hand to destitute
persons. This organization, established in March, 1865,
was primarily interested in looking after the welfare of
the newly freed Negroes. On the other hand, in the dis-
tressing days of 1865 and 1866 the Bureau fed whites as
well as blacks, aided stranded persons to return to their
homes, doctored the ill, and settled contract disputes between ex-slaves and their employers. The Bureau at one
time hoped to assign 40 acres to the head of each Negro
family. But the state and federal appropriations were so
skimpy that the Negroes never received their "40 acres and
a mule." In fact, many Negroes were eventually forced
from the lands they had simply taken over at the close of
the war. These Negroes became distrustful of all white
promises.

The Freedmen's Bureau also established numerous

schools for colored people. For teachers the Bureau relied partly on local whites and partly on outsiders from
the North. At first the schools were well attended. However, as most Negroes apparently did not realize the difficulty of an education, in time many lost interest and quit
school.

After 1866 the Freedmen's Bureau was chiefly concerned with propaganda: educating the ex-slaves to support the Republican party.

The chief criticism of the Bureau coming from white
South Carolinians was aimed at the activities of some of
its lower officials, many of whom were incompetent and
dishonest. In settling disputes between whites and blacks,
these subordinate officials were often prejudiced and unfair. They sided with the Negroes and humiliated the
former slaveholders in many ways. Yet, despite these
objections, the Bureau performed a number of useful services in South Carolina in 1865 and 1866. And the higher
officials of the Bureau, especially, were usually ex-Union
soldiers of some ability.

2. *President Andrew Johnson and His Program*

With the assassination of President Lincoln by John
Wilkes Booth, Andrew Johnson stepped into the presidential office. A North Carolinian by birth and a Ten-
nesseean by adoption, Johnson had remained loyal to the
Union during the war. As a reward Lincoln had appointed
him military governor of Tennessee, and the Republican
party nominated him as vice-president in 1864.

President Johnson wanted no harsh reconstruction.
Like Lincoln, he desired to readmit the Southern states to
the Union as painlessly as possible. As a preliminary
measure, on May 29, 1865, the President issued a procla-
mation extending pardons to ex-Confederates who would
take the oath to support the Constitution and the Union.

However, prominent ex-Confederate officials and persons of wealth were not included in this general pardon. These persons were to apply to the President individually if they desired amnesty.[4]

On June 30 the President appointed Benjamin F. Perry of Greenville as provisional governor of South Carolina. Perry had opposed secession in 1860, but once the state had left the Union, he had supported the move. He was an able lawyer and was acceptable to most of the white people of South Carolina.

Governor Perry had several interviews with President Johnson. The two men agreed that a state constitutional convention should be called. They felt the convention should abolish slavery (the Thirteenth Amendment had not yet been ratified), nullify the Ordinance of Secession, and provide for popular election of the governor and of the presidential electors.

The Convention of 1865 followed the lines laid down by President Johnson and Governor Perry. The question of Negro suffrage also arose. Governor Perry intended to recommend limited Negro suffrage, but some of his friends persuaded him to drop the proposal. Later he said that limited Negro suffrage granted in 1865 might have checked the Republicans' demand for unlimited Negro voting privileges in 1868.

The old lowcountry-upcountry rivalry flared up once more in the Convention. In the new apportionment of state senators and representatives, the lowcountry lost heavily. For example, Charleston had its number of senators reduced from ten to two.[5]

4. President Johnson, a man of humble background, disliked the Southern aristocracy. He considered himself the champion of the masses, and he hoped to see the reorganized Southern governments fall under the control of the small-farmer and worker classes.

5. Wallace, *Short History*, p. 563. The new constitution was put into effect without a popular referendum.

3. *South Carolina under Governor Orr, 1865-1868*

In the fall of 1865, the South Carolina voters elected a new legislature and chose James L. Orr as governor by a narrow margin over General Wade Hampton. Undoubtedly, the popular General Hampton would have won if he had not publicly declared that he did not want the position.

Probably the outstanding piece of legislation drawn up by the new legislature was the "Black Code," a special set of laws the assemblymen felt was needed to govern the freedmen. The "Black Code" extended many personal and property rights to Negroes, but it also restricted them in various ways. The criminal provisions of the code were severe. For instance, a Negro could be punished for a greater variety of crimes and punished more harshly than a white. Special courts were set up for Negroes. For minor offenses a guilty Negro could be fined or whipped. If the Negro could not pay his fine, the court could lease him to someone who would pay it. Furthermore, a Negro was not permitted to testify in court except in cases where he or another Negro was involved.

The "Black Code" forbade Negroes, except farmers, to own firearms or to make or sell whisky. And a Negro had to obtain a special license to engage in work other than farming or domestic service. The "Black Code" also contained elaborate provisions for contracting colored servants to white masters. Masters might "moderately" whip servants under eighteen years of age. Servants could not leave the master's premises or receive visitors without permission from the master. But the "Black Code" did try to protect Negro servants by requiring written work contracts between servant and master. Finally, the "Black Code" prohibited marriages between whites and blacks.

Northerners looked upon the "Black Code" as an underhanded attempt to re-enslave the black people. On January 1, 1866, General Dan Sickles, the Union commander in South Carolina, declared the "Black Code" illegal. He decreed: "All laws shall be applicable alike to all inhabitants." Within the next 12 months, the legislature amended some portions of the code and repealed others so that the Negroes enjoyed practically the same legal rights as the whites.

The legislature also passed a "stay law" to rescue South Carolina debtors from bankruptcy and loss of property. On the matter of debts General Sickles was sympathetic with the poverty-stricken people of the state. He cooperated with the legislature and Governor Orr, and decreed that imprisonment for debt should cease.

On April 2, 1866, President Johnson declared the rebellion officially ended. He reported that the Southern people were loyal and capable of enforcing law and order. Gradually he decreased the size of the military force in South Carolina. By November, 1866, there were less than 3000 Union soldiers remaining. In the meantime, General Sickles had turned most of the jails and prisons back to local authorities. The Union military force in the state in 1865 and 1866 for the most part cooperated with the civil authorities, and, in general, military rule was not harsh during these years.

In June, 1866, the Southern people were offered the opportunity to ratify the Fourteenth Amendment to the Constitution of the United States. The first section of the amendment defines citizenship to include Negroes, and guarantees the blacks equal civil rights with whites. Governor Orr opposed the amendment. He asked if "fair and just men" in the North desired ignorant Negroes to go to the polls and elect congressmen "who are to pass laws taxing and governing them." The South Carolina legislature turned down the amendment by an almost unanimous vote. Every other ex-Confederate legislature, except Tennessee's, likewise refused to approve the amendment.

B. RADICAL RECONSTRUCTION

1. The Radical Program

The Republican party in 1865 was divided into two factions: the Moderates and the Radicals. The Moderates supported President Johnson's program, whereas the Radicals had other plans. The chief motive of the Radical Republicans was not merely to seek vengeance against the South, but to obtain permanent control of the United States government. The Radicals realized that the Democrats might regain control in Washington if Southerners and Westerners united in support of the Democratic party. The Radicals remembered that Lincoln had won in 1860 with approximately 40 per cent of the popular vote. Consequently, if the Radicals could find some sure way to control the South's votes, they believed they could remain firmly entrenched in Washington. Their plan was simple: they would disfranchise the ex-Confederates and enfranchise the Negroes. They reasoned that the Negroes, with a little Radical guidance, would surely vote for the party that set them free.

The Radical Republicans were primarily representatives of Northern businessmen: shippers, bankers, merchants, and industrialists. So long as they controlled the federal government, they could pass laws to benefit the business group. But President Johnson's devotion to the Constitution and sympathy for the South threatened to thwart their plan. Therefore, during most of 1866 the Radicals struggled with the President to determine whose policies would be imposed upon the South. The issue was settled in the November elections when the Radicals won control of better than two-thirds of both houses of Congress.

Once assured of control over Congress for the next two years, the Radical Republicans passed several laws to reconstruct the South. South Carolina was placed under a military commander, who was ordered to register all "loyal voters," that is, all males over twenty-one, either Negro or white, provided the whites had not voluntarily aided the Confederacy. After the registration was complete, the voters chose delegates to attend a new state constitutional convention.

The Constitutional Convention met in Charleston in January, 1868. Its delegates consisted of 76 Negroes and 48 whites. This proportion was to be expected, for the colored voters outnumbered the whites. Among the Negro delegates were several unusually capable men. Probably the most notable of these was Francis L. Cardozo, a Charleston mulatto. He was a well-educated and skillful politician. Other prominent Negro delegates were Robert B. Elliott, an Eton College graduate, Richard H. Cain, future congressman, and Jonathan J. Wright, future state supreme court justice.

Among the white delegates, only 23 were native Southerners, and most of these were "scalawags" (Southerners who cooperated with the Radicals). The two outstanding men in this group were Thomas J. Robertson, a Charleston merchant, and Dr. Albert G. Mackey. Dr. Mackey served as presiding officer of the Convention and had much to do with the actual writing of the new Constitution. Several of the leaders of the Convention were "carpetbaggers" (Northerners who had come South). Some of the carpetbaggers were capable and honest; some were rascals. Three better-known carpetbaggers were Daniel H. Chamberlain, B. F. Whittemore, and J. K. Jillson.[6]

The Constitution of 1868 was more democratic than any previous one in South Carolina history. It included universal male suffrage and omitted all property qualifications for office holding. It likewise provided for popular election of many officials formerly appointed by the gov-

6. For brief sketches of many prominent Reconstruction politicians, see Simkins and Woody, *South Carolina during Reconstruction*, pp. 112-46.

ernor or the legislature. State judges were still to be chosen by the legislature, but no longer for life terms.

The new Constitution outlawed dueling and imprisonment for debt. It legalized divorce and granted women many legal rights they had never before enjoyed. Two steps were taken to encourage social equality between the two races: the schools and state militia were opened to members of both races on an unsegregated basis.

The Constitution of 1868 included a number of provisions attempting to promote economic equality between the two races, but the legislature did little to carry them out. For example, very little land was furnished the Negroes. And the elaborate school system remained largely on paper. The Constitution also revised the state's tax system, but it failed to place safeguards on the use of the state's monies. Within a few years the state's debt had risen above $25,000,000.

When the Radical Constitution was placed before the voters, they approved it by more than a two-to-one vote. The Convention, regardless of its shortcomings, had apparently done its work fairly well. The Constitution it wrote was satisfactory enough that South Carolina kept it for 18 years after the end of Radical rule.

2. Radical Government under Scott and Moses

The new legislature met in July, 1868. In the Senate, ten of 31 members were Negroes; in the House, 78 of 124 were colored. The Negro legislators remained in the majority until 1874. Very few of the white members were Democrats; most were either Republican carpetbaggers or scalawags.

The legislators, white and black, had a mixture of reasons for serving. Some were honest and public-spirited, but most apparently were either selfish or dishonest or both. The Reconstruction years were noted for dishonesty in government both in the South and in the North. Ugly scandals arose in many areas of the country. Unfortunately, many of the politicians who controlled South Carolina were in tune with the times, in this respect.

A majority of the South Carolina newspapers were in sympathy with the "lost cause" of the Confederacy. They heaped ridicule upon the Radical legislature. They called it "unlawful" and said that it was maintained only by Union troops and their bayonets. Journalists from other parts of the country visited the General Assembly to see the Negroes in action. Best known of these writers was James S. Pike, a Northern Republican. He visited South Carolina in March, 1873. As he looked in the House of Representatives, he found that the speaker, the clerk, the doorkeeper, the little pages, the chaplain, and many members were Negroes. He wrote: "They were of every hue, from light octoroon to the deep black. They were such a looking body of men as might pour out of a market-house or a court-house at random in any Southern State." Pike added that their dress was varied. Some wore the garments of a field hand, while others wore fancy but second-hand frock coats and stovepipe hats.[7]

This Negro-carpetbag-scalawag combination was not noted for distinguished service. Its achievements were small; corruption was commonplace; there was much buying and selling of votes. Large business firms paid handsome sums of money to obtain the passage of laws favorable to them. In 1872, "Honest John" Patterson was said to have paid out $40,000 to secure his election to the United States Senate over ex-Governor Robert Scott and Negro Congressman Robert B. Elliott. There was also much bribery in connection with pardons for criminals. So degenerate had the state government become that guilty officials seldom bothered even to deny the charges of dishonesty.

7. James S. Pike, *The Prostrate State: South Carolina under Negro Government* (New York: D. Appleton and Company, 1874), p. 10.

Not only was the Radical government corrupt, but it was excessively expensive. The statehouse was lavishly refurnished, unnecessary employees were placed on the state's payroll, and a free "commissary" was opened in the statehouse for legislators and their friends. There was a dishonest arrangement with the printer for the state under which the public printing bill soared thousands of dollars above normal. The legislative expenses for the 1871-72 session topped $1,500,000. By contrast, the expenses of the 1876-77 session dropped to $84,000.

The legislature's greatest expense, however, came from railroad schemes. The Radicals endorsed the bonds of several railroads. By doing so, the legislature committed the state to pay the bondholders if the railroad companies were unable to pay their own debts. This practice was the main cause of the enormous debt the state accumulated. To their credit, the Radicals increased expenditures for education and other needed state services, although this effort was small compared with the cost of waste, bad judgment, and corruption.

The state's first Radical Republican governor was Robert K. Scott, a carpetbagger from Ohio. Governor Scott served two terms (1868-72). He has been described as "not corrupt at heart" nor "devoid of common sense." But he was weak and no match for his cunning and crooked associates. Sometimes he condemned the "villainies" of the legislature, and he even vetoed several bills that he thought betrayed the best interests of the state. Governor Scott also kept the state insane asylum from closing because of lack of funds. Yet, as a result of financial mismanagement on the part of his state treasurer, Governor Scott was threatened with impeachment. He escaped by buying off the impeachers.[8]

8. Simkins and Woody, *South Carolina during Reconstruction*, pp. 113-14.

Franklin J. Moses, Jr., the second Radical governor, was a scalawag of the worst sort. He came from a well-known family and showed promise as a lawyer, but in 1867 he suddenly sided with the Radicals. During his term of office, 1872-74, he was immoral, extravagant, and without principle. He accepted bribes for pardoning criminals, appointing officials, and influencing legislation. The Radical government was at its worst under his governorship.

C. THE OVERTHROW OF THE RADICAL GOVERNMENT

1. *Early Opposition to Radical Rule*

When the Radical Republican government was organized in 1868, the pre-war Democrats were demoralized and offered feeble resistance. In 1870 a group of former Democrats held a convention and organized the Union Reform party. The new party nominated Judge R. B. Carpenter to oppose the re-election of Governor Scott.

It was in the campaign of 1870 that the Ku Klux Klan first appeared in strength in South Carolina. The Klan was loosely held together but very active in several upstate counties. These hooded night riders tried to frighten the Negroes away from the polls. In answer to the Klan, Governor Scott armed the Negro militia, which at times struck back at the sheeted Klansmen.

The Union Reform party did not have enough supporters to defeat Governor Scott, and he won re-election handily. After the election the Negro militia seemed to become bolder and more threatening. As a counter the Ku Klux Klan increased its activity. In several counties race riots and bloodshed occurred. On one occasion the Negroes threatened to burn the town of Chester. At another time hooded Klansmen lynched two Negro militiamen under arrest at Union for murder. A few weeks later (February 12, 1871), a mob of several hundred Klansmen forcibly took another eight Negro militiamen from the

Union jail and shot them after a mock military trial.   This
tragic incident was followed by mob violence in other
places.

Governor Scott next tried to preserve order by dis-
banding the Negro militia in several counties.   President
Ulysses S. Grant also intervened.   He suspended the writ
of *habeas corpus* in nine upstate counties, he sent additional
federal troops, and his officers arrested hundreds of Klansmen.   Several Klansmen were sentenced to prison, but
eventually President Grant pardoned them.   Nonetheless,
these vigorous moves by the federal government destroyed
the Klan in South Carolina before the end of 1871.[9]

The election of 1872 saw the Radicals split into two
factions, with the minority faction favoring financial reform.
The Union Reform party had disintegrated and the opponents of Radical rule, therefore, could not take advantage
of the quarrel in the Republican ranks.   Two years later another opportunity presented itself. In 1874 the state Republican convention nominated Daniel H. Chamberlain of
Massachusetts for governor.   Internal friction within the
Radical group continued, and some "Independent" Radicals
refused to support Chamberlain.   They held their own convention and selected Judge John T. Green for governor and
Martin Delany, a Negro, for lieutenant governor.   As both
Green and Delany were respected for their honesty, many
former Union Reform party members supported them.
Chamberlain won the November election, but the vote was
so close that the Radicals almost lost control of South
Carolina.

Governor Chamberlain himself realized that the Radical Republicans had to reform or face defeat in the next
election.   His past record as attorney general had cast doubt
upon his honesty.   But after becoming governor, Chamberlain seemed to be sincere in his efforts to clean up the state

9. Wallace, *Short History,* p. 582.

government. In his first year in office, he vetoed 19 bills which he considered wasteful of the taxpayers' money. Many South Carolinians who had supported the Union Reform party in 1870 and Judge Green in 1874 now looked with favor on Governor Chamberlain.

Unfortunately for Governor Chamberlain, the Radicals in the legislature sometimes completely disregarded his wishes. They paid no heed to some of his proposed reforms, and they elected as circuit judges two of the worst politicians in the state: ex-Governor Moses and W. J. Whipper, a Negro legislator. Although Governor Chamberlain was eventually able to keep the two men from taking their seats on the court, their election had greatly angered many former Democrats. The Charleston *News and Courier* wrote of the legislature: "They have run over Governor Chamberlain, as they have run over any other Republican who strives to check them in their mad career." *The News and Courier* said that the only answer was for the pre-war Democrats to reorganize their party.[10] Shortly afterward the Democratic party was reborn.

2. *The Campaign of 1876*

The feud between Governor Chamberlain and the Radical legislature over the appointments of Whipper and Moses clearly revealed that the Republican rift of 1872 had not been healed. It was only after a bitter intra-party fight that Chamberlain won renomination for governor.

In the meantime, the reorganized Democrats were undecided about what course to follow. Part of them ("Fusionists") wanted to support Governor Chamberlain. They felt that so long as the Negroes voted Republican the Democrats stood little chance of winning. The Republicans simply had a majority of the voters. The other Democrats

10. *The News and Courier* (Charleston, S.C.), December 21, 1875, as quoted in Simkins and Woody, *South Carolina during Reconstruction*, pp. 479-80.

("Straightouts") opposed such an alliance, no matter how honest Governor Chamberlain might be.

The issue of Straightout or Fusion was settled by events arising in Edgefield County. There race relations were tense. The Negroes controlled the county government and the militia. Even Republican Judge T. J. Mackey denounced the corruption and unfairness of the Radical rule in Edgefield. From this situation erupted the Hamburg riot. It arose over a minor personal difficulty between two white men, Thomas Butler and Henry Getzen, and a Negro militia captain, Doc Adams. The Negro captain, drilling his company on Hamburg's main street, obstructed the passage of the white men's buggy. Although violence almost occurred on the scene, the whites contented themselves with swearing out a warrant for the arrest of Adams. On the day of the scheduled hearing, July 8, large groups of both blacks and whites appeared in Hamburg.

General Matthew C. Butler, counsel for the white men, conferred at length with Doc Adams and Trial Justice Prince Rivers, a Negro. General Butler offered to drop the prosecution if the Hamburg Negro militia gave up its arms and returned them to the governor. As the day wore on, however, it became evident that no solution would be reached.

Late in the afternoon, firing broke out between whites and the Negro militia, the latter having taken refuge in a large brick warehouse. After one white man was killed in an assault upon the warehouse, the Negroes became demoralized and deserted their strong fort, only to be hunted down by angry whites. In the end seven Negroes were slain, some in cold blood after capture. But for the intervention of General Butler, more blacks might have died.[11]

The Hamburg Riot was a test between white and Negro

11. Alfred B. Williams, *Hampton and His Red Shirts: South Carolina's Deliverance in 1876* (Charleston, S.C.: Walker, Evans and Cogswell, 1935), pp. 27-30.

over the continuation of Radical Reconstruction. Irate
Edgefield whites were determined to resort to force. Of the
Negro captain's trial, Benjamin R. Tillman later wrote:
"It was our purpose to attend the trial to see that the young
men [Getzen and Butler] had protection and, if any opportunity offered, to provoke a row, and if one did not offer,
we were to make one."[12]

The Democrats accused Governor Chamberlain of sid-
ing with the Negroes in the Hamburg riot. This catastrophe
cemented the Democratic opinion, and the Straightouts won
a complete mastery of the party. There was henceforth no
more talk of fusion with Governor Chamberlain. Under
the leadership of Generals Martin W. Gary and Matthew C.
Butler, the Democrats nominated General Wade Hampton
for governor. According to Alexander C. Haskell, Hampton won the nomination because he was "a reform man,
who was eminently conservative, and who would be able
to unite the two races better than anyone else in the state."
In his acceptance speech, Hampton promised that if elected
he would be "Governor of the whole people, knowing no
party, making no vindictive discriminations, holding the
scales of justice with firm and impartial hand." During the
campaign he appealed to the Negro for his vote and promised fair treatment for the colored race. By contrast, the
inflexible Martin Gary preferred to drive the Negroes from
the polls. He scorned reconciliation between the two
races.[13]

As the campaign shaped up, General Hampton's form-
ula for victory was "force without violence." Large bodies
of Democrats roamed the state in defense of their candidate.
Wearing red shirts and armed with pistols and shotguns,

12. Francis B. Simkins, *Pitchfork Ben Tillman, South Carolinian*
(Baton Rouge, La.: Louisiana State University Press, 1944), p. 62.

13. The most complete account of Hampton's racial policy is in
Hampton M. Jarrell, *Wade Hampton and the Negro: the Road Not
Taken* (Columbia, S.C.: University of South Carolina Press, 1949).
See especially pp. 52-62.

they appeared at Republican meetings and demanded equal speaking time. The solemn appearance of hundreds of mounted "Red Shirts," as they were soon called, frightened many Negroes away from the Republican rallies.[14]

The campaign reached its height in the late summer and early fall. Hampton's supporters did not always adhere to his "force without violence" policy. In fact, both sides were guilty of occasional violence, not to mention much fraud and intimidation. Several political rallies were broken up altogether. The worst riots occurred at Ellenton, September 16-19, and at Cainhoy, October 16. At Ellenton one or two whites and possibly as many as 40 or 50 Negroes were killed. At Cainhoy five whites were killed and several other whites wounded. Miraculously, it seems, there was no bloodshed on election day in November.

3. The Disputed Election

When the votes were counted, it appeared that General Hampton had defeated Governor Chamberlain by a narrow margin, while the Republican candidate for president, General Rutherford B. Hayes, had narrowly carried the state. Over the accuracy of these results, there occurred one of the most confusing political fights South Carolina has ever known. Each party claimed victory in both state and national contests. Each justly accused the other of fraud. Some people had traveled around and voted several times on election day. Because of such shenanigans the Republicans demanded that the votes in Edgefield and Laurens counties be thrown out.

14. The term "Red Shirt" arose as an aftermath of the Hamburg Riot, when on September 5 a monster torchlight procession was held in Aiken in honor of the whites facing trial for their part in the riot. "A. P. Butler, one of the defendants, commanded a company wearing homespun shirts colored red with paint. This was the grimly derisive answer of the 'Butchers of Hamburg' to Senator Morton's bloody-shirt speeches and Republican reliance on the bloody shirt as a pre-eminent political weapon." Thus began the use of red shirts. Williams, *Hampton and His Red Shirts*, p. 133.

From this confused situation emerged two legislatures. The Democrats claimed 65 of the 124 members of the House of Representatives. They organized and, to avoid bloodshed, followed their leader, General William A. Wallace, out of the statehouse and over to Carolina Hall. As 65 was a majority of the total House membership, the Democrats asserted that they had a quorum and were the legally constituted House of Representatives.

The Republicans, with 59 members, controlled affairs in the statehouse. They declared there had been no legal elections in Edgefield and Laurens counties, and that their 59 members, therefore, were a majority of the 116 that they claimed had been legally chosen. But the Republican cause suffered a great blow when five of their number deserted their ranks and joined the Democrats at Carolina Hall.

On November 30, the Democratic portion of the legislature (called the Wallace House) moved back to the statehouse, where the Republicans (called the Mackey House) were in session. Both parties claimed victory in the quarrel, and both refused to give up the statehouse. The impasse was ridiculous, yet grave. For four days Democrats and Republicans ate and slept in the legislative chamber. To add to the confusion, each group tried to conduct regular legislative business. Outside the statehouse, friends of both parties gathered in large numbers. One false move could easily have led to a riot. In view of the tense situation, Speaker Wallace withdrew his Democratic Legislators from the chamber for a second time.

On December 6, the South Carolina Supreme Court declared Wallace the legal speaker of the "lawfully constituted House of Representatives." Nevertheless, the Republican representatives still held the statehouse. They proceeded with the inauguration of Daniel Chamberlain as governor. Chamberlain was supported by federal troops.

As a counter to this military support, General Hampton solemnly warned that if he was not able to serve as governor, the state would be forced back under military rule.

In the meantime, the presidential election remained unsettled because of disputed votes from several Southern states, including South Carolina. The Southerners finally agreed to accept the election of Republican candidate Hayes in return for several concessions. One was Hayes's promise to remove the federal soldiers from the South. On April 10, he ordered the Union troops out of South Carolina. This move doomed the Republican government in the state. Governor Chamberlain and the Mackey House then yielded the statehouse to Governor Hampton and the Wallace House. Thus ended the long, trying period of Reconstruction.

4. Results of Reconstruction

In spite of the political turmoil of Reconstruction, there were worthwhile accomplishments. The Constitution of 1868 was more democratic than earlier ones. The Radical Republicans laid the groundwork for the modern school system. They organized local governments to meet the changing needs of the people. They rebuilt most of the state's railroads.

But these good points were offset by many evils. The Radicals were guilty of much dishonesty, and for nine years they dominated the ex-Confederates. The ex-Confederates saw their tax monies unwisely or dishonestly spent on costly projects. In addition, these people found themselves denied the right to vote and subjected to military rule.

In some ways the South Carolina Negroes were also harmed by Radical rule. It is true that the war brought them freedom and that the Fourteenth Amendment gave them citizenship. On the other hand, many of the carpetbaggers and scalawags pretended to befriend the Negroes only to use their votes for selfish purposes. The Negroes especially wanted land; they received very little. Instead, they were given the privilege to vote and hold office, something that only the educated Negroes appreciated. Some Negro leaders were wise enough to see the harm done to their race by scheming whites, but they seemed powerless to prevent it.

The Negroes, unaccustomed to freedom and having few possessions, frequently drifted from one town to another. Their crime rate rose, and their health became poorer. The whites were also guilty of an increasing number of violent crimes. The Ku Klux Klan encouraged disrespect for law and order, and much lawlessness continued after Reconstruction. For many years, race relations were tense in South Carolina, and occasionally bands of lawless white people resorted to "lynch law" to "keep the Negro in his place."[15]

In spite of many difficulties, the Negro race made some progress during Reconstruction. New jobs opened up to Negroes, and many for the first time in their lives had an opportunity to go to school. By 1900, more than 15,000 Negroes had acquired farms of their own. A lesser number became successful operators of business firms, and a few entered other professions. In some cases Negro citizens became rich or highly influential members of their communities.[16]

Finally, Radical Reconstruction ruined the Republican party in South Carolina. Native whites remained bitter about the carpetbaggers and their unscrupulous use of the Negro vote. In fact, the Republican party's reputation suffered so greatly in the state that as recently as 1950 that party received only a handful of South Carolina votes.

15. Lynching increased in the 1880's and reached its peak in 1898, when 15 persons were murdered by mobs. Wallace, *History of South Carolina,* III, 400.

16. George B. Tindall, *South Carolina Negroes, 1877-1900* (Columbia, S.C.: University of South Carolina Press, 1952), pp. 121-22.

Chapter Two

South Carolina under Democratic Party Rule, 1877-1917

Influenced by nostalgia for the "lost cause" and bitterness over Reconstruction, South Carolina remained staunchly Democratic from 1877 to 1917. This intense Southern patriotism was encouraged by the "unreconstructed" older people and was slow to subside. James M. Dabbs, born in 1896 in the South Carolina "black belt," long remembered that no American flag floated over the school he attended, while the inner walls were adorned with Confederate banners, and the children sang Confederate songs. He added: "I grew up on Two Little Confederates; and once I almost came to blows with my older brother over the question whether we had ever been beaten in war. I said we had, he said we hadn't."[1]

Within the Democratic party, the moderate faction (Conservatives) at first held the upper hand, but in 1890 the agrarian reformers won control of the party and elected Benjamin R. Tillman governor. By 1903 the Tillman movement had run its course: the Conservatives were back in power. Gradually, however, the latter were forced to make concessions to urban progressives. This budding liberal movement, after a four-year setback under Governor Coleman L. Blease (1911-15), reached its zenith during the first gubernatorial administration of Richard I. Manning (1915-16).

A. RETURN OF THE CONSERVATIVES, 1877-1890

1. The Hampton Program of Moderation

The Civil War and Reconstruction retarded South Carolina's economic growth for a number of years. In addition to the problems of war damage and Radical waste and corruption, a nation-wide depression struck in 1873. Re-

1. James M. Dabbs, *The Southern Heritage* (New York: Alfred A. Knopf, 1958), pp. 7-8.

pair work was slowed or halted, money became scarce, prices dropped, and all classes suffered. The state government was shackled with a heavy debt, and the campaign of 1876 left much racial bitterness.

This was the situation facing Governor Wade Hampton in spring, 1877. When he called the General Assembly into a special session, the newly elected governor found the Democrats divided on several matters of policy.

First, there was the question of paying the state's debt. While in office, the carpetbaggers had sold bonds to raise money for their various programs but primarily for their railroad schemes. Because of the state's poor credit, some of these bonds had been sold for no more than 50 per cent of their face value. The carpetbaggers had then proceeded to squander much of the hard-earned revenue. By 1873 the debt had soared above $25,000,000, whereupon the carpetbaggers themselves decided to reduce it. Their funding measure of that year was later endorsed by a state-wide taxpayers' convention, and the Democratic executive committee in 1876 agreed to abide by that settlement. On the other hand, there were those who favored further reduction because of a legislative report that some fraudulent bonds had been included in the settlement of 1873. Leading the opposition to the funding measure was General Martin W. Gary, who declared the debt ought to be canceled. He publicly accused the legislature of being under the "magical influence" of "oily-tongued bond holders, bond speculators, bankers and members of the financial boards."[2] This prolonged battle soon took on the appearance of an upcountry-Charleston feud because many of the bondholders were residents of Charleston.

For his part, Governor Hampton, while discountenanc-

2. Hampton M. Jarrell, *Wade Hampton and the Negro: the Road Not Taken* (Columbia, S.C.: University of South Carolina Press, 1949), p. 126.

ing fraud, urged moderation. He and his Conservative allies at first were able to block all extreme attempts at canceling but in the end were forced to accept compromises. By the time refunding was virtually complete, in October, 1882, the state's debt stood at $6,500,000.[3]

In the special legislative session of 1877, General Gary opposed Governor Hampton on other matters. The former favored the popular General Samuel McGowan for chief justice of the state supreme court, while Hampton backed the candidacy of Associate Justice A. J. Willard, a Northerner and a Republican. This was in line with the Governor's policy of reconciling all factions. After a lengthy tussle in the Democratic caucus, the Governor's will prevailed. Gary suffered further frustration when the legislature bypassed him in favor of General M. C. Butler for a seat in the United States Senate.

Establishing a policy toward the Negroes that would be fair and at the same time acceptable to the Democratic voters was the thorniest problem that Governor Hampton had to face. Hampton attributed his election in 1876 in no small measure to 17,000 colored voters and was insistent on redeeming his pledge to the Negroes. He declared, "I felt that I was the governor of the colored people as much as the white people, and that their rights would be protected as fully as the others." He therefore hoped to win the Negroes' trust and support by granting them justice, security, education, and fuller economic opportunities. In manifestation of his good faith he appointed a number of Negroes to office.[4]

In his conciliatory racial policy, Governor Hampton had the backing of moderates like General Johnson Hagood and a number of newspapers, including *The News and*

3. David Duncan Wallace, *The History of South Carolina* (4 vols.; New York: American Historical Society, 1934), III, 326-27.
4. Jarrell, *Wade Hampton and the Negro*, p. 123.

Courier. So successful was his wooing of the blacks that in 1878 a move in the Republican state convention to endorse Hampton's program nearly succeeded. As events turned out, the Republicans failed to nominate a state ticket, thus conceding the election to the Democrats. During the campaign the Governor frequently reminded the voters of his 1876 pledge to treat all men as "equal before the law," and he left no doubt that he clearly intended to honor the pledge. Most of the Negro voters took him at his word, for Hampton won re-election by 169,550 to 213 votes. Two days later the governor was gravely injured in a hunting accident when the mule he was riding crushed his leg against a tree. But while he lay dangerously ill the legislature selected him to fill the Senate seat of "Honest John" Patterson, a notorious Radical.[5]

In his appeal to the Negroes, Governor Hampton hoped to obliterate political divisions drawn along racial lines. Though Hampton and his supporters had no intention of jeopardizing white supremacy, they foresaw that if the Negro vote were eliminated by fraud and violence, a return of Federal troops and a renewal of Republican rule would surely follow. Complete elimination of the Negro vote was exactly what General Gary and his faction favored. These dissidents openly claimed that their policy of violence, not Hampton's conciliatory approach, had been responsible for Democratic victory in 1876. So long as Hampton remained chief executive, however, his moderate racial policy prevailed. According to one historian, in two years Hampton "accomplished more for both races and more nearly harmonized the two" than any other leader, North or South. This harmony was achieved in spite of ten preceding years of fear, hatred, and suspicion. However, "Gary probably came closer than Hampton to expres-

5. *Ibid.,* pp. 140-48.

sing the convictions of a majority of the white voters of the state, and he was defeated because of his opposition to Hampton rather than because of his political views."[6]

In 1880 the frustrated and disappointed Gary attempted to win the nomination for governor as a self-styled "poor man's friend." To thwart this challenge from Gary, Hampton, it was reported, threatened to resign from the Senate and run for governor himself unless the Democrats nominated a Conservative like General Johnson Hagood. Such drastic action was unnecessary, for the unfortunate Gary carried only ten delegates to the state convention. The following year Gary died and with him died all real opposition to the Conservatives until Ben Tillman entered politics to challenge the so-called "Statehouse Ring."[7]

As soon as he took his Senate seat in Washington, Wade Hampton's political influence within his state began to decline. He saw his generous Negro suffrage plan altered by others of his party who were more inclined toward Martin Gary's extreme position. In 1882 the General Assembly enacted the "eight box" election law. This measure required that candidates for different offices be listed on separate ballots and that each ballot be dropped in the appropriate box. This was, in effect, a literacy test for voting. It was therefore easy for election officials to confuse illiterate voters by repeatedly shuffling the boxes around.

The "eight box" law did not defraud all Negroes, nor was the law universally supported by the whites. It was a compromise between the Hampton and Gary policies. Probably 10,000 to 15,000 Negroes continued to vote, and until 1900 Negroes were elected to the legislature (mainly from Georgetown, Berkeley, and Beaufort counties). Also, one congressional district in lower South Carolina elected

6. *Ibid.*, pp. 127, 150.
7. *Ibid.*, p. 153; Wallace, *History of South Carolina*, III, 328-30.

a Negro to Congress nearly every two years until 1896. In no state-wide election, however, did a Negro win office after 1876.[8]

During the 1880's the governor's office was held successively by General Johnson Hagood, by Hugh S. Thompson, a dark-horse candidate who had previously served as state superintendent of education, and by John P. Richardson, a representative of the well-to-do planter class. Richardson was a member of the famous Richardson-Manning family, six of whom served as governors of South Carolina.

In addition to questions of the state debt and the political rights of Negroes, several other issues arose to harry Hampton's successors. The legislators representing the poorer classes wanted a usury law to prevent creditors from charging exorbitant rates of interest. The General Assembly finally agreed to reduce interest rates to a reasonable level. On the other hand, the "poor" lost their battle against the growing demand for a fence law. The necessity of stock control to preserve and develop better breeds of cattle, and to reduce cattle fever and similar diseases, was a powerful argument for the value of fencing livestock. Those who favored enclosure did not gain victory easily, for it was not until 1921 that the entire state was placed under a fencing law for livestock.

Not to be classed as a "rich versus poor" statute was the antidueling law of 1881. It disqualified from eligibility for public office any person who had participated in dueling as a principal or in any other way. This measure was the result of a duel (July 5, 1880) in which Colonel E. B. C. Cash killed Colonel W. M. Shannon. The dispute leading to the fatal encounter was complicated and involved several persons. It arose over a lawsuit brought by Conrad Weinges against Robert Ellerbe. Under the influence of

8. Jarrell, *Wade Hampton and the Negro*, pp. 158-59; George B. Tindall, *South Carolina Negroes, 1877-1900* (Columbia, S.C.: University of South Carolina Press, 1952), pp. 309-10.

alcohol Ellerbe had assaulted Weinges. Colonel Cash, who was Ellerbe's brother-in-law, and Colonel Shannon, who was a lawyer representing Weinges, were drawn deeper and deeper into the quarrel, and eventually decided to settle the affair on the field of honor. This was the last formal duel in South Carolina in which one of the participants was killed. So intense was the resentment against Cash for killing the popular Shannon that a small mob threatened to lynch him.[9]

In retrospect, the views of Hampton, Hagood, Richardson, and their associates were generally in keeping with the political philosophy of the dominant economic group of the 1880's—the merchants and the rising captains of industry. These new business leaders were the wealthiest men in the state and the most prominent members of their communities, and their power weakened the social prestige and political influence of the ante-bellum planters. The latter therefore found it advantageous to ally themselves with the merchants and industrialists in what might be described as a union of aristocracy and military glamour on one side and newly-created wealth on the other.[10] This Conservative coalition favored low taxes, laissez faire, and a general maintenance of the status quo. Shortly, however, the Conservative alliance was rudely shaken by voices of protest from discontented agrarians.

2. The Farmers Rise against Conservative Rule

Although grumbling mainly to themselves, the farmers were in an angry mood by the mid-eighties. To their traditional grievances were added the economic difficulties

9. Wallace, *History of South Carolina*, III, 330-32. According to Bernard Baruch, his father, Dr. Simon Baruch, persuaded the posse not to attempt to lynch Cash. Bernard M. Baruch, *Baruch, My Own Story* (New York: Henry Holt and Company, 1957), pp. 38-39.

10. This view is partly upheld by Francis B. Simkins, *Pitchfork Ben Tillman, South Carolinian* (Baton Rouge, La.: Louisiana State University Press, 1944), pp. 73, 80.

brought on by low prices and several bad crop years. These conditions were universal throughout the farm belt in the South and the Midwest. From this situation emerged an agrarian leader of great talent, Benjamin Ryan Tillman.

Ben Tillman ("Pitchfork Ben") was born (August 11, 1847) and reared in Edgefield County. His family was noted for violent and stirring action. Before young Tillman had reached his nineteenth birthday, his father and five brothers were dead, four by violence of war or personal encounter. Meanwhile, his older brother, George, had served a prison term for manslaughter.

Although he was eighteen when the Civil War ended, young Tillman did not serve in the Confederate Army. A long and painful illness had left him blind in one eye. He did, however, take an active part in the Red Shirt campaign of 1876. Afterwards he retired to his farm in lower Edgefield County.[11]

As a farmer, Tillman was progressive for his times, but he gambled on continuing prosperity by extending his operations with borrowed capital. Then the bad crop years of the mid-eighties struck him and "failure after failure in the cotton crop left nothing with which to pay interest."[12] In view of his economic distress, Tillman decided to organize a farmers' society in his home county in 1884. Although the society was not very successful, Tillman himself received some notice in farm circles.

The following year, Tillman addressed a state-wide meeting of farmers and mechanics at Bennettsville. In an electrifying speech, the Edgefield farmer gave his listeners a gloomy picture of farming conditions in South Carolina and condemned the legislature for failure to render proper services to the tillers of the soil.[13] Ben Tillman's address

11. Tillman's life through the campaign of 1876 is covered in *ibid.*, pp. 22-69.
12. *Ibid.*, p. 89.
13. *Ibid.*, pp. 93-94.

created a stir throughout the state, and during the next few months he followed it with a series of letters to the Charleston *News and Courier*.

Dedicated to his cause, Tillman from 1886 to 1890 busied himself with pushing the farmers into action against the "lawyers in the pay of finance," "the Columbia Club," the "polluted atmosphere" of the statehouse—against aristocrats in general and Charlestonians in particular. He organized and led the Farmers' Association, addressed its conventions, and sought to promote a moderate agricultural program, including reform in the use of federal funds for agricultural education. However, Tillman was unable to secure support for his measures from any of the Democratic gubernatorial aspirants in 1886 or 1888, and the Conservative Democrats in the legislature effectively throttled most of his program.[14]

Declining to run for office himself, Tillman was about to give up active politics when Thomas G. Clemson's death on April 6, 1888, gave him new hope. Clemson's will left the state a fund of $80,000 and the John C. Calhoun estate of 814 acres for the establishment of a separate agricultural college, a project dear to Tillman. The founding of Clemson College the following year was a signal victory for the farmers.

In 1890 Ben Tillman, after consultation with the farm leaders, decided to run for governor. A formal statement of his intentions ("Shell Manifesto") was published in the newspapers on January 23, 1890. The farmers were called upon to elect delegates to a convention scheduled for March 27. The convention would, in turn, designate candidates for Democratic nomination later in the year. The Shell Manifesto also made it clear that the farmers intended to work within the framework of the Democratic party.

14. *Ibid.*, pp. 92-137.

The March convention was well attended. Tillman spoke in behalf of his candidacy for governor, and he concluded: "The Reform element of South Carolina has reached the Rubicon. If you don't cross it now, you may as well go home and better never come back here."[15] Nevertheless, it was only through the skulduggery of Tillman's skillful lieutenants J. L. M. Irby and W. Jasper Talbert that the convention was persuaded to endorse the idea of separate nominations ahead of the state Democratic convention. The March convention designated Tillman for governor and Eugene B. Gary for lieutenant governor. In the end Tillman had the support of his own Farmers' Association, the rival Farmers' Alliance—active in South Carolina after 1888—and a minority of lawyers who were "out" with the powers in control. Tillman was further aided by the state Democratic executive committee's decision, made under pressure, to grant a joint debate in each county seat among the several candidates for state offices.

It was well known that the Conservative choice for governor would be Joseph H. Earle, a calm and able candidate, and for lieutenant governor General John Bratton, a planter with a distinguished war record.

Quickly the campaign degenerated into bitter diatribes, slanderous remarks, near-violence, and howling mob action. Earle and Bratton were hooted down at Laurens, Tillman at Winnsboro, and General Wade Hampton at Aiken. At Barnwell it briefly appeared that Tillman would have a personal collision with an opponent who called him a "black liar." And at Columbia a hostile crowd tried to intimidate the one-eyed farmer. He stood his ground, defended his program, denounced his opponents in his usual violent terms, cleared the Tillman name with regard to Confederate service, and bitterly declared, "When any man comes here

15. *Ibid.*, p. 145.

and talks about my record, I simply spew him out of the mouth."[16]

Defending the status quo and pleading for party unity, the Conservatives were generally a poor match for Tillman's vitriolic onslaughts. Hoping for better results, they belatedly and unsuccessfully sought to replace the convention with a direct primary as the method of nominating a gubernatorial candidate. When the state Democratic convention met in August to make the rules for the party and again in September to nominate candidates, the Tillman forces were in firm control both times. The entire Reform slate of candidates was nominated.

Some of the Conservatives were unwilling to abide by the distasteful results of the convention. They called a convention of their own for October and nominated Alexander C. Haskell as Tillman's opponent in the November election. Only four or five newspapers supported the Haskellites, known as "Straightout Democrats," and the Tillmen leaders never regarded the rebellion seriously. The Haskellites won Republican endorsement and sought Negro support, but the latter shied away from them, distrusting their promises and fearing Reformer retaliation. The outcome was that Tillman triumphed by 59,159 votes to Haskell's 14,828.[17]

Why was Tillman able to exert such great influence upon the white masses of the state? His biographer writes: "An explanation is that the farmers for the first time in the history of South Carolina were given an opportunity of being led by one who looked upon life from their angle, who was like them in personal appearance, speech, and manners, and who expressed their ideals and prejudices. His humorous and coarse speech appealed to a majority no more delicate than he in matters of taste."[18]

16. *Ibid.*, p. 159.
17. *Ibid.*, pp. 163-68; Wallace, *History of South Carolina*, III, 349-50.
18. Simkins, *Pitchfork Ben Tillman*, pp. 131-32.

B. The Tillman Era, 1890-1914

1. *Tillman Takes over the Government*

Benjamin Ryan Tillman was inaugurated governor on December 4, 1890, before a large audience of enthusiastic supporters.   In his inaugural address, the new governor called his election a victory for democracy "unparalled in its magnitude and importance."   He assured his listeners that the "whites have absolute control of the State government, and we intend at any and all hazards to retain it." The main portion of his speech, however, was concerned with special reforms he had advocated during the campaign. As it turned out, Tillman's address was not only pleasing to his friends but was also respected by his enemies.

Before long the Conservatives became embittered over Tillman's move to unseat United States Senator Wade Hampton.   This elderly Confederate hero and victor in the famous 1876 gubernatorial campaign was forced into retirement for having opposed Tillman's election.   In his place the legislature chose J. L. M. Irby, a Tillman crony who exhibited great political finesse, but whose "virtues were overshadowed by sensational vices" of violence and drunkenness.[19]

Governor Tillman next turned his attention to a number of legislative proposals.   He was successful in securing adoption of several of his pet plans.   For example, the legislature established Winthrop College for girls at Rock Hill, reorganized the University of South Carolina, and pushed the construction of Clemson College.   The lawmakers adjusted taxes so that small landowners paid relatively less while corporations paid relatively more.   They increased appropriations for state institutions and reorganized the insane asylum, placing a prominent doctor in charge.   The legislature re-apportioned its seats so that the more populous upstate counties were proportionately

19. *Ibid.*, p. 187.

represented in the House of Representatives. Charleston County, long the ruler of South Carolina, lost one-third of its House members. To secure these results Tillman at times dealt harshly and profanely with recalcitrant legislators.

The Governor's dictatorial and arbitrary tactics were resented by some of his own partisans and eventually led to the defeat of part of his program. Tillman was further embarrassed by the exposure of his acceptance of a free railroad pass (he admitted his mistake and ceased to use the pass) and the refusal of Columbia society to invite the Tillman family to balls and teas.

Dissatisfied with his incomplete success and still believing in his ability to charm his rural supporters, to stir up hatred against Columbia and Charleston, and to capitalize on white supremacy, Governor Tillman asked the voters to give him a new legislature in place of the "driftwood" lawmakers sent to the capital in 1890.

To oppose Tillman in the 1892 election, the Conservatives put up for governor John C. Sheppard, a lawyer-banker and former governor, and for lieutenant governor James L. Orr, the Anderson cotton mill president and son of the famous Reconstruction governor of the same name. The 1892 campaign witnessed Tillman's endorsement of most of the Farmers' Alliance program, his feud with his brother George after the latter's defeat for re-election to Congress, the emergence of the anti-Tillman Columbia *State* under N. G. Gonzales' editorship, and a series of joint debates more bitter than those of 1890.

At Greenville Tillman exclaimed: "I had rather follow the majority to hell than these men to heaven." At Walterboro no speaker on either side could secure an uninterrupted hearing. At Florence "a bloody riot seemed imminent several times." And at Edgefield pistols were drawn and bloodshed seemed certain until the sheriff and some women rushed between the two hostile groups.[20]

Tillman profited more from these disturbances than his opponents, and he was largely responsible for the ugly displays of temper. Yet he stood up to bullying with calmness and refused to be drawn into anything more violent than a verbal onslaught. In the end the Tillmanites won a sweeping victory in the legislature, and the Governor was returned to office with increased prestige and power. Subsequently, as Tillman sought to round out his program, he became more tyrannical and overbearing than during his first term of office.

After his second inaugural, Tillman plunged ahead with his reforms, which included reduction of taxes, refundment of the state's debt, an increase in Confederate veterans' pensions, closer regulation of the railroads, introduction of the primary system for nominating Democratic candidates for office, and limitation of working hours in the textile industry to 66 per week. Prior to the passage of this last measure, the 72-hour work week was common in textiles.

The Dispensary Act, another of the Governor's measures, calls for special attention. For many years South Carolinians had debated various methods of controlling the manufacture and sale of liquor, but agreement on any one method was lacking. Large numbers of South Carolinians favored outright prohibition. Others believed that prohibition would be difficult to enforce and would lead to increased lawlessness. This controversy was raging when Ben Tillman moved into the governor's office. Tillman soon expressed his preference for state control rather than prohibition, and some of his friends by parliamentary trickery pushed a law through the legislature setting up a dispensary system modeled closely after the one employed in Athens, Georgia.

20. *Ibid.*, pp. 209-14.

The Dispensary Act established state liquor stores (dispensaries) in which no children or habitual drunkards were to be permitted to make purchases. All buyers had to register before purchasing liquor, and they could not open bottles on the premises. Moreover, the dispensaries could sell alcohol only in the hours between sunrise and sunset. The act was to go into effect on July 1, 1893, after which date no private citizen could lawfully manufacture or sell whisky.

The Dispensary Act was never popular. The Tillmanites who wanted prohibition did not like it, while many Conservatives opposed it because it was a Tillman measure. Consequently, many persons refused to cooperate with the "spying" constables appointed to enforce the law. Bootlegging flourished in spite of Tillman's firm warning that the law would be enforced "to the limit." To the Governor the dispensary system became a near obsession. He declared, "I will make the places that won't accept the Dispensary dry enough to burn. I will send special constables if I have to cover every city block with a separate man."[21]

Governor Tillman's attempt to enforce the Dispensary Act led to bloodshed at Darlington on one occasion. The Governor had sent a small group of constables there to uncover a ring suspected of organized resistance to the law. There was ill feeling on both sides, and when a constable killed a local citizen during a heated quarrel, a riot broke out in which several persons were killed or wounded. In a flurry of gunfire, a mob of angry Darlingtonians drove the state policemen from the town. The crowd then destroyed the local dispensary and threatened to lynch any constable they might catch.

When news of the "Darlington War" reached Columbia, mob action also threatened the capital city. Governor

21. *Ibid.,* pp. 242, 246.

Tillman called out three companies of Columbia militia, only to have them refuse to go to Darlington. Companies from Manning, Sumter, and Charleston likewise defied the Governor's orders. Undaunted, Tillman declared Darlington and Florence counties in a state of insurrection, took over railroads, the telegraph, and the Columbia police force, and called out more militia. Led by three companies from Edgefield, loyal rural militia came to the Governor's rescue. However, before his troops could reach Darlington the mob dispersed and the town settled down. During the "War," so intense was the hatred against the dispensary system that some of the leading Conservative newspapers openly sided with the Darlington mob. Tillman quite naturally blamed these journals, rather than his constables, for causing the bloodshed. Dr. D. D. Wallace has written that the "War" was "one of the ugliest manifestations of defiance to authority in South Carolina history."[22]

2. The Senate and the Constitutional Convention

In 1894 Governor Tillman launched his campaign for a seat in the United States Senate. By that time he had become a champion of free silver and a vigorous opponent of President Grover Cleveland.[23]

Tillman's adversary in the senatorial race was Matthew C. Butler, long allied with the Conservatives. In the canvas, Butler tried to woo both Conservatives and Tillmanites. Compared with the usual Tillman campaign, the contest was dull, however, and Butler's defeat was early foreseen. It was during the senatorial contest that Tillman won his sobriquet "Pitchfork Ben." At Winnsboro he called President Cleveland "an old bag of beef," and declared, "I am going to Washington with a pitchfork and prod him in

22. *Ibid.,* pp. 247-61; Wallace, *History of South Carolina,* III, 362.
23. Cleveland had refused to let Tillman control federal patronage in South Carolina. Simkins, *Pitchfork Ben Tillman,* pp. 312-13.

his old fat ribs." The newspapers immediately seized upon the statement and gave Tillman a new title.[24]

In the 1894 elections, the South Carolina voters not only sent "Pitchfork Ben" to Congress, but also, by a vote of 31,402 to 29,523, approved the calling of a constitutional convention. Through it Tillman hoped to eliminate Negro suffrage and thereby to destroy the "unholy alliance" between the Negroes and dissident Conservatives. His narrow victory in having the convention called was due to Negro and Conservative opposition, and also to some Tillmanite objection in the upcountry, where disfranchisement of poor and illiterate whites as well as Negroes was feared. The Conservative opposition came from the many lowcountry whites who simply did not share the Governor's almost pathological fear of "Negro rule." The Columbia *Daily Register* was probably the only daily newspaper in the state that staunchly supported the calling of the convention.[25]

As previously noted, a few Negroes served in the legislature and in other offices from the end of Reconstruction until the 1895 Constitutional Convention. Fraud and trickery, such as the "eight box" election law, kept the colored vote down, but legally there were about 120,000 potential Negro voters in the state. Their outright disfranchisement was blocked by the Fifteenth Amendment of the United States Constitution. The Tillmanites intended to devise some way around the Fifteenth Amendment without specifically seeming to violate it.

Before the delegates were elected to the Convention, Tillman agreed with Conservative leaders to divide the representation equally between the Conservatives and Re-

24. *Ibid.*, pp. 315-16. In Tillman's stead, John Gary Evans won the nomination for governor over William H. Ellerbe. Both men were Reformers. Evans, of course, was elected.
25. *Ibid.*, p. 282; George B. Tindall, "The Campaign for Disfranchisement of Negroes in South Carolina," *Journal of Southern History*, XV (May, 1949), 232-33; V. O. Key, Jr., *Southern Politics in State and Nation* (New York: Alfred A. Knopf, 1949), p. 548.

formers. This agreement threatened to produce a rebellion, led by Senator Irby, within Tillman's own ranks and eventually caused Tillman to repudiate his own pledge. Some compromises were effected, but not to the point of threatening Reformer control of the Convention.

When the Convention of 1895 assembled on September 10, Senator-elect Ben Tillman was in complete control. His new plan for voting requirements received little opposition except from the six Negro delegates in the body.[26] According to the new regulations, any male over twenty-one could vote if he had established residence, had registered and paid his taxes due, and could read and write the state constitution, provided that he was not an idiot, a pauper, insane, or confined to prison, and had not been convicted of any one of a long list of crimes. A pardon from the governor could remove disqualification for crime. Voters who registered before January 1, 1898, merely had to be able to "understand and explain" to the satisfaction of their county registration boards any section of the state constitution, rather than to read and write it. The registration boards consisted of "three discreet persons" in each county. After January 1, 1898, a voter who could not meet the literacy requirements would be exempted from them if he had paid all collectible taxes during the previous year on property valued at $300 or more.[27] Tillman himself opposed adding a "grandfather clause," for he feared that federal courts would declare it in conflict with the Fifteenth Amendment, a prediction which eventually came true in 1915. In sum, the suffrage provisions closely resembled those of the Mississippi Constitution of 1890, which, ac-

26. There were five Negroes elected from Beaufort and one from Georgetown counties. At the convention these men spoke ably in defense of Negro rights. The whites listened respectfully but remained unmoved by their arguments.

27. Inez Watson (ed.), *Constitution . . . of the State of South Carolina as Amended, April 2, 1954* (Columbia, S.C.: State Budget and Control Board, 1954), Art. II, Sects. 3-6.

cording to one writer, were phrased "to exclude from the franchise not Negroes, as such, but persons with certain characteristics most of whom would be Negroes."[28]

After the Constitution of 1895 went into effect, the Republican vote gradually dropped from a normal 15,000 to 20,000 ballots to less than 5000. The general elections in November, therefore, became almost meaningless. At the same time, a state-wide primary in 1896 replaced the state convention as a system for nominating Democratic party candidates for office. Before long Negroes were excluded altogether from Democratic primaries and could only vote in the general elections.

Aside from the suffrage provisions, the new Constitution enforced customary Jim Crow practices and separate, but not necessarily equal, educational systems for the two races. Tillman had no desire to educate the masses of South Carolina blacks. The Constitution also included a weak antilynching clause, more rights for women, and prohibition of racial intermarriage. On the other hand, Tillman was unable to persuade the Convention to legalize divorce.

As for the remainder of the Constitution, the state's leading historian concluded that it "merely perpetuates the usual American system of a split up executive department, with a Governor denied power to execute the laws he is sworn to uphold; a legislature encumbered with local legislation, and so shackled with limitations that it is frequently straining its morals to circumvent the restrictions it has sworn to observe, and a judiciary hamstrung in its race against crime and legal delays. . . ."[29] The Convention adjourned on December 4 after providing that the Constitution would go into force January 1, 1896, without a popular referendum.

28. Key, *Southern Politics*, p. 538.
29. Wallace, *History of South Carolina*, III, 374.

The new Constitution complete, Tillman then directed his attention to his position in the Senate. He shortly delivered a lengthy speech in defense of free silver and in opposition to President Cleveland. His style on the Senate floor was no different from his accustomed stump-speaking manner, in which he ranted and heaped wordy abuse upon his opponents. The speech gained the new senator instant, nation-wide notoriety but little influence.

At the Democratic national convention in 1896, Tillman launched another intemperate attack against President Cleveland and the "moneyed interests" of the East. This divisive harangue pained Democratic leaders, several of whom hastened to disavow Tillman's stand. In the end, the Senator was gratified that free silver was endorsed by the convention, and he went forth to battle vigorously for the party's standard bearer, William Jennings Bryan.

Back home, Senator Tillman's tight hold on the voters temporarily seemed to loosen a little. His inept and unpopular candidate for the second South Carolina seat in the United States Senate, John G. Evans, suffered defeat at the hands of the capable Joseph H. Earle, an erstwhile political opponent of Tillman's in the 1892 gubernatorial contest. Earle embraced enough of Tillmanism to win a considerable Reform vote. Nevertheless, despite Evans' defeat, the voters returned a pro-Tillman legislature and a pro-Tillman governor, William H. Ellerbe.

The following year Earle died and was succeeded in the Senate by Congressman John L. McLaurin, long a close friend of Tillman. Thus, in 1897 the senior Senator was riding high. "The government of South Carolina was in friendly hands, and the Senator's personal popularity was so great that no one dared raise a hand against him."[30]

30. Simkins, *Pitchfork Ben Tillman*, pp. 341-42.

3. The Spanish-American War and the End of "Reform"

In 1895, the year that "Pitchfork Ben" entered the Senate, long-standing Cuban discontent against Spanish misrule broke into open revolt. In their struggle for independence, the Cuban rebels won the sympathy of the American people. Newspapers increased American interest by playing up stories of Spanish brutality.

In January, 1898, the United States government sent the battleship *Maine* to the Havana harbor to protect American lives. The story is well known. On February 15 a mysterious explosion ripped through the vessel, sinking it and killing about 260 crew members. Although the cause of the disaster was never discovered, many Americans at that time blamed the Spanish government. An outcry arose demanding American intervention to set Cuba free. In April, 1898, President William McKinley asked Congress to intervene.

Governor William H. Ellerbe quickly organized two regiments of volunteers in South Carolina, but the war was of such short duration that neither South Carolina regiment saw battle action. However, several South Carolinians served with distinction in other units. These included Major Micah Jenkins of the "Rough Riders," Captain G. H. McMaster of the regular army, and Lieutenant Victor Blue of the navy. N. G. Gonzales, editor of *The State* and son of a Cuban revolutionary general, served with the Cuban rebels, and M. C. Butler, an ex-Confederate general, was appointed major general in the United States Army. After the war, former Governor John G. Evans acted as mayor of Havana.

With Ben Tillman in the Senate, the attention of the country centered about the war in Cuba, and the return of agricultural prosperity, reform was gradually forgotten in South Carolina. Many of Tillman's henchmen began to think only of the spoils of office and personal gain. Contests for office often developed into mad scrambles among the Tillmanites with corruption becoming commonplace.[31]

In Washington Senator Tillman spoke often, loud, and long. He particularly won attention by his bold and brutal speeches on racial issues. Tillman declared that Negroes were biologically inferior to whites, that lynching for rape was justified, and that Yankees were hypocritical about their views toward the Negro race. He further claimed that Reconstruction had demoralized the blacks. He opposed Negro education, favored repeal of the Fourteenth and Fifteenth Amendments, and urged the arming of Southern whites. Senator Tillman openly admitted defrauding the Negroes of their vote. But he also admitted that he did not know how to settle the race issue and could see no end to racial troubles.

An especially unpleasant episode in his senatorial career was his feud with his colleague John L. McLaurin. After the Spanish-American War Senator McLaurin decided that South Carolina needed more industry. In support of a program he labeled "Commercial Democracy," McLaurin cooperated with President McKinley and the Republicans on several measures, including the high tariff policy and the movement to annex the Philippine Islands. In return, the President consulted McLaurin about federal patronage in South Carolina. This infuriated Tillman. He turned against his fellow senator, challenged him to a series of debates, accused him of selling out to the Republicans for "a mess of pottage," and finally maneuvered him into a position whereby both senators resigned their seats. The governor, however, refused to accept either resignation.

Hatred between the two South Carolina senators grew until the two men came to blows on the Senate floor on February 22, 1902. Tillman had charged that Philippine

31. For examples, see Wallace, *History of South Carolina,* III, 384, 387, 390-92.

annexation was accomplished by the Republicans through "improper influence" on McLaurin. The latter, absent at the moment of the accusation, returned to call it a "willful, malicious, and deliberate lie." Whereupon Tillman leaped at him and fists flew. Officials wrenched the two men apart, but not before Tillman's nose had been bloodied.[32]

A short time later, Tillman persuaded the state Democratic executive committee to deny McLaurin the right to be a candidate for renomination in the Democratic primary. Tillman's plea for party unity and his appeal to white fear of revived Negro voting carried the day.

The Tillman-McLaurin fisticuffs brought formal Senate censure upon Tillman. As a result, the White House withdrew an invitation for Senator Tillman to attend a state dinner honoring Prince Henry of Prussia. Tillman was humiliated and helpless. From that day on, he was an implacable enemy of President Theodore Roosevelt, and, with rare exception, fought the chief executive on all important issues.

In 1903 Ben Tillman became involved in the defense of his nephew, James H. Tillman, who was on trial for the murder of N. G. Gonzales. Riding on his uncle's reputation, Jim Tillman had worked his way up to the office of lieutenant governor in 1900. He eyed the governor's chair in 1902. At this juncture Gonzales, through repeated editorials in his newspaper, *The State,* sought to expose the Lieutenant Governor as a "proven liar, defaulter, gambler and drunkard." Gonzales achieved his purpose, but at fearful cost. The embittered and brooding Tillman killed the editor in cold blood on January 15, 1903.

Although innocent of inciting his nephew to murder, the Senator felt constrained to defend him. His influence was probably not inconsequential in bringing about Jim Tillman's acquittal by a Lexington County jury.[33]

32. Simkins, *Pitchfork Ben Tillman,* pp. 8-9.
33. *Ibid.,* pp. 380-85; Wallace, *History of South Carolina,* III, 412-14.

4. The End of the Dispensary

In the 1902 state elections, the Conservatives won control of the legislature, and Duncan Clinch Heyward was elected governor. Heyward's victory came as a surprise, for the genial and aristocratic rice planter was an amateur in politics and little known outside his native Colleton County. He, in turn, attributed his election to a "clean and sincere" campaign.[34]

The new executive advocated improvements in the state's educational system, the elimination of child labor in factories, and the encouragement of foreign white immigration. He believed the latter measure would ease racial tensions and improve agriculture. Governor Heyward likewise proposed changes in state finance to place the government on an annual "pay-as-you-go" basis and to remove certain county financial offices from politics. Above all, he advocated strict law enforcement.

The Governor realized only a portion of this ambitious, progressive program. Nevertheless, he was popular, being re-elected in 1904 without opposition, and he laid the foundations for future achievement. His greatest difficulty lay in the enforcement of the Dispensary Act.[35]

There had been opposition to the dispensary system from the beginning. There was the "Darlington War" while Ben Tillman was still in the governor's chair. In time the opposition to "Ben Tillman's Baby," as the dispensary system was called, grew even stronger. Constables found the law almost impossible to enforce, and some judges

34. In the first primary in 1902, Heyward led W. Jasper Talbert, the nearest of four rivals, by 36,551 to 18,685 votes. In the runoff, Heyward won by 50,830 to 40,494. Margaret Ola Spigner, "The Public Life of D. C. Heyward, 1903-1907" (Master's thesis, University of South Carolina, 1949), pp. 4-6, 14-15, 67-69.

35. Heyward was unable to secure a compulsory school attendance law, and his immigration proposal failed to win widespread support. Nor did he achieve any permanent reform in the state's fiscal policy. *Ibid.*, pp. 60-66, 70-71.

openly condemned it. Often juries would acquit offenders, and the officers would then find themselves involved in lawsuits with those whom they had arrested.

The opponents of the dispensary system fell into three main groups: those who wanted complete prohibition of the sale of alcoholic drinks; those who disliked Ben Tillman and any of his measures; and those who wanted no government control of alcoholic beverages whatever. Too few people were interested in the success of the Dispensary Act for it to be workable.

The dispensary system fell into further disrepute when an investigation uncovered corruption among dispensary officials. The board of commissioners that operated the system was subject to great pressure from various dealers to buy particular brands of liquor. The distillers were ready to bestow handsome gifts in return for "right" deals. Also, local dispensers and constables were sometimes bribed to overlook "blind tigers," or illegal saloons. The city of Charleston seems to have been the worst offender against the Dispensary Act. In 1896 Governor Evans had placed the city temporarily under special state police control. For a time afterwards, violations in Charleston were lessened, but within a few years they were as frequent as ever.

The conditions just described made it difficult even for a conscientious governor to enforce the Dispensary Act. In spite of Governor Heyward's good intentions, an official investigation in 1905 showed that violations of the law were still common. By that time the move for state-wide prohibition had gained much headway in South Carolina, and Senator Tillman, growing more conservative, submitted to the dispensary system's inevitable extinction. The election of 1906 settled the issue. Though Tillman was re-elected to the Senate, the new governor, Martin F. Ansel, was a prohibitionist. The following year the legislature voted to repeal the Dispensary Act. Thereafter, each county was free to continue its own dispensary system or to adopt total prohibition. In 1915 the "drys" won a state-wide referendum, ending all legal sale of alcohol within the state. The "wets" were not left completely thirsty, for the referendum did not repeal the "Gallon-a-Month" law, which permitted importation into the state of one gallon per person per month.[36]

5. *The Governorship of Coleman Livingston Blease*

During the relatively quiet years from 1903 to 1910, a "new Tillman" emerged in South Carolina politics. He was Coleman Livingston Blease, an ambitious, sociable lawyer from Newberry. He had served in the legislature as a Tillman supporter in the 1890's. In 1904 he was elected to the state Senate, and in 1906 and 1908 he unsuccessfully ran for governor.

In 1910 Blease entered his third governor's race. By that time the old Tillman forces had split into two main groups: the more prosperous farmers with their ties to Clemson College and its agencies, and the poorer tenant farmers, from whose ranks were recruited many cotton mill workers.[37] Blease had the support of the latter group, which was more numerous. His opponents, like Tillman's in 1890, underestimated Blease's voter appeal. Their wild, and often unsubstantiated, statements about his character boomeranged to Blease's credit. He triumphed over the Conservative candidate Judge C. C. Featherstone, a prohibitionist, by some 5000 votes. Governor Blease was re-elected in 1912 and in 1924 was sent to the United States Senate for one term. When out of office, Blease entered

36. *Ibid.,* pp. 34-52; Wallace, *History of South Carolina,* III, 412-14; Robert M. Burts, "The Public Career of Richard I. Manning" (Ph.D. dissertation, Vanderbilt University, 1957), pp. 234-35. Ansel, who lost in the first primary in 1902, defeated Richard I. Manning in a runoff contest in 1906, 47,556 votes to 37,089. *Ibid.,* p. 145.

37. *Ibid.,* pp. 526-27.

a campaign either for governor or for senator nearly every two years until his last race in 1938.

What was Cole Blease's voter appeal? Dr. D. D. Wallace, long a close observer of South Carolina politics, wrote that Blease's popularity was due to his personality and the view he presented. He spoke for the sharecroppers and mill workers while denouncing the aristocrats. The relatively inarticulate masses therefore felt that "Coley" was making them an important political force in the state.[38]

In spite of mill-worker and tenant-farmer support, Blease developed no specific program for the welfare of these classes. In fact, he followed no consistent policy at all. He seemed to be strictly an opportunist who knew how to play on race, religious, and class prejudices to obtain votes. Professor Francis B. Simkins says that Blease represented the worst phases of Tillmanism, or what "Pitchfork Ben" himself called "Jim Tillmanism." Blease was frequently accused of gambling, drinking, and licentious living, and of consorting with the lawless elements in the state. "Tillman was intellectual, harsh, ascetic, careless in dress; Blease was unread, affable, intemperate, meticulous. . . . Both were self-centered, dictatorial, and potentially jealous of each other."[39]

Besides the support of the poorer classes, Cole Blease usually had the backing of the whisky and gambling interests. When Charlestonians defied the law of 1912 prohibiting horse racing and protests arose, Governor Blease exclaimed: "Do they expect me to dress up like a preacher and beg them not to race?" He ignored the violations, and except for some of the ministers, no one in the port city seemed to care.

Blease believed in complete white supremacy. In

38. David Duncan Wallace, *South Carolina: a Short History, 1520-1948* (Chapel Hill, N.C.: University of North Carolina Press, 1951), pp. 655-56.
39. Simkins, *Pitchfork Ben Tillman*, pp. 489-91.

violent speeches he frequently abused the Negro race, encouraged lynching, and opposed education for Negroes at white taxpayers' expense. He went so far as to condemn one of his political opponents for acting as a trustee of a Negro school.

Governor Blease was likewise harsh in his criticism of the newspaper fraternity, which he called a "dirty set of liars," and he praised his erstwhile crony Jim Tillman for murdering Gonzales. Blease vetoed a bill to modify the state's severe libel law and recommended imprisonment for reporters or editors publishing candidates' speeches so as to give false impressions.

At times Blease's messages to the legislature were dignified, but his erratic course is evident from his legislative program: he favored more aid to schools; he abolished the textile mill in the state penitentiary as unhealthy; he established a state tuberculosis sanitarium; and he had the Medical College of Charleston adopted as a state institution. Contrariwise, he opposed compulsory school attendance and physical examinations for school children; he opposed factory inspections designed to ensure safe and healthful working conditions; and he opposed any law reducing working hours for factory laborers. Blease pretended to know more about cotton-mill workers than labor leaders did, and he said a man ought to be permitted to work under any conditions he chose.[40]

As chief executive of the state, Blease sometimes defied the courts, and he frequently squabbled with the legislature. Several times in the legislative chambers Governor Blease and his opponents almost came to blows. When his Negro chauffeur was twice fined for speeding in Columbia, the Governor pardoned him. He clearly abused his power to pardon criminals. He once said, "I love the pardoning power. I want to give the poor devils a chance. I hope to

40. Wallace, *History of South Carolina*, III, 428-30.

make the number an even thousand before I go out of office."[41]   Blease surpassed his goal, for during his two terms as governor, he freed between 1500 and 1700 convicts, many of whom were guilty of murder or other serious crimes.   It was rumored that any friend of "Coley" was safe from punishment.   Some of his enemies even accused him of receiving fees from those he pardoned.

In 1912, when Governor Blease ran for a second term, Senator Tillman was also up for re-election.   The latter had been in poor health since he had been struck with partial paralysis in 1908, and a cerebral hemorrhage in February, 1910, had almost ended his political career.   The once fiery Senator had taken no active part in the 1910 election that brought Cole Blease into the South Carolina executive mansion, but at the last minute before the 1912 primary he published a letter endorsing Blease's opponent, Judge Ira B. Jones.   By that time Tillman was convinced that Blease was morally unworthy of the governor's office and had injured the good name of the state.   On the other hand, Tillman openly opposed Blease with reluctance, for he feared he would thereby bring about his own political demise.   The Governor was greatly angered by this "eleventh-hour stab."   He derisively declared, "I fear no evil from Senator Tillman's letter except that possibly his mind has become more diseased of late than it was when I had my last talk with his confidential physician."

The primary results brought victory for both Governor and Senator.   Strangely, Ben Tillman was now catering to those very persons he had opposed in 1890.   His biographer writes, "He had, in a sense, surrendered to the Haskellites."

In 1914 Cole Blease tried to move from the governorship to the United States Senate by ousting Ellison D. Smith, running for a second term.   The enfeebled Tillman

41. *Edgefield Chronicle* (S.C.), January 21, 1915, as quoted in Burts, "Richard I. Manning," p. 167.

opposed Blease in another "eleventh-hour stab." This time Tillman was successful. Not only did Blease fail, but so did his candidate for governor, John G. Richards. For the next ten years Cole Blease was out of office, though not out of politics.[42]

6.   *The Progressive Administration of Richard I. Manning*

The winner of the 1914 gubernatorial contest was Richard I. Manning, prominent Sumter County planter, banker, farmer, and legislator, and unsuccessful candidate for governor in 1906. Manning's biographer believes that Governor Cole Blease's two administrations "produced a wave of revulsion that made possible both Manning's election as governor in 1914 and his achievement of reforms previously rejected." Viewed in broader terms, Manning's victory marked South Carolina's effort to catch up with the progressive currents sweeping the nation.[43]

In his first inaugural, Manning outlined a program for reform and then took up his cudgel to ensure that much of it passed the legislature. Few of the proposals were original with him. Some were the "fruition of seeds sown during the Heyward administration"; some were Populist planks; some were reforms already adopted by other states. Nevertheless, Manning was probably the first South Carolina governor to recognize the seriousness of the new social and economic problems created by the advent of industry. He believed the government should attempt to assure the economic welfare of all its people and should undertake those functions which individual citizens or smaller governmental units could not efficiently perform, such as care of the distressed, delinquent, and handicapped, establishment

42. For the Blease-Tillman feud, see Simkins, *Pitchfork Ben Tillman*, pp. 492-504.
43. Burts, "Richard I. Manning," p. iii.   Of 11 candidates in the first primary, Richards led with 26,594 votes, while Manning received 25,289.   In the second race, Manning won by 73,969 to 45,099.   *Ibid.*, pp. 180, 188.

of a state highway system, and promotion of free education for all children.[44]

Governor Manning first directed the attention of the General Assembly to the pathetic conditions at the State Hospital. An investigation showed that approximately 1700 imbeciles, idiots, tuberculous patients, and mental cases were crowded in dilapidated, unsanitary firetraps. The food was poor, the patients were not satisfactorily classified or treated, and the hospital had only two full-time and two part-time doctors. The legislature approved a complete reorganization under the direction of Dr. C. Fred Williams.

Next, the Governor's forces, against opposition from many business firms, pushed a new tax law through the General Assembly that provided for the establishment of a three-man tax commission. The commission was authorized to equalize tax assessments throughout the state. Other legislative achievements in Manning's first term were the passage of a local option law for compulsory school attendance, the creation of the Board of Charities and Corrections, the introduction of the Australian ballot for the Democratic primary in Richland and Charleston counties, and the enactment of several labor laws to prevent employers from defrauding employees.[45]

In 1916 Manning supported and secured additional labor legislation: a three-man conciliation board, a workmen's compensation act, a measure requiring textile mills to adopt a weekly payday, a revised railway employer's liability act, and a child labor law raising the minimum work age from twelve to fourteen.[46]

The Governor's sincere interest in the welfare of the workers, including their right to organize, frightened the textile mill owners, and his attempts to mediate several labor disputes increased their resentment. His Bourbon back-

44. *Ibid.*, pp. 196, 527-29.
45. Manning's 1915 program is fully covered in *ibid.*, pp. 201-29.
46. *Ibid.*, pp. 277-80.

ground, his honesty, and his stern but impartial enforcement of the law, however, held their support in his fight for re-election against veteran Cole Blease in 1916. Editor William Watts Ball viewed the election as a contest "between government and misgovernment." He added: "If I had a son in the pen, I have no doubt I would be a Bleaseite." By contrast, Blease, always a favorite on the stump, had the support of the workers, for whom he had done next to nothing. He made political capital of Manning's having sent troops to Anderson earlier that year to enforce a court eviction order against strikers at Brogon Mill. And, as usual, he played up Manning's aristocratic background.[47]

The closeness of the contest foreshadowed frustration for Manning, for the large number of newly-elected Blease-ite legislators were ready to block further progressive reforms. In 1917 the General Assembly refused to adopt a single Manning suggestion for changes in governmental organizations and functions. The legislators, moreover, refused to heed his advice on many other measures, some of which later became law. The only noteworthy legislative achievement was the revision of an ill-advised insurance law of 1916 which had driven most of the fire-insurance firms from the state.[48] The progressive movement had already passed its peak when the United States government decided to intervene in the European War in April, 1917. Domestic issues were quickly shunted to the rear in South Carolina in favor of "The Great Crusade" abroad.

47. In the first primary the votes were as follows: Blease, 49,925; Manning, 33,538; and Robert A. Cooper, 25,196. Two other candidates received a total of about 500 votes. The mill executives probably preferred Cooper to Manning, but Manning to Blease. In the runoff, Manning won by 71,489 votes to 66,785. Senator Tillman openly supported Manning. *Ibid.*, pp. 310-20.

48. Manning suggested a single, four-year term for governor, biennial legislative sessions, a pardon board which would administer the governor's pardoning powers, elimination of county chain gangs, a state finance commission to investigate the possibility of establishing a budget system, increased salaries for state officials, and coordination of effort and funds among state charitable, mental, correctional, and penal institutions. *Ibid.*, pp. 305-6, 385-88.

Chapter Three

From World War I to World War II

During the years 1917 to 1941, the Democratic party continued its ascendancy in South Carolina. The beginning of the era was almost coincidental with the death of Benjamin R. Tillman (July 3, 1918) and its end with the passing of Cole L. Blease (January 19, 1942).

A. SOUTH CAROLINA AND THE WAR

1. The State Works for Victory

With the outbreak of war in Europe in August, 1914, the United States government followed a tortuous path of questionable neutrality until April, 1917. When President Woodrow Wilson asked Congress for a declaration of war against Germany, the entire South Carolina delegation, except Fred H. Dominick, voted for the resolution. Dominick was a recently elected congressman from Newberry and a law partner of Blease.

From the outset, Blease, Dominick, John G. Richards, John P. Grace, ex-Senator John L. McLaurin, and other Bleaseites harassed Governor Manning. Organizing a new "Reform" movement, the Blease forces accused the Governor of discriminating against Bleaseites in appointing the selective service boards and of trying to build up a personal political machine. They questioned his competence and his patriotism and condemned his sons for "strutting about in pretty uniforms and holding commissions" in positions of safety.

Blease personally led the attack. In July, 1917, he

openly charged that Manning was worse than the Reconstruction governors. He said: "They stole the money but Manning is stealing the souls and bodies of your boys." The fiery ex-Governor denounced the Selective Service Act as unconstitutional and accused the "Manning faction" of drafting "Reform" boys into military service. Although admitting that the war had to be won since the United States was in it, Blease declared he religiously believed "that on the final judgment day every American citizen who is killed in this war off of American soil will be charged against the President of the United States and the members of Congress of the United States who voted for it."[1]

In 1918 Blease began to soften his criticism, for he had failed to get the desired reaction and was eager to win a Senate seat. Moreover, he apparently feared a recently enacted federal sedition law. His tactics availed him nothing. In the August primary, Nat B. Dial administered one of the most ignominious political defeats Cole Blease ever suffered.[2]

While the Bleaseites were publicly castigating Manning's administration, the Governor went about his task of marshaling the state's resources for war. He acted promptly to establish a selective service administration for each county and regional appeals boards, to improve transportation and communication facilities, to secure military training camps for the state,[3] and to combat vice in the military

1. For the story of the Bleaseite opposition, see Robert M. Burts, "The Public Career of Richard I. Manning." (Ph.D. dissertation, Vanderbilt University, 1957), pp. 441-45; and David Duncan Wallace, *The History of South Carolina* (4 vols.; New York: American Historical Society, 1934), III, 445-47. The slur on the Manning sons' war service was grossly unfair. Several of them saw battle action, and one, William Sinkler, was killed in the Argonne Forest on November 6, 1918.

2. Bleaseite editor William P. Beard was sentenced to prison for sedition, and John P. Grace's *Charleston American* was temporarily banned from the mails. In the 1918 election, Manning and President Wilson supported Dial, who carried 42 of 45 counties. *Ibid.,* pp. 449-52; Burts, "Richard I. Manning," pp. 438-40, 446, 486-87.

3. Governor Manning opposed the training of Negro troops in South

areas. The Governor set up a State Council of Defense, under the chairmanship of David R. Coker. The Council, through newspapers and pamphlets, promoted Liberty Loans, economy in food consumption ("meatless Tuesdays"), and increased food production ("victory gardens"), aided the Red Cross, and constantly urged the people to greater productive effort in industry.[4]

The Governor faced a special problem due to a serious coal shortage in the winter of 1917-18. B. B. Gossett, state fuel administrator, did what he could to secure additional coal supplies and to distribute existing stocks where most needed. In spite of his efforts, some factories were forced to close temporarily, and many civilian homes were without coal. Gossett received much criticism for this situation. He, in turn, blamed the coal dealers, some of whom he said were "utterly unable to think of anyone but themselves." By midwinter the shortage had ended, though in the spring the state was briefly inconvenienced by a gasoline shortage.[5]

For their efforts, Governor Manning and the Council of Defense were amply rewarded. In agriculture, although many able-bodied youths entered military service, crop production rose from an annual average of $121,000,000 (1912-16) to $446,000,000 in 1918. Part of this increase, however, was due to a rise in farm prices. This increased farm income relieved many tenant farmers of heavy debts and enabled them to get a "fresh start" in life.

South Carolina industry—mainly textiles—likewise

Carolina, and he repeatedly warned Washington authorities, by way of Congressman A. F. Lever, that racial troubles might erupt if Negro soldiers from other states were sent to South Carolina. He especially opposed Northern Negro troops. The Governor feared that persons unfriendly to the Wilson administration might purposely provoke race riots simply to discredit the government. As a result of his pleas, the War Department at first sent no out-of-state Negroes to Camp Jackson. *Ibid.*, pp. 395-97.

4. *Ibid.*, pp. 392-424.
5. *Ibid.*, pp. 412-16.

"went to war." Production soared in value from $168,-000,000 in 1916 to $326,000,000 in 1918. Like the farm youths, many young men of the mill villages entered the armed services. The mill superintendents were forced to recruit teen-agers, women, and elderly men to keep the plants running. And urgent war contracts for tenting and uniforms strained the resources of the entire textile industry.

South Carolinians subscribed more than $120,000,000 to United States war bonds and saving stamps. Thousands of others aided the American Red Cross at various military bases within the country, while a few volunteered for overseas work.[6]

A South Carolinian whose war service deserves special notice is Bernard M. Baruch, a close friend of President Wilson. Baruch acted as an informal adviser to the President on many matters, especially those dealing with economic problems. He was so well informed that the President nicknamed him "Dr. Facts." At one time President Wilson offered Baruch a cabinet post, but the modest Jew declined the position.

Early in the war President Wilson set up the War Industries Board to be responsible for the output of war materials and for the allocation of labor in war industries. Baruch served as chairman of this important board, and when the war was over he served as an economic advisor to the President at the Paris peace conference.[7]

Meanwhile, thousands of South Carolinians entered the armed forces either as soldiers, sailors, or marines. For training they were sent to all parts of the United States, but

6. Statistics on production and war loans are to be found in *Fourteenth Annual Report of the Commissioner of Agriculture . . . 1917* (Columbia, S.C.; Gonzales and Bryan, 1918), pp. 5-8; *Fifteenth, 1918,* pp. 3-18; *Sixteenth, 1919,* p. 14.

7. See Margaret Coit, *Mr. Baruch* (Boston: Houghton Mifflin Company, 1957). Until 1957 Baruch owned a large plantation, "Hobcaw Barony," just off Highway 17 between Georgetown and Murrell's Inlet. Here Baruch was host to many famous persons, including President Franklin D. Roosevelt in 1944.

most were eventually connected with one of four army divisions—the Thirtieth, the Forty-Second, the Eighty-First, and the Ninety-Second. Nearly all the South Carolina Negro troops were assigned to the latter.[8]

2. *Training Troops in South Carolina*

As South Carolinians traveled to various camps throughout the nation, the federal government began to set up training posts within the state itself. The main army posts in the state were Camp Jackson, Columbia; Camp Sevier, Greenville; and Camp Wadsworth, Spartanburg. In 1917 and 1918, thousands of soldiers were trained at each of these posts. Marines were trained at stations on Parris Island and in Charleston.[9]

A typical story of an army training post is that of Camp Wadsworth.[10] This base was conceived by Spartanburg civic leaders and city officials who put up $200,000, thereby persuading the War Department to establish a camp near the city. The final agreement was reached on July 6, 1917. Immediately, the Southern and the Piedmont and Northern railways began to build sidings to the camp site; the Spartanburg Water Works Commission laid nine miles of 12-inch water main; the army began to pave roads to and in the camp area; and 4500 workmen feverishly constructed camp buildings—1000 within six or seven weeks.

8. In a feud with the War Department, Governor Cole Blease had disbanded the South Carolina National Guard. Governor Manning reorganized the guard and mobilized two regiments in June, 1916. Both regiments saw service on the Mexican border that fall. Burts, "Richard I. Manning," pp. 306-9.

9. Columbia was the first South Carolina city to offer a definite site for a camp: 2000 acres with guaranteed lights, power, and other utilities. Local citizens subscribed $50,000 toward the purchase of the site. Charleston and Aiken unsuccessfully competed for camps. *Ibid.*, pp. 391-92.

10. The Camp Wadsworth story is told in Fronde Kennedy (supervisor), *History of Spartanburg County* (Spartanburg, S.C.: Spartanburg Branch of American Association of University Women, 1940), pp. 236-58.

The first troops arrived on July 27 and within two months 20,000 soldiers were in training at Wadsworth. Most of these men were members of the Twenty-Seventh Division, a New York National Guard unit under the command of Major General John F. O'Ryan. This Division included a number of celebrities, most famous of whom was Colonel Cornelius Vanderbilt.

The training was rapid and tough—simulated trench warfare under the direction of veteran French and British instructors. The troops, who lived in tents, suffered from the cold in the winter of 1917-18 because of a coal shortage; the following summer the camp was without an adequate supply of ice. The entire area throbbed with activity; troops were constantly coming and going. "Hearts burned when old companies and regiments were broken up or done away with. A regiment would parade for the last time; officers and men would have a dinner, gifts and compliments would be exchanged, and the members would report to new assignments or adopt new numbers as their insignia."[11]

Spartanburg did its best to be hospitable to the troops. The city raised a fund of $27,500 for War Camp Activities. The Red Cross, the YMCA, the YWCA, the Chamber of Commerce, the civic clubs, the fraternal clubs, the churches—all of the city's agencies worked wholeheartedly at the effort to relieve the monotony of camp life. These agencies sponsored parties, dances, banquets, concerts, singing conventions, watermelon cuttings, musical shows, and other recreational activities. Local theaters offered vaudeville and motion picture shows, some of which were called indecent by more conservative members of the community. However, the task was almost insuperable—there were too many soldiers. Places of recreation and relaxation were overcrowded; inns could not take care of all would-be

11. *Ibid.*, p. 245.

guests; rents soared; soldiers stood in block-long lines to get to soda fountains; transportation facilities between the camp and the city were inadequate; and the hastily built roads did not stand up well under the stress of heavy traffic and bad weather. These conditions, plus the scarcity of some consumer goods, caused some friction between the soldiers and civilians, but nothing of a serious nature.

The army itself made every effort to furnish recreation for the troops and their civilian visitors. Regimental bands were organized and gave concerts both on and off the post. The audience always responded to the strains of "Over There." There were parades, drills, and teas. Civilians were given conducted tours of the trenches and other training areas. And dances were held every Saturday night at whatever places were available. The army maintained a Hostess House with a cafeteria in the center of the camp, and the enlisted men operated their own club ("Rock Cliff"). The soldiers organized several newspapers: *The Bee Hive, The Gas Attack,* and others; while *Trench and Camp,* appearing in October, 1917, at Columbia, was the official paper of Camps Jackson and Wadsworth. The "Over There Club," an enlisted men's organization of former Harvard, Columbia, and Yale students, presented a musical comedy, "Swat the Spies," with Private Cornelius Vanderbilt, Jr., in the leading role.

The Twenty-Seventh Division slipped quietly out of camp in April, 1918, to be replaced shortly with the Sixth Division and later the Ninety-Sixth Division. In the summer of 1918, the camp population was above 40,000 troops.

Camp Wadsworth was quarantined in September, 1918, due to a diphtheria epidemic in Spartanburg. The following month influenza broke out, but apparently was never severe among the Camp Wadsworth soldiers.[12] The quarantine

12. The epidemic, complicated by pneumonia, took 3820 lives in the state between September, 1917, and March, 1919. It pointed up the fact that most South Carolina counties were without an adequate health

ended five days before the Armistice, November 11. On that occasion the camp and city, in common with the rest of the United States, went wild with joy. Every noise-making instrument in the vicinity sounded off. Spartan-burg's Mayor John Floyd, with hand on whistle, rode a switch engine up and down the tracks.

The second winter at Camp Wadsworth was one of gloom as the men only thought of getting home for Christmas. The camp, though receiving some convalescents at its hospital, was rapidly demobilized, and official head-quarters was closed March 25, 1919.

3. South Carolinians in Battle Action

Altogether, more than 64,000 South Carolinians joined the armed forces. Of these, 2085 died while in service, 460 directly in battle or of battle injuries.

The Forty-Second ("Rainbow") Division was the first outfit containing South Carolina troops to reach France. The state supplied a battalion of engineers and a regimental commander for the Forty-Second. Although the engineers' chief work consisted of building roads and bridges, several times they fought as infantrymen.

The Eighty-First ("Wildcat" or "Stonewall") Division was trained at Camps Jackson and Sevier. One of its regiments, made up mainly of South Carolinians, aided in smashing the mighty Hindenburg Line south of Verdun. This action took place just before the war ended.

South Carolina's star shone brightest in the notable exploits of its men in the Thirtieth ("Old Hickory") Di-vision. Most of the Division's South Carolinians served in the 118th Infantry Regiment, commanded by Colonel Peter K. McCully of Anderson. "Old Hickory" reached France in May, 1918, and after some training and fighting, it was sent up against the Hindenburg Line at Bellicourt. At that

---

organization. Wallace, *History of South Carolina.* III, 477; Burts, "Richard I. Manning," pp. 493-94.

point the Germans considered their defense system almost perfect. Making use of a four-mile-long tunnel through which a canal flowed, they constructed elaborate shelters to house their soldiers. Above ground their position was protected by rows of barbed wire and by numerous machine-guns in camouflaged concrete pillboxes.

The Thirtieth Division attacked in the early morning of September 29. It broke through the Hindenburg Line, took the trenches and the tunnel, defeated two German divisions, and captured over 1400 prisoners. For the first time in the war, the Hindenburg Line had been penetrated. This action by the Thirtieth was called one of the great feats of the conflict. The Thirtieth remained on the battlefront during most of the remainder of the war. Altogether, it captured 3848 enemy troops while suffering losses of 1055 killed and 4936 wounded.[13]

The Thirtieth won a disproportionate share of battle honors. Its members were awarded 12 Congressional Medals of Honor, three more than any other unit of like size. Of these 12 medals, South Carolinians of the 118th Infantry Regiment received six. Only New York with ten and Illinois with eight received more Congressional Medals of Honor than did South Carolina. The state's six army heroes were Sergeant Gary Evans Foster, Inman; First Lieutenant James C. Dozier, Rock Hill; Sergeant Richmond H. Hilton, Westville; Sergeant Thomas Lee Hall, Fort Mill; Corporal James D. Heriot, Providence; and Corporal John C. Villepigue, Camden. Besides South Carolina's army heroes, navy Ensign Daniel Sullivan of Charleston won a Congressional Medal of Honor for valiant service aboard the U.S.S. *Christabel*. Sergeant Hall and Corporal Heriot were killed in action.[14]

13. Battle action of South Carolinians is covered in Wallace, *History of South Carolina*, III, 452-57.
14. For citations, see Department of the Army, *The Medal of Honor of the United States Army* (Washington: Government Printing Office,

Typical of these heroes were Sergeant Foster, Sergeant Hilton, and Corporal Villepigue.

Sergeant Foster, who won his medal on October 8, 1918, gave the following account of his action: "I was about a hundred yards ahead of the company when I ran across a machinegun nest down in a ditch, which looked like an abandoned road. I had my rifle with me and told them to come out and be captured. I think I killed three or four of the Germans, and the rest just came on out with their hands up crying *Kamerad* and some other German talk that I couldn't understand." Officially Sergeant Foster was credited with killing three and capturing 25, single-handed.[15]

Sergeant Hilton won his Medal of Honor for bravery in action October 11, 1918. The official account states that on that day his company was held up by intense enemy machinegun fire coming from a nearby village. Leading a few men, Sergeant Hilton advanced toward the position. With his rifle and pistol, he personally killed six of the enemy and captured ten others. Sergeant Hilton was severely wounded during the fight.

Corporal Villepigue's Medal of Honor came as a result of gallant action on October 15, 1918. He was scouting about 500 yards in advance of his platoon when he ran into a small group of the enemy. With a hand grenade he killed four. Advancing a few yards farther, Corporal Villepigue encountered a machinegun nest. He rushed it and killed four more enemy soldiers. Six others immediately surrendered.

In addition to the Congressional Medals of Honor, South Carolinians won 88 Distinguished Service Crosses. Five of the state's high ranking officers were awarded the

1948), pp. 262-65; and U. S. Bureau of Naval Personnel, *Medal of Honor, 1861-1949* (Washington: [Government Printing Office, 1950]), p. 125.

15. Kennedy, *History of Spartanburg County*, p. 261.

Distinguished Service Medal: Brigadier Generals T. Q. Donaldson, Johnson Hagood, and Frank Parker, and Colonels J. M. Kennedy and R. C. Richardson.

4. *Other Wartime Achievements*

During the war Governor Manning did not forget the need for further reform. Although the results of the 1917 legislative session disappointed the Governor, his program met with better success in 1918. The legislature was generous in its appropriations for the schools, colleges, and most of the agencies of public welfare. It broadened the use of the Australian ballot for the Democratic primary to include all but the rural precincts; it created a training school for the feeble-minded and an industrial school for girls; and it fought off the farmers' attempt to kill the Tax Commission, then in the process of reassessing farm property. Manning wrote that the General Assembly was sensitive to the need of social legislation and accomplished more than he had expected.[16]

B. THROUGH PROSPERITY AND DEPRESSION

1. *Problems during the Prosperous 1920's*

South Carolina's four governors from 1919 to 1931 were Robert A. Cooper (1919-22), Wilson G. Harvey (1922-23), Thomas G. McLeod (1923-27), and John G. Richards (1927-31). Governors Cooper and McLeod were each elected twice to two-year terms. Before Governor Richards was inaugurated, the South Carolina voters amended the state constitution to increase the governor's term of office to four years, while at the same time making the governor ineligible for two successive terms.[17]

16. In contrast, the General Assembly, following Manning's advice, refused to ratify the women's suffrage amendment. Wallace, *History of South Carolina*, III, 438-44; Burts, "Richard I. Manning," pp. 447-71.

17. For the 1920's, I have relied mainly on Wallace, *History of South Carolina*, III, 457-70. Harvey became governor upon the resigna-

Governor Cooper continued Manning's progressive program, but during his second term a nation-wide depression struck. It was particularly severe in agriculture. Cotton prices dropped from a wartime high of 40 cents a pound to less than half as much. Throughout the twenties the cotton growers suffered. Eventually the price of cotton rose to 25 cents but only because the boll weevil and two or three years of drought cut the crop.

The farmers' hardships increased while Governor McLeod held office. McLeod, a kindly and gentlemanly official, was slow to take action in the farmers' behalf. He promoted no positive measures to ease the cotton growers' burdens and seemed to feel that his only duty was to furnish efficient and honest government. In Washington, Republican President Calvin Coolidge was unsympathetic with the farmers' troubles, vetoing the McNary-Haugen bills designed to bring relief to the farmers in the cotton and wheat belts.

The end of World War I brought other problems for South Carolina governors to face. The increase in the use of automobiles caused the public to demand good roads. More and more the State Highway Department was given authority to regulate the road traffic, while the legislature increased appropriations for the building of highways. By the end of Governor McLeod's second term, highways connected all the state's larger cities, although few miles of these new roads were as yet surfaced. Commercial buses—seven- or eight-passenger touring cars at first—also began to appear on the public highways.

Throughout the 1920's, the prohibition amendment was the object of great controversy in South Carolina as in the rest of the nation. The law was difficult to enforce and bootlegging flourished. This was due in part to the nig-

tion of Cooper on May 20, 1922, to accept a position in the Federal Land Bank in Washington.

gardliness of federal, state, and local governments in hiring revenue agents, but the bootleggers were encouraged to violate the law by the failure of most citizens to cooperate with the enforcement officers. In many cases violators were well known to members of the communities in which they lived and carried on their illegal business. Despite its shortcomings, the prohibition amendment seems to have reduced the consumption of alcohol in South Carolina except in the larger cities.

Another post-war problem was the increase in racial tension. World War I had given many Southern Negroes opportunities for better jobs, increased pay, and a higher social position than they had enjoyed heretofore. This was especially true for those who joined the armed services or who migrated North to work in industry. For the first time in their lives, thousands of Southern Negroes were able to escape "Jim Crow." When the war ended they naturally did not wish to give up their newly acquired social and economic gains. But in the postwar readjustment, unfortunate race riots erupted in St. Louis, Washington, and other cities where whites and blacks were crowded together. The whites of South Carolina likewise feared trouble.

The more extreme whites joined the Ku Klux Klan in an effort to frighten Negroes as the Klan had done in Reconstruction days. The newly organized Klan did not stop at anti-Negro agitation. It was anti-Catholic, anti-Jewish, anti-socialistic, and anti-foreign. It became so powerful an organization in some states that many prominent politicians supported its program. The Klan's influence was probably never that great in South Carolina, despite rumors that several legislators were secretly members. While the legislature refused to pass a law driving the Klan into the open, this failure to act may have resulted from a lack of interest in the Klan rather than fear of the hooded organization.

As evidence of Klan violence against both whites and

blacks came to light, public opinion gradually turned against the organization. By 1930 its power had greatly declined throughout the United States.

Governors Cooper, McLeod, and Richards believed in liberal financial support for the state's public schools, and all three advised revision of the state's tax system because they believed it to be unfair to some taxpayers. Governor Richards created a problem of his own when he tried to enforce the state's "Blue Laws," old statutes originally designed to prohibit public entertainment on Sunday. The Governor not only instructed the law enforcement officials to clamp down on public amusements, but he ordered them to prohibit the sale of all commodities except ice, milk, coffee, tea, drugs, medical supplies, meals in restaurants, gasoline for emergencies, and newspapers. Beginning with Sunday, February 26, 1927, the state experienced a number of puritanical Sabbaths. Before long, however, the rigid enforcement of the "Blue Laws" broke down in the face of hostile newspaper sentiment, adverse court decisions, and juries sympathetic to violators.[18]

2. *The Fight over the Highway System*

When the South Carolina government began to spend large sums of money for road building, a lengthy dispute broke out over the method of financing the highway expansion. Governor Richards favored a more rapid system of road construction than the pay-as-you-go plan then in force. He and his supporters suggested the sale of $65,000-000 worth of bonds. With the proceeds from the sale he hoped to build an elaborate road system immediately.

The legislature approved the road bond issue in 1929

18. *Anderson Daily Mail* (S.C.), February 22, 26, March 5, 7, 1927. In 1959 a wave of protest, led by theater owners, arose against restrictions on Sunday movies. By January 1, 1960, legal prohibition of Sunday movies had broken down throughout the state while sheriffs awaited a final judicial verdict regarding the constitutionality of the "Blue Laws."

but did not submit it to a popular referendum, as the state constitution required whenever an act increased the state's debt. In reviewing the case, the state supreme court, by a three-to-two vote, ruled the bond issue unconstitutional However, a split decision by the court on a constitutiona question requires the submission of the matter to the circui judges. The latter overruled the supreme court and, on a technicality, decided the bond issue was legal without a popular referendum.[19]

For six years South Carolinians fought and arguec about the bond issue. The chief opposition seems to have come from the upper part of the state, where roads were in better shape than in the lowcountry. The opponents rallied around Olin D. Johnston of Spartanburg in the governor's race of 1930. Johnston lost a close battle to Ibra C Blackwood, who polled an enormous majority in Charleston. Johnston then claimed that the Charleston vote had not been fairly counted, and many of his supporters were likewise convinced of fraud. After a brief hearing, the executive committee of the state Democratic party ruled that there was no evidence of dishonesty in the Charleston voting. This failed to allay the suspicions of the Johnston forces, who noted that the Charleston ballots were quickly burned, making further investigation impossible.[20]

Blackwood's victory enabled the State Highway Commission, under the able guidance of Ben Sawyer, to move ahead rapidly with the state's road building program. By June 30, 1933, there were almost 6000 miles of highways in the state system, of which over 3200 had been surfaced. The entire system of roads and bridges cost almost $100,-000,000.[21]

19. David Duncan Wallace, *South Carolina: a Short History, 1520-1948* (Chapel Hill, N.C.: University of North Carolina Press, 1951), pp. 680-81.
20. H. S. Commager, "A South Carolina Dictator," *Current History*, XLVII (March, 1936), 568-72.
21. *Annual Report of the South Carolina Highway Department* . . .

Olin D. Johnston did not accept his defeat as final. In 1934 he easily won the governorship against the veteran Cole Blease. Johnston's platform of a $3 automobile license fee was appealing to the poor, but no doubt many people voted for him because they felt that he had been cheated out of victory in 1930.

As a youth Governor Johnston had worked in a cotton mill. Later he worked his way through Wofford College and the law school of the University of South Carolina. He was proud of the fact that he came from humble origins and was a self-made man. Said he: "My election as Governor did not meet with the approval of the blue-bloods and aristocrats of this State, to whom I am obnoxious simply because I had come from poor but honorable parentage." Many cotton mill hands and poor farmers who had previously supported Blease now turned to this new champion.

Governor Johnston quickly learned that he could not change the bond issue. Not to be outdone, he reasoned that he could change the State Highway Commission. He immediately tried to replace several of its members with men of his own choosing, but the courts ruled his actions illegal. Finally, in October, 1935, the Governor resorted to the use of force. He called out the national guard, declared martial law, drove the Commission from its offices, and seized highway funds from several Columbia banks. This hasty and high-handed action aroused much ill will. The legislature passed resolutions rebuking the Governor, while the courts again ruled his methods unlawful. The Governor yielded.[22]

Ben Sawyer remained on the Commission and in control of the Highway Department until his death in 1940. In spite of his trouble with Governor Johnston, he greatly

---

June 30, 1933 (Columbia, S.C.: General Assembly of South Carolina, 1933), pp. 8, 127.

22. *Time*, XXVI (November 11, 1935), 12; Wallace, *Short History*, pp. 680-82; Commager, "South Carolina Dictator."

improved the South Carolina road system. At the time
of his death nearly every village in the state was reached by
at least one paved highway.

3. *South Carolina and National Affairs*

In the 1920's South Carolinians carried little weight in
national Democratic party councils, notwithstanding the
fact that in presidential elections the voters regularly gave
the Democratic nominee an overwhelming endorsement
Even Alfred E. Smith, the "wet," Catholic New Yorker
polled 91.4 per cent of the state's votes in 1928. South
Carolina whites were so thoroughly wedded to Democratic
party solidarity as a means of maintaining white supremacy
that they were seldom influenced by the credentials of the
Democratic nominees.[23] With the advent of the depression
in 1929 and the election of Franklin D. Roosevelt in 1932
a slow ferment began to take place in South Carolina politics. The depression was accompanied with much unem
ployment, falling prices, and real privation. Moreover
farmers in South Carolina had not been prosperous in the
"prosperous twenties." Agricultural crop production
dropped from $446,000,000 in 1918 to $156,000,000 in
1929. Thereafter, the depression pushed the figure to an
estimated low of $63,000,000 in 1932.[24] So desperate
were some farm laborers that they gladly worked for room
and meals only.

The depression also affected almost everyone else. The
state's leading industry, textiles, was especially hard hit
Many cotton mills closed down, while nearly all the remainder greatly reduced hours and wages. Unskilled mill
hands, if lucky enough to have jobs, commonly received ten
cents per hour in 1932. In addition to the usual and ex-

23. B. L. Poole, "The Presidential Election of 1928 in South Carolina," *Proceedings* of the South Carolina Historical Association, 1953
pp. 15-16.
24. *Year Book of the Department of Agriculture . . . 1932-1933*
(Columbia, S.C.: General Assembly of South Carolina, 1933), p. 12

ected difficulties, a particularly heavy blow was dealt the outh Carolina economy when the People's State Bank hain of 44 banks failed to open its doors on January 2, 932.

Governor Blackwood and the legislature were unable o cope with the economic crisis. They were forced to rely n the federal government for relief funds. However, President Hoover was too slow to comprehend the true ature of the depression. The Republican "prosperity-is-ust-around-the-corner" attitude drove millions of voters nto the Democratic party, thus assuring Roosevelt's elec-ion in 1932.[25]

The new President quickly won the confidence of most Americans through his dramatic speeches and his "New Deal." He gave hope to the underprivileged and the un-mployed and reassured the country that it had "nothing o fear but fear itself."

President Roosevelt's cabinet included one South Caro-inian, Daniel A. Roper, as Secretary of Commerce. As the Democrats controlled both houses of Congress, some South Carolinians, because of their seniority, attained important ommittee assignments.[26]

Probably the three outstanding New Deal measures to ffect South Carolina were the Agricultural Adjustment Act (AAA), the Works Progress Administration (WPA), and he National Industrial Recovery Act (NRA).

The AAA eventually put cotton, wheat, tobacco, and everal other farm products under a quota system, whereby ndividual farmers were limited in the amount that each ould grow. This was intended to cut production and elim-

25. Roosevelt polled 98 per cent of the total vote cast in South Carolina in 1932.

26. Between 1933 and 1942, Congressmen John J. McSwain, Allard I. Gasque, and Hampton P. Fulmer headed important House com-mittees at various times, while Ellison D. Smith was Chairman of the Senate Committee on Agriculture and Forestry.

inate large crop surpluses. The federal government would guarantee the farmer a minimum price for his products just as long as he did not exceed his allotment. Although grumbling arose over "unfairness" in setting quotas, and the red tape and inefficiency involved, many a South Carolina farmer admitted the AAA saved him from bankruptcy as cotton rose from five to ten cents a pound.

The WPA furnished wages for workers on such public projects as city, county, or state governments would undertake. Some of the projects, such as road building, park construction, and slum clearance, were worthwhile; other projects were of questionable value. Be that as it may, the WPA provided subsistence for otherwise jobless people, both white and black.

The NRA aided the struggling textile industry to standardize wages at a minimum of 30 cents per hour and to regulate working hours. In general, working hours were reduced from 55 to 40 per week. The NRA also encouraged laborers to organize unions. Immediately, the United Textile Workers branched out and won many new members in South Carolina. There were some labor disturbances in 1933, and in 1934 the United Textile Workers staged a large-scale strike for higher wages. The strike was accompanied with violence and bloodshed in several places. In the end the strike failed, and many of the new members deserted the union.

As the New Deal continued, President Roosevelt remained immensely popular with the poorer people. His "fireside chats" over the radio and his winning smile won him greater popular support than any of his Republican opponents could muster. None the less, shortly after his re-election in 1936 President Roosevelt began to face significant opposition among some members of his own Democratic party. Conservative Democrats feared that expanding governmental regulation of business would eventually destroy free enterprise. Because they looked to the Supreme Court as the champion of property rights, the President stirred up a hornet's nest in January, 1937, with his proposal to reorganize the Court. The President hoped to retire all justices over 70 years old or to add additional justices in order to change the sentiment of the Court toward his New Deal. Several South Carolina congressmen staunchly fought against the "packing" bill, which in the end was defeated.

Other South Carolinians turned against President Roosevelt because of his liberal labor policy. But it was his civil rights program that stirred up more opposition in South Carolina than any other issue. There arose a feeling among white South Carolinians that the national Democratic party was merely trying to break down segregation in order to win the Negro votes in the North. Mrs. Roosevelt's excursions throughout the nation as a social worker were resented in South Carolina, for she too seemed to favor racial equality. Under pressure from Negro leaders, the President in 1941 set up a Fair Employment Practices Committee (FEPC), but Southern congressmen successfully blocked all radical attempts to alter traditional racial patterns. The FEPC remained largely inoperative in the South.

Despite these differences, President Roosevelt never lacked loyal support in South Carolina. His opposition, though highly vocal, was decidedly in the minority. Evidently, most South Carolinians seemed to feel that more good than harm came from the New Deal. In 1936 Senator James F. Byrnes pointed out that the state had received $242,000,000 from various New Deal agencies in return for $10,000,000 in taxes.[27] When President Roosevelt was elected for a third term in 1940 and for a fourth term in 1944, he carried the state by large majorities.

27. *Time*, XXVIII (August 26, 1936), 18.

4. The Senatorial Careers of Cole Blease and "Cotton Ed" Smith

After serving two terms as governor (1911-15), Cole Blease made his first bid for the United States Senate, unsuccessfully trying to unseat freshman Senator Ellison D. Smith. Blease blamed his defeat on an "eleventh hour stab" by senior Senator Ben Tillman.[28] Two years later Blease suffered further frustration as he tried to oust Richard Manning from the governor's position. Undaunted by two successive losses, Blease eagerly tried for the Senate in 1918 after Tillman's death. Once more he lost, this time in a stiff contest to N. B. Dial.

In 1922 Blease entered the race for governor against Thomas G. McLeod. Defeated again, the former governor changed his method of campaigning and challenged Dial when the latter came up for re-election in 1924. Blease softened his violent language and talked of the "fatherhood of God and brotherhood of man." He supported prohibition "because my state wants it" and made the usual hazy promises to mill workers and tenant farmers. The Bleaseites circulated a catchy little phrase: "Roll up yer sleeves and say what cha please; the man fer the office is Cole L. Blease." Blease's tactics were successful. He eliminated Senator Dial in the first primary and defeated Congressman James F. Byrnes in the runoff contest.[29]

During his six years in Washington, Cole Blease was a great declaimer. He spoke loud and often, especially whenever a filibuster occurred. His chief claim to notoriety was his constant readiness to defend the right to filibuster as the South's best remedy for blocking unfavorable legislation.[30]

Cole Blease's victory in 1924 was his last. In 1930 he

28. Francis B. Simkins, *Pitchfork Ben Tillman, South Carolinian* (Baton Rouge, La.: Louisiana State University Press, 1944), p. 503.
29. O. L. Warr, "Mr. Blease of South Carolina," *American Mercury,* XVI (January, 1929), 25-32.
30. *Ibid.*

lost his seat to James F. Byrnes. But Blease never quit campaigning. In 1932 he again tried to oust "Cotton Ed" from the Senate, and in 1934 and 1938 he made futile bids for the governorship. It was only in his last race that he failed to win enough votes to enter the runoff primary. By that time he was an elderly, white-haired man who had lost most of his dash and fire. He calmly asked the voters to read their Bibles and "then think carefully and sanely how you are going to cast your vote." Burnet R. Maybank of Charleston won the contest.[31]

Until the 1938 election, Cole Blease could almost always count on 50,000 votes from the poorer classes. Many of these people now turned their allegiance to other candidates. Blease probably holds some kind of record for the largest number of close but unsuccessful races for high offices in South Carolina. Between 1906 and 1938, he ran for governor eight times and senator five but emerged victorious only three times. With his death in 1942, there passed from the scene one of the most colorful and controversial men in the history of South Carolina politics.

The man who served longer in the United States Senate than any other South Carolinian was Ellison D. Smith, an unforgettable character better known as "Cotton Ed." First elected in 1908, "Cotton Ed" held his Senate position until his death on November 17, 1944.

In his first race "Cotton Ed" set the pattern for all his later political battles. He rode to speaking contests atop a wagon load of cotton bales and he wore a cotton boll in his coat lapel. He caressed the boll and loudly proclaimed: "My sweetheart, my sweetheart! Others may forget you, but you will always be my sweetheart!"[32] If the price of cotton went up just before election day, Senator Smith took

31. *Newsweek,* XII (August 22, 1938), 14.
32. Robert R. McCormick, "He's for Cotton," *Collier's,* CI (April 23, 1938), 48.

credit for its rise. If cotton prices dropped, he blamed Wall
Street speculators. For over 30 years his platform remained unchanged: states' rights, white supremacy, and
a tariff for revenue only. Always an able stump speaker,
"Cotton Ed" was seldom bested by hecklers. Furthermore,
during his long stay in the Senate he never built up a political machine on which to lean in election years.

In his early years Senator Smith introduced several
measures beneficial to the farmers, but later he seemed more
interested in talking than acting. Perhaps it was not altogether his fault, for, as his nephew related, "Sometimes he
became serious, but they would not have it. A voice called
from the crowd, 'Cut that out and tell us a story.' They
cheerfully helped him corrupt a brilliant mind and turn a
gay and charming nature to devious ends."[33] He ceased
to perform any constructive service for the cotton and tobacco growers of his state. Instead, from his position as
Chairman of the Senate Committee on Agriculture and
Forestry, "Cotton Ed" spent most of his time fighting those
New Deal measures which he did not like. And there was
his constant battle for white supremacy. He seldom lost an
opportunity to capitalize on the issue. For example, at
the Democratic national convention in Philadelphia in 1936
he walked out of the hall when a Negro appeared to offer
the invocation. Later the Senator dramatized the incident
in this manner: "And he started praying and I started walking. And as I pushed through those great doors, and walked
across the vast rotunda it seemed to me that old John Calhoun leaned down from his mansion in the sky and whis-
pered in my ear, 'You did right, Ed.' " In sum, as one
national magazine phrased it, Senator Ellison D. Smith was
"a conscientious objector to the 20th century."[34]

33. John A. Rice, *I Came out of the Eighteenth Century* (New
York: Harper and Brothers, 1942), p. 15.
34. Harry S. Ashmore, *An Epitaph for Dixie* (New York: W. W.
Norton and Company, 1957), p. 101; *Time,* XLIV (August 7, 1944), 18.

Because of "Cotton Ed's" opposition to much of the New Deal program, President Roosevelt used his powerful influence against the crusty old South Carolina spellbinder in the 1938 senatorial race. The Senator's chief opponent was Governor Olin D. Johnston. The President backed Governor Johnston with the statement that "one of these candidates thinks in terms of the past and governs his actions accordingly. The other thinks in terms of 1938, and 1948, and 1958 as well." During the campaign, the special train in which F.D.R. was riding from Warm Springs, Georgia, to Washington stopped in Greenville for a few minutes to give the Johnston candidacy a boost. For some unexplained reason the President was delayed in making an appearance. Finally he showed up, in company with the Governor, but had hardly begun to speak when the train pulled out of the station, leaving behind a large crowd of disappointed hearers.[35]

Out on the stump Johnston called Smith a "sleeping Senator." He added: "We have two Senators. They remind me of a team of mules. One of them, Byrnes, . . . goes forward with the Administration. The other one, Smith, . . . hangs back on the singletree." Smith acidly replied: "Johnston imitates my voice. What wouldn't he give to imitate my brain!"[36]

Most of the South Carolina newspapers favored the re-election of "Cotton Ed," while Senator Byrnes and Burnet R. Maybank, the governor-to-be, quietly aided him. It was also rumored that some of Roosevelt's advisers on South Carolina affairs double-crossed the President and furnished Smith clandestine support. In any event, Roosevelt's public pronouncements in behalf of the Governor failed to produce an unseating of "Cotton Ed." The majority of the South Carolina voters evidently agreed with the elderly

35. *Anderson Daily Mail,* August 12, 1938; *Newsweek,* XII (September 5, 1938), 7.
36. *Ibid.* (August 22, 1938), p. 14.

Senator that people generally resent outside interference with their politics.

On election night Senator Smith and a group of his ardent admirers appeared in Columbia clad in red shirts reminiscent of General Wade Hampton's famous campaign of 1876. In front of the statehouse and under the statue of Hampton, the Smith forces held a rally, with their candidate giving a rousing speech. When the morning papers reported his smashing victory, "Cotton Ed" proudly proclaimed: "I may be a heathen but, by gad, I'm still a fightin' man."[37]

5. *End of an Era*

With the outbreak of World War II in September, 1939, state politics was gradually pushed to the inside pages of the newspapers. In the 1940 elections interest was centered mainly on the presidential contest, as there was no gubernatorial or senatorial race in South Carolina that year. Senator Smith showed his contempt for the national administration by refusing to attend the Democratic convention. On the other hand, Senator Byrnes attended and played an important role in party councils. At this time and for several years thereafter, Byrnes was probably the most influential South Carolina political leader in Washington since John C. Calhoun.[38]

"Jimmy" Byrnes first entered the Senate in 1931, was re-elected handily in 1936, and supported most New Deal legislation, though he did seem to waver slightly about the middle of the President's second term. By 1940 he was one of Roosevelt's most trusted advisers. In return for his skillful parliamentary leadership, the President appointed

37. *Time*, XXXII (August 29, 1938), 11; XXXII (September 12, 1938), 26. Also, V. O. Key, Jr., *Southern Politics in State and Nation* (New York: Alfred A. Knopf, 1949), p. 145.

38. During the Wilson administration, Congressman A. Frank Lever from Lexington was very influential in Washington political circles.

Byrnes an associate justice of the United State Supreme Court in 1941. As his replacement in the Senate, the South Carolina voters chose Governor Burnet R. Maybank. A few weeks later the Japanese struck Pearl Harbor, bringing the era to an abrupt end.

Chapter Four

The Industrial Revolution Comes to
South Carolina, 1865-1941

In 1939 there were 1331 manufacturing establishments in South Carolina, employing 127,000 workers and manufacturing products valued at $397,000,000. Forty-two of the state's 46 counties had at least ten industrial plants each. The leading counties were Greenville with 118 establishments, Spartanburg with 104, Charleston and Richland with 92 each, and Anderson with 51. Of all the industries in South Carolina, textiles was by far the leader. It employed 95,000 workers and turned out products valued at $266,000,000. Compared with the other states, South Carolina ranked twenty-eighth in manufacturing. Of the 11 ex-Confederate states, South Carolina ranked seventh.[1]

A. THE RISE OF THE COTTON MILLS

1. Cotton Mill Expansion

It was in textiles that rapid industrial development first took place in South Carolina. William Gregg, Vardry McBee, and a few other pioneers began operating small mills before 1860. Together, these plants were valued at less than a million dollars, had a total of only 31,000 spindles, and employed fewer than 1000 workers. Thus, one large cotton mill of 1941 had more capital, employed more workers, and operated more spindles than all the mills in the state before the Civil War.[2]

1. *Manufactures, 1939* (3 vols.; Washington: [Bureau of Census] Government Printing Office, 1942), I, 42-45; III, 942-43. Also, *Blue Book of Southern Progress, 1941* (Baltimore: Manufacturers Record, 1941), p. 30.

2. For an industrial survey of South Carolina before 1860, see E. M. Lander, Jr., "Manufacturing in South Carolina, 1815-1860," *Business History Review*, XXVIII (March, 1954), 59-66.

Because of the war and Reconstruction, there was only very moderate cotton-mill growth between 1860 and 1880. William Gregg increased the size of his Graniteville plant, and other businessmen built mills of considerable size at Piedmont, Langley, and Camperdown (Greenville). By 1880, the total capital invested in South Carolina mills was $2,750,000, while the number of workers was above 2000. After 1880, however, expansion increased rapidly. The accompanying table indicates the speed of the development.

TABLE 1
SOUTH CAROLINA TEXTILES

	1860	1880	1900	1910	1920	1930
Number of Mills	17	14	115	167	184	239
Capital (Millions)	$.801	$2.77	$39.26	$76.6	$140.3	$209.8
Value of Product (Millions)	$.713	$2.89	$29.72	$69.4	$286.15	$225.3
Spindles	30,890	82,424	1,908,652	4,088,782	4,997,406	5,689,642
Number of Workers	891	2053	30,201	....	54,629	94,756

Sources: Agriculture Yearbook, 1930, pp. 71-73; Handbook of South Carolina, p. 467; South Carolina, a Handbook, pp. 57-58; South Carolina: Resources and Population, Institutions and Industries, p. 579.

A comparison of the textile industry of 1880 with that of 1920 shows that the number of mills increased 13 times, the number of spindles 60 times, the number of workers 26 times, and the value of annual output 100 times. After 1920 textile expansion began to slow down because of foreign competition, development of synthetic fibers, overproduction, and a depression.

The importance of textiles to South Carolina may be noted from the fact that the South Carolina mills since 1920 have annually manufactured about one-fourth of the nation's output of cotton yarn and cotton cloth. And as seen, in 1939 about three-fourths of South Carolina's 127,000 industrial workers were employed by the textile industry.[3]

3. In 1939, South Carolina had 5,500,000 of 24,700,000 active spindles in the United States, but South Carolina mills operated one-fourth of

By the outbreak of World War II, the textile industry was centered largely in Spartanburg, Greenville, and Anderson counties, though a few plants were widely scattered throughout the state, especially along the fall line and the Catawba River. Much of the textile expansion after 1900 was aided by the introduction of hydroelectric power.[4]

A few of the entrepreneurs who helped to bring the mills to South Carolina deserve special mention. Outstanding among the Spartanburg County industrialists were Dexter Converse, Augustus W. Smith, John B. Cleveland, and the Montgomerys—John H., Walter S., and Victor. In Greenville County were the Hammetts, the Geers, the Woodsides, the McBees, and Captain Ellison Smyth. In the Anderson region were Robert E. Ligon, James L. Orr, D. P. McBrayer, and James P. Gossett. Elsewhere, there were Colonel Leroy Springs at Lancaster and Lewis W. Parker at Columbia. At one time Lewis Parker was president of five mills near Columbia and another at Greer.[5]

Probably the best-known promoter in both North and South Carolina was Daniel A. Tompkins of Charlotte. Under his leadership scores of mills were constructed, while through his publicity and news articles dozens of other influential persons became interested in textiles.

2. *The Reasons Why the Mills Came to South Carolina*

South Carolina had several advantages over New England as a center for cotton manufacturing. First, there was a slight advantage in having the mills close to the cotton fields. The textile manufacturer could save on shipping

---

the spindle hours. *Statistical Abstract of the United States, 1942* (Washington: Government Printing Office, 1943), p. 942.

4. For the 1865-1907 period, I have relied largely on August Kohn, *The Cotton Mills of South Carolina* (Columbia, S.C.: State Department of Agriculture, Commerce and Immigration, 1907); and *Handbook of South Carolina* (Columbia, S.C.: State Department of Agriculture, Commerce and Immigration, 1907), Chap. XI.

5. Kohn, *Cotton Mills,* pp. 213-17.

charges if the raw cotton was grown close at hand. Yet, in time this saving was relatively small, for many South Carolina mills had to buy their cotton from Alabama and Mississippi. There was little difference in the cost of shipping cotton by water from New Orleans to Massachusetts or by rail from Vicksburg to Spartanburg. Also, the New England mills had their finished goods close to the New York market.

A second advantage was the willingness of South Carolina's state and local governments to give the new mills special tax exemptions for several years.

A third factor (the most important) was the abundant supply of cheap, non-union labor. The mill proprietors found that many poor farmers from the piedmont and the mountains were eager to move to the mill villages. These new factory workers were suspicious of labor unions, and they would not band together to seek higher wages and better working conditions. As recently as 1930, South Carolina textile mill wages were from 30 to 40 per cent lower than textile wages in New England.[6] But even at these wages, most cotton mill operatives considered themselves better off in the mill than on the farm.

A fourth advantage for the South Carolina mill owners was the laissez-faire policy of the state government, which lagged well behind the New England states with regard to labor legislation. Not until 1892 did the General Assembly enact a maximum hour law for textiles, then put at 66 per week. Fourteen years later, after much wrangling, the legislature agreed to reduce the maximum hours to 62 beginning January 1, 1907, and to 60 January 1, 1908. These accomplishments were secured in the teeth of stern opposition from the textile magnates, led by James L. Orr, Ellison Smyth, and Lewis Parker.

Concerning restriction of child labor, a bill to that end

6. *Monthly Labor Review,* XL (May, 1935), 1170-80.

was introduced in 1884. Thereafter, it was almost an annual fight. But as late as 1901 there seemed little prospect
of success, for "the mill owners had command of the situation." These men secured thousands of workers' names to
petitions opposing restrictive measures—signatures secured
through intimidation, it was claimed by the advocates of
child-labor control.

The fight reached its climax between 1901 and 1903,
when *The State,* under N. G. Gonzales' editorship, and
Governor McSweeny both strongly supported the move to
eliminate child labor from South Carolina factories. Other
forces in the fight were the American Federation of Labor
with its few members in Aiken and Spartanburg counties,
and the National Child Labor Committee. Orr, the mill
spokesman, informed the legislature that many children of
necessity had to work to obtain food and clothing. He
said, "It is therefore an actual condition, and not a humani-
tarian theory you are to deal with." He warned that "hasty
legislation" might drive workers to other states and check
South Carolina's industrial growth. Nevertheless, in 1903
the legislature, with the blessing of Governor Heyward, enacted a law prohibiting factory and mine work for children
under twelve, special cases excepted.

Soon investigations revealed numerous violations of the
law, while at the same time agitation was begun to raise
the minimum age to fourteen and to place severe restriction
on night work for children. The manufacturers repeatedly
proposed tying any child labor bill to a compulsory school
attendance law for all children under working age. Their
opponents denounced this move as a subterfuge, saying
that the owners knew full well that a compulsory attendance
law would never pass. Such a measure would also educate
Negro children, a goal not desired by Tillman, Blease, and
many of their followers. Hence, the manufacturers, fighting tenaciously from a strong defensive position, forestalled

any major change until 1916. Then, with Governor Manning's endorsement, the legislature passed a fourteen-year bill to go into effect January 1, 1917.[7]

In the early years of the South Carolina industry, the advantages just named were somewhat offset by the lack of skill of the workers. Furthermore, many of the workers were unreliable and unaccustomed to factory discipline, and the managers found it necessary to keep a number of spare hands around at all times. Also, the South Carolina mills had to furnish schools, churches, and recreational facilities that the New England mill proprietors did not provide. Finally, in 1938 another advantage disappeared when both state and national governments raised the minimum age limit for workers to sixteen years and lowered the work week to 40 hours.

3. Raising the Capital

In spite of obvious advantages that South Carolina (and other Southern states) had to offer the textile manufacturers, raising the capital for a mill was no easy task. At first, local organizers might call a town meeting, offer their proposal, and ask for investments. There were several occasions when ministers of the gospel preached the need of cotton mills. Once public interest was aroused, some persons invested as a matter of community spirit.

Sometimes promoters collected the capital on the installment plan and, as a special attraction to small investors, made individual payments as low as 25 cents per week. Whenever one cotton mill was successfully established in a community, quite often the momentum resulted in the organization of a second or a third plant.

Besides local investors, many businessmen from Charleston put money into cotton mills. The important factories

7. This entire struggle is covered by Elizabeth H. Davidson, *Child Labor in the Southern Textile States* (Chapel Hill, N.C.: University of North Carolina Press, 1939), pp. 89-101, 178-93.

at Piedmont, Pacolet, Clifton, and Pelzer were aided by Charleston capital. Some of the Charleston businessmen offered not only their money but also their services to run the mills.

Another source of capital was Northern businessmen. Frequently, New England machinery manufacturers and New York marketing agents furnished capital for Southern mills, but usually on the condition that the local entrepreneurs put up part of the necessary funds. Such terms were not always satisfactory for the local promoter, for whenever an outside agent furnished a large share of the capital, he usually controlled the policies of the company. And sometimes the outsider was more interested in commissions for his agency than profits for the cotton mill.

Regardless of the source of their money, some South Carolina textile plants began operations with too little capital. This necessitated operating "on a shoestring" and often with obsolete machinery. With the first financial difficulty, mills of this sort collapsed. Contrariwise, the well-organized and well-managed factories made handsome profits between 1880 and 1920. Successful managers expanded their plants, added new machinery, and diversified their products. They hired more and more workers and progressed steadily. The money invested in South Carolina cotton mills increased from less than $3,000,000 in 1880 to $140,000,000 in 1920. By that time, the factory owners and managers constituted an important and powerful new class.

4. Life in the Mill Villages

In reviewing life in the mill villages prior to 1900, we may note that most villagers originally came from the farm. Dishearteningly poor conditions in South Carolina agriculture for many years before 1900 caused thousands of tenant farmers to give up their struggle to wrest a living from the soil. Whole families often flocked to nearby mill villages. Mainly poorly educated workers of Anglo-Saxon descent, these people were naïve and countrified. Captain Ellison Smyth later recalled that one old woman at Pelzer insisted on blowing her horn at noon to call the children from the mill to dinner. Another family moved away from Pelzer after a few weeks because they believed electric lights were unhealthy.[8]

A few foreigners also came to South Carolina, and for a short time some factory owners tried using Negro labor. Foreigners never became numerous, however, and soon the Negroes were discharged from all but a few menial tasks.

When a new worker reached the mill village, he saw an imposing brick structure, two to four stories high, in the center of the town. This was the factory. If the building was old, it might be covered with ivy. Nearby was the mill village, consisting of several rows of box-like four-room houses. These grey or white dwellings rested on brick or stone pillars, and each had a front porch. The interior walls, ceilings, and floors were usually made of pine. At first none of the houses had electricity, gas, plumbing, or running water. A privy was situated several yards to the rear of each dwelling.

Public wells were centrally located in the village streets. Every house had adjacent land for a garden plot, and most companies furnished pasture land and hog pens for those families who wished to keep cows and pigs. In some villages (Monaghan and Piedmont, for instance), over 50 per cent of the mill families owned cows. Houses rented for about 50 cents per room per month, but many services were furnished free of charge.[9] Generally, the mill companies sold wood and coal at low cost to their employees.

8. Letter from Smyth to Miss Will Lou Gray, November 10, 1937. Cited in James F. Miles, "Economic Survey of South Carolina Textiles" (Master's thesis, University of South Carolina, 1939), pp. 67-68.

9. Kohn, *Cotton Mills,* pp. 52-55.

The actual condition of the homes was a matter left entirely to the individuals who rented them. As in other communities, some of the factory people kept their homes looking neat and attractive. The overseers and other officials lived in larger homes that were usually set apart from the remainder of the village.

As for wages, before 1900 they ran as low as 25 cents per day for small children. After the turn of the century the minimum wage in most factories was about 50 cents a day. The average daily pay of all South Carolina textile workers in 1902 was approximately 75 cents, and it rose to $1.10 in 1907. Some skilled workers earned as much as $3.00 per day. [10]

For these small wages hours were very long. A 12-hour work day, six days a week, was common until Ben Tillman's 66-hour law passed the legislature in 1892. On work days, each mill blew a whistle or rang a large bell about an hour before starting time. This was the rising signal. A second bell or blast came about 15 minutes before starting time. At the third signal work began.

A former resident of Graniteville said there were a few $3-a-day men in Graniteville in the 1880's. They were known as the town dandies. One dandy boasted of buying cigars by the box; another said he took his sweetheart to dinner in Aiken on Sunday; another claimed to have owned the first bicycle ever seen in Graniteville. These men could afford to rent buggies and travel to Augusta, where they purchased clothes and enjoyed the entertainment of the city.[11]

The average worker could not enjoy such pleasures. He had no horse and buggy, and little money to spare. In mill villages located beyond walking distance from a large

10. *Ibid.*, pp. 32-36.
11. Life in Graniteville in the 1880's is described in W. E. Woodward, *The Way Our People Lived* (New York: E. P. Dutton and Company, 1944), Chap. X.

town like Greenville or Columbia, he seldom yielded to the lure of the "bright lights." For recreation, most of the mill people depended largely on picnics, fishing, swimming, occasional traveling minstrel shows, and informal get-togethers for music.

Many villagers learned to play musical instruments. The boys and men especially liked fiddles, accordions, and harmonicas; the womenfolk played organs whenever their families could afford to buy them. Most young people liked to dance, but generally the older people regarded dancing as sinful. Consequently, public dances were forbidden in many mill villages.

In the absence of recreational facilities, some mill workers indulged in drinking sprees on Saturday nights. The factory owners tried to discourage the use of alcohol and fired the worst offenders. The owners built churches and furnished ministers. Some two or three times a year the mill church conducted a religious revival, featuring a visiting evangelist who delivered a series of rousing sermons on the evils of sin and the torment of hell-fire. The type of sermon usually appealed to the villagers, most of whom were either Baptists or Methodists.

The mill officials also built schoolhouses and offered free education to all village children too young to work in the factory. Until the 1920's many of the mill schools were superior to the state-supported schools. As a result, illiteracy was almost stamped out among the younger people of the mill communities.

In comparing life in a mill town with that on a farm, one poorly-educated Graniteville worker put it this way: "I like it here. We live in a nice house, lots better'n than [*sic*] that cabin in the country. And there's always people around to talk with. Me and my gals—between the four of us we make from twenty-five to thirty dollars a week, and that ain't to be sneezed at, lemme tell you. And we get it in good, hard cash every Saturday, without any ifs and ands about it."[12]

Life in a mill village underwent considerable change by the twenties.   One of the most significant changes was the development of organized recreation.   Most of the companies began to support semi-professional baseball and basketball teams.   Numerous big-league baseball players got their start with mill teams.   Many textile companies also began to furnish Saturday night movies and Sunday afternoon band concerts.   But probably the greatest change was wrought by the coming of the automobile.   This permitted the mill folk, as well as the farmers, to escape their isolation.   In the late twenties, Model-T Fords were common sights on mill-village streets.

With the passage of the "6-0-1" school law in 1924, public schools were improved to such an extent that the mills began to close their private schools.   The state also made high schools available for mill children.   Henceforth, a few boys and girls from the villages began to go to college. Education was further aided by the fact that after 1920 every village was reached by a daily newspaper,.   Two additional changes of importance were, first, that children under fourteen were not permitted to work in the mills after January 1, 1917, and second, that factory hours for workers were lowered by law in 1921 to a maximum of 55 per week.

Of interest is the following information from the Saxon mill village at Spartanburg.   In 1926 there were 178 families in the Saxon village.   Of these, 79 owned phonographs, 39 automobiles, and 23 pianos, and 18 were sending their children to institutions of higher learning.   In the same year, 155 families subscribed to a daily newspaper. Throughout the textile region, most of the workers were natives either of North Carolina or South Carolina, but few remained in one village for long.   A survey of 156 homes

12. *Ibid.,* p. 341.

in four villages in 1939 revealed that 90 families had been living at their present locations less than four years.[13]

By the thirties most mill villages had running water and electricity. Radio aerials were as common then as television antennas became in the fifties. A few villages, such as that built by James C. Self in Greenwood, consisted of attractive brick bungalows.

In sum, the average villager of 1930 was better educated and better paid for his work than his 1890 counterpart. His working hours were shorter; he enjoyed more conveniences, better recreation facilities, and better health; and he was less provincial. In a few factory towns the companies owned everything from the grocery store to the graveyard, but these towns were no longer in the majority.

With the coming of the great depression of the 1930's, the South Carolina textile people suffered along with the other economic groups. The unrest and hardship caused by the depression gave labor unions an opportunity as never before to organize the mill workers. In the early thirties, the United Textile Workers, an affiliate of the American Federation of Labor, sent organizers into the piedmont textile area. These labor leaders achieved considerable success within a short time. By 1934 possibly one-half the textile workers in the state were listed on the union's roll.

A number of labor-management disputes flared up between 1929 and 1934, but there was no industry-wide trouble until September, 1934. At that time, the UTW, under the guidance of Francis J. Gorman, struck for a 30-hour work week with no reduction in pay. The previous

13. Marjorie Potwin, *Cotton Mill People of the Piedmont* (New York: Columbia University Press, 1927), p. 66; Miles, "Economic Survey," p. 82. A survey of the Whitmire village in 1926 revealed that one-third of the families owned automobiles and one-half subscribed to newspapers. *Ibid.*, pp. 77-78.

year the NRA textile code had set a minimum wage of $12 for a 40-hour week, which was a noteworthy increase in the minimum paid by most South Carolina factories. Gorman's strike therefore seemed ill advised, notwithstanding the fact that it was widely supported throughout the United States.

About two-thirds of the South Carolina workers walked out. They organized "flying squadrons" to swoop down on plants still in operation. In a few cases there were riots and bloodshed. Six strikers were killed at Honea Path when panicky mill guards fired into a crowd of agitators outside Chiquola Mill. Governor Blackwood ordered the national guard into action in several towns to preserve order. In the end the strike was broken, and the UTW failed to gain its objective.[14] This failure dealt the union a mortal blow. Its membership dropped sharply, and unionization among South Carolina mill hands has not been strong since.

By 1941 the worst of the depression was over. South Carolina mills were back on full time, and wages were about twice as high as in the spring of 1933.[15]

B. OTHER INDUSTRIES IN SOUTH CAROLINA

One of the oldest and most important industries was sawmilling. It was significant even in colonial days. After 1900, sawmilling with power machinery became one of the state's top producers of wealth. Statistics show that the products of sawmills in 1939 were valued at over $16,000,-000. This figure does not include the hundreds of little

14. An impartial, day-by-day account of the strike was carried by *The New York Times*. See especially the issues of September 7 and 9, 1934.

15. Textile wages, industry-wide, averaged 21.4 cents per hour in April, 1933, and 41.2 cents in 1940. In September, 1940, the Northern average was 46.9 cents per hour, the Southern 38.5 cents. The Fair Labor Standards Act of 1938 required a minimum of 32.5 cents in 1940. Most South Carolina mills complied. *Monthly Labor Review*, LIII (December, 1941), 1490-1502.

TABLE 2
OTHER INDUSTRIES, 1939

Type	Number of Workers	Value of Product
Bread and bakery products..............	1266	$ 5,873,000
Brick and hollow structural tile...........	882	1,379,000
Cottonseed oil, cake, meal, and linters......	1020	7,586,000
Fertilizer...............................	1931	11,702,000
Household furniture.....................	1557	2,879,000
Wholesale meat-packing..................	472	3,949,000
Non-alcoholic beverages..................	996	7,279,000
Planing mills (not connected with sawmills)....	1096	4,449,000
Plywood mills...........................	786	1,630,000
Sawmills, veneer mills, cooperage, etc.........	10,402	16,567,000
Paper and allied products.................	2809	19,923,000
Other finished lumber products.............	1735	5,576,000
Ice....................................	805	1,801,000
Prepared feeds for fowls and animals.........	144	1,145,000
Ice cream and ices......................	209	1,204,000
Textile machinery.......................	530	1,558,000
Wooden boxes..........................	762	1,229,000

Source: Census of *Manufactures, 1939,* III, 946-49.

"woodpecker" mills which employed fewer than five workers each. These small mills moved rapidly from one place to another, leaving piles of sawdust behind as tokens of their activity. Closely connected with sawmilling was the manufacture of furniture, wooden boxes, tool handles, coffins, plywood products, and the like.

During the 1930's, the manufacture of wrapping paper and cardboard, made primarily from the pulp of small pines, was initiated within the state. This industry was primarily developed in coastal South Carolina. Another forest industry once very important in South Carolina was turpentine and rosin production. But, since the "bleeding" of pines for turpentine ruins them for lumber, by 1939 the turpentine and rosin industry had declined.

The manufacture of commercial fertilizer was one of the state's largest industries in 1939. Shortly after the Civil War, beds of rich phosphate rock were discovered in the Charleston area. Quickly a number of firms sprang up to mine the ore and process it for agricultural use. The peak of the industry was reached in 1885 when 673,000 tons of rock were produced, valued at over $4,000,000. Unluckily for the state's phosphate miners, richer beds were discovered in Florida, Tennessee, and elsewhere about 1890. Thereafter, mining operations were gradually discontinued in South Carolina. The Charleston firms, however, continued to manufacture fertilizer, depending on rock mined elsewhere and shipped in mainly via water.[16]

Closely allied to industry since 1900 has been hydroelectric power. The first plant built in the state "for the transmission of power over a distance of several miles for use by the general public" was at Portman Shoals on the Seneca River. Its successful operation, begun in 1897, inspired Dr. W. G. Wylie to try a similar project on the Catawba. With the aid of W. C. Whitner and William S. Lee, Dr. Wylie had the Catawba plant ready for operation in 1904. These men then interested the North Carolina tobacco millionaire James B. Duke in their work. Duke agreed to finance a string of hydroelectric power dams along the Catawba.[17]

Henceforth, the development of electric power in South Carolina grew rapidly. In 1940 there were 23 hydroelectric, 13 steam electric, and 5 internal combustion engine stations which generated and purchased over two billion kilowatt-hours of electricity. Slightly less than that amount was sold to 149,000 customers for over $22,000,-000.[18]

C. SOUTH CAROLINA GETS OUT OF THE MUD

A system of rapid and cheap transportation is an indispensable characteristic of a specialized economy. Quite

16. *South Carolina, a Handbook* (Columbia, S.C.: State Department of Agriculture, Commerce and Industry, 1927), pp. 84-89.
17. *Ibid.*, pp. 42-43.
18. *Year Book of the Department of Agriculture . . . 1940-1941* (Columbia, S.C.: General Assembly of South Carolina, 1941), p. 247.

naturally, therefore, the growth of industry in South Carolina was accompanied by a great improvement in the state's system of transportation.

The Civil War had completely disrupted transportation facilities in South Carolina. Marauding armies had burned bridges, torn up miles of track, and destroyed much of the railways' rolling stock. Inland water transportation had likewise reached a standstill; the common roads and causeways were in poor condition. About the only available transportation in 1865 consisted of a few army wagons and ambulances. Horses and mules were scarce, and feed for livestock seemed even scarcer.[19] South Carolina was really "stuck in the mud," as General Sherman himself was ready to attest.

The first system of transportation to recover was the railroads. The state's river and canal traffic never attained its pre-war importance, and its roads showed no significant improvement before the coming of the automobile.

1. The Railroads

During the Reconstruction era, the Radical government of South Carolina spent lavish sums of money rebuilding railroads and constructing new lines. The fraud and wasteful methods of finance noted earlier made this a costly enterprise, and many of these state-supported lines were soon plunged into bankruptcy. As a result, a general reorganization of the South Carolina railroads took place at the close of Reconstruction, but with new construction continuing. "Main-line" railroad mileage in the state increased from 992 in 1860 to 1356 in 1877, 2842 in 1900, and 3811 in 1924.[20]

19. Francis B. Simkins and Robert H. Woody, *South Carolina during Reconstruction* (Chapel Hill, N.C.: University of North Carolina Press, 1932), pp. 9-10.
20. *Twenty-Second Annual Report of the Railroad Commissioners . . . of South Carolina* (Columbia, S.C.: State Company, 1901), pp. 4-5; *South Carolina, a Handbook* (1927), p. 220.

TABLE 3
SOUTH CAROLINA RAILROADS

	SINGLE TRACK (main-line) MILEAGE		
	31 Dec 1924	31 Dec 1941	31 Dec 1952
Alcolu Railroad Co.....................	25.00	....	....
Atlantic Coast Line...................	912.94	910.61	791.38
Augusta Northern R'y. Co..............	11.20	11.20	....
Bamberg, Ehrhardt and Walterboro R'd. Co...........................	14.40	....	....
Bennettsville and Cheraw R'd. Co.......	44.50	23.44	....
Blue Ridge R'd. Co....................	44.00	44.20	....
Branchville and Bowman R'd. Co........	11.12	....	....
Buffalo, Union-Carolina R'd. Co.........	19.20	19.20	....
Carolina, Clinchfield and Ohio R'y. Co. of S. C............................	18.09	18.09	18.18
Carolina and Northwestern R'y. Co......	37.00	37.00	81.07
Carolina Western Railroad..............	6.00	6.00	4.50
Charleston and Western Carolina R'y. Co.	320.68	320.68	320.68
Charlotte, Monroe and Columbia R'd. Co.	17.16	....	....
Chesterfield and Lancaster R'd. Co.......	35.26	31.75	....
Columbia, Newberry and Laurens R'd. Co.	75.00	75.00	75.00
Due West R'y. Co.....................	5.00	....	....
Georgia and Florida R'd. Co.............	....	56.43	57.03
Greenville and Northern R'y. Co.........	19.00	23.20	19.00
Hampton and Branchville R'd. & Lumber Co........................	24.00	47.67	47.67
Lancaster and Chester R'd. Co...........	28.92	28.91	28.99
Marion and Southern R'd. Co............	1.63	....	....
Northwestern Railroad Co. of S. C.......	80.50	....	....
Pickens Railroad Co...................	9.30	....	9.30
Raleigh and Charleston R'd. Co..........	21.34	19.91	....
Seaboard Air Line R'y. Co..............	795.00	761.75	735.97
Rockton and Rion R'y. Co..............	....	12.00	12.00
Seivern and Knoxville R'd. Co...........	25.14	....	....
Southern Railway Co...................	1,102.96	891.53	1,045.63
Ware Shoals Railroad Co...............	5.00	5.00	5.17
Piedmont and Northern R'y. Co.........	101.20	129.55	101.56
Total......................	3,810.54	3,473.12	3,353.13

Sources: Annual Report of the Railroad Commission, 1925, p. 172; Annual Report of the Public Service Commission, 1941-42, p. 18; Annual Report of the Public Service Commission, 1952-53, p. 13.

South Carolina Railroads, 1867. Drawing by David E. Martin from map in Simkins and Woody, *South Carolina during Reconstruction,* opposite p. 22.

The table and map show that the three most important railroad lines in South Carolina by the 1920's were the Southern Railway System, the Atlantic Coast Line, and the Seaboard Air Line. The Southern was the largest. Organized in 1894, the Southern owned about 8300 miles of track throughout the South by 1925. Its main route was from Washington to New Orleans, by way of Spartanburg and Greenville. The Southern's other chief routes inside South Carolina extended from Spartanburg to Charleston, and from Charlotte to Savannah. These two lines crossed each other at Columbia. The Southern also established important repair shops at Hayne, on the outskirts of Spartanburg.

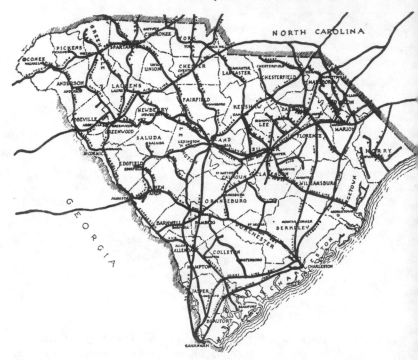

South Carolina Railroads, 1926. From *Year Book of the Department of Agriculture . . . 1926*, opposite p. 46.

In 1898 a number of small railroad companies were combined to form the Atlantic Coast Line. For several years this company expanded until it was serving the entire Atlantic coastal region from Virginia to Florida. In 1925 it completed a double-track line from Richmond to Jacksonville, running through Florence, Kingstree, and Charleston. Florence became the location of large Atlantic Coast Line repair shops. By 1925 the entire Atlantic Coast Line system contained 4925 miles of track.

The third great railroad system, the Seaboard Air Line, was also organized shortly before 1900. The Seaboard's main route, also from Richmond to Jacksonville, passed through Cheraw, Camden, and Columbia. Its secondary

ɔute, from Monroe, N.C., to Birmingham, ran through
ʰester, Clinton, Greenwood, and Abbeville.[21]

As the accompanying map shows, all three of these large
ailroad systems established several branch lines. In addi-
on, many of the smaller companies, such as the Piedmont
nd Northern (P&N), the Charleston and Western Carolina
C&WC), and the Columbia, Newberry, and Laurens
CN&L), came under the control of larger companies.

Before the mid-twenties, nearly all heavy freight moved
y rail, and most travelers relied on the numerous passenger
ains. The larger companies furnished comfortable diners
nd pullmans. South Carolina's dependence on the rail-
ays was impressively seen in 1908 when an August flood
ashed away or damaged several railroad bridges and some
ack.[22] For several days travelers were stranded and freight
ovements at a complete standstill in some areas.

In the late twenties, growing competition from buses,
ucks, and automobiles forced the railroads to reduce their
ervice. The depression of the thirties added to their fi-
ancial difficulties. Several smaller companies went into
ankruptcy, and the larger roads discontinued service on
ɔme of their branch lines. Between 1925 and 1941, there
as a reduction of almost 500 miles of track in the state.[23]

Hardest hit of all railway traffic was the passenger serv-
e, especially the "locals." These three- and four-coach
ains traveled short distances, followed slow schedules, and
opped at every hamlet. Some of the smaller lines met
ιe reduction of passenger traffic by hitching a coach to
ιe rear of a freight. Such a move was met with a further
ıss in customers, for few enjoyed the ordeal of riding a

21. A brief history of these three railroads is in *ibid.,* pp. 215-20.
22. *Fifth Annual Report of the Commissioner of Agriculture* . . .
ᵗ08 (Columbia, S.C.: Gonzales and Bryan, 1909), pp. 45-52.
23. *Sixty-Fourth Annual Report of the Public Service Commission*
. . *1941-1942* (Columbia, S.C.: General Assembly of South Carolina,
ᵗ42), p. 18. The 500 discontinued miles of track include electric
ʳeet railways.

passenger-freight combination. For instance, a round trip from McCormick to Anderson (120 miles) in 1935 required at least ten hours, usually longer. At each of a dozen stops the passengers—if there were any—idled the time as best they could while the locomotive slowly shifted freight cars onto sidings.

2. The South Carolina Highways

The first automobiles came to South Carolina about 1900. Oldsters tell hair-raising tales about the early cars and the terrible roads they traveled on.

Interest in improving roads began in 1895, when the South Carolina government adopted a system of using convict labor to build and repair them. Three years later a "Good Roads Association" was organized and began to agitate for improved roads. A survey in 1904 showed that the state had only about 300 miles of roads surfaced with crushed rock, shells, or stone. There were another 1575 miles of sand-clay roads. When kept in repair, the sand-clay roads were reasonably satisfactory for horse-drawn vehicles. But there were no paved roads in South Carolina and the state annually spent much less than one million dollars on its roads.[24]

The reaction of a small country boy when he first saw an automobile was described by J. M. Eleazer of the Dutch Fork community many years after the incident:

The first automobiles came through our stone hills about 1902. I can just remember it. I was about six. The old folks doubtless read of 'em, for we took *The State*. But we younguns knew nothing of them.

There were three of 'em in this first batch. We were sitting on the porch after dinner. The dusty road a hundred feet out front afforded us glimpses through the bushes that lined it. Here they came chugging along, making a powerful racket and kicking up such a dust it scared us, as we peeped out from behind the skirts of older relatives.

24. *Handbook of South Carolina* (1907), pp. 332-39.

After they had passed, we ventured out to look at their strange tracks and to see that curtain of red dust that floated off down the road.

It was later we learned of the runaway horses that twisted two buggies around trees and tore the harness up.[25]

By the time the United States entered World War I, automobiles were becoming fairly numerous in South Carolina—40,174 motor vehicles were registered that year. During the war, army trucks constantly moved across South Carolina's roads, ever pointing up their inadequacy for handling heavy traffic. One editor commented: "The roads of this state resemble the condition described in the first chapter of Genesis—'without form and void.' "[26]

In 1917 the General Assembly established the State Highway Commission and followed shortly with many changes in the state's highway program. The legislature levied gasoline taxes (two cents a gallon in 1922), motor vehicle taxes, and additional property taxes to support a highway construction program. Through federal legislation in 1917 and 1924, the national government also offered financial aid on a "matching" basis.

In 1925 there were 170,422 registered motor vehicles in South Carolina, and the state highway system then included 4740 miles of roads, 3100 of which were classed as "improved." Yet, only 228 miles of the improved roads were paved. Up to that time, the Highway Department had concentrated on the construction of better dirt roads and the bridging of rivers. The Department built 139 bridges in 1923 and 1924 alone.[27] Previously, there was not a single span across the Santee or across the Savannah

25. J. M. Eleazer, *A Dutch Fork Farm Boy* (Columbia, S.C.: University of South Carolina Press, 1952), pp. 38-39.
26. *The Columbia Record* (S.C.), December 8, 1918, as quoted in Robert M. Burts, "The Public Career of Richard I. Manning" (Ph.D. dissertation, Vanderbilt University, 1957), p. 464.
27. *Annual Report of the State Highway Commission . . . 1924* (Columbia, S.C.: General Assembly of South Carolina, 1925), pp. 20, 47, 82.

between Augusta and Anderson. A traveler from Conway to Charleston via McClellanville had to ferry the Pee Dee, the Black, the Sampit, the Santee, and the Cooper, as well as to cross several miles of "corduroy" roads in the swampy approaches to these streams.

The county roads were usually in poorer condition than the state highways, with the notable exception of Sumter County. At an expense of $4,000,000 this county had paved 137 miles of its roads by 1925.[28]

A trip across the state in 1925 was a slow and tiresome venture. If during the journey the driver strayed from the main road only once or twice, had no flat tires or engine trouble, and reached his destination the same day he started, he considered himself fortunate. In rainy weather it was best not to try to travel at all in most parts of the state. The upcountry roads were too muddy; the lowcountry roads were flooded in swampy areas. In reasonably dry weather, the "corduroy" swamp roads, although rough, were passable.

With the passage of the "Pay-As-You-Go" Highway Act of 1924, the chief burden of financing and maintaining the roads was transferred from the counties to the State Highway Department. Immediately, the road improvement program picked up, particularly with regard to paving. In 1929 the legislature further accelerated the program by adopting a "build-now-pay-later" policy. To help finance this stepped-up building program, the legislature also increased the gasoline tax, which in time became the chief source of revenue for the State Highway Department.

By 1941 the Highway Department had eliminated most "dead man" curves and treacherous railway crossings; it had marked all highways carefully and established a highway patrol. There were 9682 miles of roads in the state

28. Anne K. Gregorie, *History of Sumter County, South Carolina* (Sumter, S.C.: Sumter County Library Board, 1954), pp. 481-82.

South Carolina's Crazy-Quilt, Disconnected System of Paved Roads, 1929. Drawing by David E. Martin from map in *Annual Report of the South Carolina State Highway Department, December 31, 1928,* opposite p. 48.

highway system, of which 6596 were paved. There was hardly a town in South Carolina not reached by a paved highway. The entire highway system, including bridges, was valued at $157,000,000. The system was clearly necessary, for in 1941 there were 361,523 registered motor vehicles in South Carolina, or slightly more than double the number in 1925.[29]

29. *Annual Report of the State Highway Department, 1940-1941* (Columbia, S.C.: General Assembly of South Carolina, 1941), pp. 108, 181, 195-99, 208. A gasoline tax of three cents in 1925 yielded $2,357,171 in income; the tax of six cents in 1940 yielded $11,290,519.

Chapter Five

South Carolina Agriculture, 1865-1941

A. FROM THE WAR TO 1900

1. Effects of the War and Reconstruction on South Carolina Agriculture

The Civil War brought much destruction to rural as well as city property in South Carolina. Many farmers returned from the war to face a desolate homestead. Burned-out buildings and torn-down fences were common wherever troops had been. Thousands of farms suffered simply from neglect, which led to erosion of hilly land, flooding of bottom land, and destruction of dikes and drainage ditches. At the close of the war, livestock and farm tools were scarce, and in many instances the master of the farm had perished in the conflict.

During Republican rule, the South Carolina farmers received little help from the state government. Furthermore, the farmers had to work out a new system of white-black relations. At first this was no easy task, for the freedmen were little inclined to work. Thousands wandered aimlessly and a few even returned to Africa. Nevertheless, before the end of Reconstruction most of the former plantation slaves had again settled down to work.

In view of these and other difficulties, many farmers, both large and small, were unable to meet their financial obligations and consequently lost their lands to banks or other creditors. To add to the agrarian woes, a nation-wide depression struck in 1873, and a wave of bankruptcies followed.

The dispossessed farmers were now forced into tenancy. Since few Negroes had property of their own, most of the ex-slaves likewise became tenants. Some tenants rented land for cash, and a few simply became wage hands. The largest portion of them, however, became sharecroppers, deferring until the harvest their share of the crop.

Farm tenancy was supported by the country merchant. He advanced food, fertilizer, and other supplies while the tenant cultivated the crop. To guard against losses, the merchant took a lien on the future harvest, and when it was ready for market he handled its sale. But the crop lien was risky. Whenever the crop failed or the tenants deserted, the merchant suffered the loss. To protect himself against such misfortunes, the merchant charged a high rate of interest (20 to 75 per cent) on the supplies he advanced. He furthermore insisted that the tenants plant a non-perishable staple for which there was a ready market—cotton, for example.

While it is true that some merchants became rich, others were ruined by the hazards of the system, for cotton production was generally unprofitable from 1873 until 1900. In this era the country suffered from two severe depressions, and during the second cotton dropped to less than five cents a pound ($25 a bale). At that price no matter how hard a tenant family worked they were lucky to have anything left after they met their expenses. Few sharecroppers escaped the unfortunate system into which they had fallen, and other farmers sank to the same economic level. By 1900 approximately 61 of every 100 South Carolina farmers were tenants.[1]

An entirely different type of tenancy existed among the

1. *Thirteenth Census, 1910, Abstract . . . with Supplement for South Carolina* (Washington: [Bureau of Census] Government Printing Office, 1913), p. 608.

Negroes on the Sea Islands. The "two-day" labor system was common in that region. The tenant worked for a landlord for two days per week for ten months each year. In return the tenant received a house, some fuel, and six acres of land for his own use. Each tenant family customarily owned a pig or two, a few chickens, a cow, and perhaps a mule. The Sea Island Negroes planted corn, sweet potatoes, and a little cotton on their plots. To work their crops they depended more on the hoe than the plow.

In the years immediately following the Civil War, the Sea Islanders frequently worked for the railroad or in the phosphate diggings to supplement their small farm income. Their lot was also eased by the plentiful supply of fish and game at hand and by the absence of severe winters.[2]

2. Life on the Farm

Before 1900 farm life was not easy. The work day was long and the work strenuous. The South Carolina farmers, like the textile workers, had no modern conveniences. Nearly every task had to be performed by hand: drawing water, milking cows, churning butter, "chopping" and picking cotton, feeding livestock, and cutting wood. Besides, many farmers tanned their own leather, shod their own mules and horses, ground their own corn meal, and made their own soap.

From early spring to late fall, the farmer began his day's work before sunup and ended it after sundown. His wife usually worked even longer hours than he. She was busy preparing breakfast before he arose. And after supper she often sat up late sewing, churning, cleaning the kitchen, and preparing food for the next day. If she had small children, her lot was doubly hard.

Doctors' visits were rare, and farm folk depended on

2. *South Carolina: Resources and Population, Institutions and Industries* (Charleston, S.C.: [State Board of Agriculture] Walker, Evans and Cogswell, 1883), pp. 29-30.

home remedies and each other for medical care. Nearly all babies were born at home, and many small children died of typhoid fever, diphtheria, pneumonia, and other diseases now no longer common. Malaria was prevalent in the low country, hookworm infected thousands of barefoot school children, and pellagra plagued many farm families whose diet consisted largely of meat, meal, and molasses ("three m's").

No rural home boasted of a central heating plant. The children usually slept in icy rooms in the winter, and his was a painful task who had to arise first and build the fires. In the summertime only those farmers who lived close to towns or railroads enjoyed the luxury of ice. The scarcity of ice and the absence of electric refrigeration forced farm people to rely much on salt meat. Fowls were eaten the same day they were killed. Frequently, farmers organized "beef clubs" in which several families pooled their resources and divided the meat whenever one of their group slaughtered a cow or calf. Hogs were butchered in cold weather ("hog killing time"). To kill, clean, and prepare a hog for the table was an all-day affair in which the entire family, and sometimes neighbors, took part.

In the upcountry, "spring houses" were widely used. These were small latticework sheds built around natural springs. In these sheds families were able for short periods of time to keep milk, butter, and other perishable food from spoiling. Below the fall line, natural springs were not very common. Instead of spring houses some farm families used their wells. Milk and butter were placed in tight jars and lowered by rope into the cool water.

The farm children customarily shared in the work of the home. At an early age boys milked cows, fed the livestock, plowed, and chopped cotton. Even the girls worked in the cotton fields. Rural schools ran at most about four or five months each year, and education interfered little with farm children's work.

Rural recreation in South Carolina was generally conditioned by two significant factors: poor transportation facilities and a scarcity of ready cash. Thus most formalized entertainment was restricted to inexpensive pleasures on week ends in good weather. And most country children's games were those which required no "store bought" equipment. During the slack seasons ("lay by" time, Christmas, etc.), rural folks enjoyed picnics, fishing, swimming, hunting, church suppers, weddings, family reunions, community singing conventions, and religious revivals.

Of course, there were large planters whose lives did not fit into the pattern just described. Some of these families survived the Civil War with their holdings intact. Others were the *nouveaux riches* who had acquired property in the confusion of the Reconstruction era.

With a retinue of household servants the planter class enjoyed leisure that the less fortunate rural folk could not afford. The planters entertained lavishly in a style reminiscent of the ante-bellum period. Their sons and daughters went to college, if they wished, and usually "married well." Moreover, the well-to-do planter was a social and political leader in his community. Tenants and small independent farmers looked to him for guidance.

In sum, before 1900 most farmers worked hard, earned little cash money, and enjoyed very few of the comforts that were commonplace in 1960. More than one-half of them did not even own the soil that they tilled.

3. *Attempts to Improve Farm Conditions*

The poor economic condition of South Carolina agriculture was partly responsible for the organization of the Patrons of Husbandry (the Grange). In 1866 Oliver H. Kelley toured the South in order to report on conditions to President Andrew Johnson. Kelley discovered that the farmers needed increased social relationship with one another to relieve them of the monotony of their work and to enable them to work together for their common benefit. He therefore organized the Patrons of Husbandry, and in time the movement swept over the South and Midwest.

Dr. Daniel Harrison Jacques was responsible for the Grange's coming to South Carolina. He began publication in 1869 of *The Rural Carolinian,* a magazine devoted to "agriculture, horticulture, and the industrial arts." Within two years, Dr. Jacques, with Kelley's encouragement, had organized the Ashley Grange No. 1, the first subordinate Grange to be set up in the South.[3]

The Patrons progressed slowly in South Carolina until the energetic D. Wyatt Aiken entered the picture. Aiken, an ex-Confederate colonel, a newspaper writer, and a successful Abbeville County farmer, was appointed deputy-at-large for the Southern states in December, 1871. He plunged wholeheartedly into the cause and by February, 1873, there were more than 100 active Granges in the state.

The Granger movement reached its height in South Carolina in 1875, when there were 332 Granges and more than 10,000 members. That same year the Patrons held their national convention in Charleston.

The Patrons held meetings once or twice a month, usually in churches, schoolhouses, or regular Grange halls. A part of each program was designed to be instructive —an essay, a lecture, a debate. Grange meetings also provided recreation—sings, picnics, suppers, and the like. Women were welcomed to membership. The majority of the Grange members, however, joined in the hope of material benefits from the organization. The Patrons in South Carolina, as

3. For activities of the Grange in South Carolina, see Solon J. Buck, *The Granger Movement* (Cambridge, Mass.: Harvard University Press, 1913); J. H. Easterby, "The Granger Movement in South Carolina," *Proceedings* of the South Carolina Historical Association, 1931, pp. 21-32.

elsewhere, emphasized the advantages of farmers' cooperatives for buying supplies and selling farm produce. Many more visionary projects were planned than were actually attempted. *The Rural Carolinian's* columns were filled with discussions of cooperative ventures.

The political influence of the Grange was limited, partly due to the fact that the order had begun to decline before Reconstruction ended in South Carolina. Nevertheless, the Patrons were instrumental in securing the establishment of the office of Railroad Commissioner (1878) and the South Carolina Department of Agriculture (1879). Several later measures for the benefit of the farmers were due to Grange influence. Meanwhile, in Washington, Congressman D. Wyatt Aiken became the chief sponsor of the bill, adopted in 1889, which raised the Bureau of Agriculture to cabinet rank.

The Grange decline in South Carolina was due to several circumstances: disagreement with the national headquarters over matters of policy, failure of the cooperatives to produce expected benefits, hard times following the Panic of 1873, the absorption of the farmers in politics in 1876-77, and finally, general apathy.

Notwithstanding its decline and eventual failure, the Grange had some lasting significance. The farmers gained experience in cooperation in both politics and business. And especially worth noting is the fact that the movement was essentially one of farmers rather than planters, and one of upcountry farmers rather than lowcountry farmers. The Patrons of Husbandry presaged a greater farm revolution to come in the late 1880's, headed by the Farmers' Association under Tillman and by the Farmers' Alliance.

Tillman and the Farmers' Association were primarily interested in politics,[4] but the Farmers' Alliance, entering South Carolina in late 1887, was mainly concerned with

4. See Chapter II.

sponsoring economic reform divorced from political action. The moving force behind the organization of the Alliance in South Carolina was Colonel L. L. Polk, an Alliance leader from North Carolina. The first state meeting was held in June, 1888, and Colonel Eli T. Stackhouse, Marion County, was chosen president. Within two years the organization had spread to every county in the state and counted 37,000 members. Its leaders participated in the councils of the national organization.[5]

The Alliance's first battle was directed against the jute-bagging trust in 1888. This fight was carried out on a South-wide basis. Jute prices at 11 cents a pound were considered exorbitant by the farmers. The Alliance therefore boycotted the jute trust and by using substitutes forced the price back to two cents a pound the following year. The same year the Alliance actively supported the move to establish Clemson College. Several members of the first Clemson board of trustees were Alliance men.

In other economic schemes the South Carolina Alliance was not so successful. Attempts at state-wide buying of fertilizer and selling of cotton broke down because the county Alliances could not agree to pursue common methods. The largest undertaking of the Alliance was a state exchange, set up in November, 1889, under the elaborate control of nine directors, a president, a secretary-treasurer, and a business manager. Its permanent location was in Columbia, where it was chiefly directed during most of its brief history by D. P. Duncan, the business manager after 1892.

By 1894 the state exchange boasted of $225,000 capital and a surplus of $17,000. Its business dealings were mainly with various county exchanges and on a cash basis. But

5. For Alliance beginnings in South Carolina, see Joseph Church, "The Farmers' Alliance and the Populist Movement in South Carolina (1887-1896)" (Master's thesis, University of South Carolina, 1953), pp. 14-23.

after 1896 business declined rapidly and the exchange suspended operation in 1899. Its failure was probably due to the parallel decline of the Alliance, the inability of Duncan to devote full time to its management, and the scarcity of cash held by county exchanges.

Working in cooperation with the white Alliance was a Colored Alliance, established in South Carolina in June, 1889, under the guidance of a white superintendent. Although the Colored Alliance boasted of 40,000 members, it attempted only one cooperative enterprise of which there is record, a state colored exchange in Charleston.[6]

With regard to politics, the white state Alliance consistently followed an official non-partisan attitude, but several county Alliances came out for Tillman after the Democratic convention of August, 1890. And many Alliance members were candidates for office on the Democratic ticket. After the 1890 election, there were approximately 55 Alliancemen in the General Assembly. A few, however, classed themselves as Bourbon or Conservative Democrats.[7]

At the Alliance state convention in July, 1891, Ben Tillman and an Alliance spokesman from Texas, Ben Terrell, debated the Southern Alliance program and the feasibility of organizing a third party. The debate was held behind closed doors on the last day of the convention. Tillman voiced his opposition to a third party, the subtreasury plan, and government ownership of the railroads. Reports filtered out that only six delegates voted for the Tillman view. The next year Tillman found it politically expedient to endorse the Alliance's economic program. In the meanwhile, however, many Tillmanites had departed from the Alliance. The Alliance was further damaged when a few of its members joined the Populist Party. Subtreasury was a dead issue shortly, and when the Democrats

6. The Alliance economic programs are described in *ibid.*, pp. 24-32.
7. *Ibid.*, pp. 47-48.

adopted "free silver" in 1896, the Alliance had little further appeal. Its economic program had largely failed, and politics had torn it apart. The South Carolina Alliance disintegrated, as did the national organization.[8]

B. TWENTIETH CENTURY CONDITIONS

1. Returning Agricultural Prosperity, 1900-1921

Despite hard times and considerable political agitation among the farmers, the state showed some agricultural progress between 1870 and 1900. During those years, cotton production rose from 224,000 to 837,000 bales per year; the oat crop increased fourfold, the corn crop doubled, rice production increased 47 per cent; and the hay crop increased by 20 times. Furthermore, about 1890 F. M. Rogers of Florence introduced the cultivation of the bright-leaf tobacco. Within ten years this new crop was annually worth over a million dollars.[9]

With the turn of the century South Carolina farmers began to enjoy renewed prosperity. The establishment of Clemson College also bore fruit. At its opening in 1893, Clemson, with 446 students, had the largest student body of any college in the state. Two outstanding examples of the results of agricultural education for South Carolina men were the awards won by A. J. Tindal, a Clemson-educated farmer of Clarendon County, and Jerry Moore, a Florence County schoolboy. Tindal won a world prize offered in 1906 by *The American Agriculturalist* for growing 182 bushels of corn per acre. Four years later young Moore also won a world prize for growing corn—228.75 bushels per acre.[10]

8. *Ibid.*, pp. 51-52, 75-76.
9. *Handbook of South Carolina* (Columbia, S.C.: State Department of Agriculture, Commerce and Immigration, 1907), p. 249; David Duncan Wallace, *The History of South Carolina* (4 vols.; New York: American Historical Society, 1934), III, 397.
10. *South Carolina, a Handbook* (Columbia, S.C.: State Department of Agriculture, Commerce and Industry, 1927), p. 136.

The teaching program of Clemson College and the experimental work of the United States Department of Agriculture (USDA) did not at first reach many of the farm tenants and small independent farmers. Seaman Knapp, a prominent agriculturalist working in Texas, believed that the reason Southern farmers were not nearly so prosperous as those in the North was that many did not know about the latest methods of scientific agriculture. He therefore persuaded the General Education Board, a charitable educational organization, to establish demonstration farms throughout the South. The USDA aided the program.

Under Seaman Knapp's program, a number of farmers were asked to volunteer their farms for the cultivation of crops according to the methods approved by the USDA. Their neighbors were then invited to witness the results and learn accordingly. Those farmers who volunteered their farms were, in return, guaranteed against money losses. By 1913 nearly every South Carolina county had one or more demonstration farms.[11]

Next, Clemson College entered into an agreement with the USDA to provide supervision of all types of agricultural demonstration work then conducted in the state. The demonstration method of teaching was made nation-wide in 1914 by the Smith-Lever Act, named in honor of Congressman A. Frank Lever of South Carolina and Senator Hoke Smith of Georgia. Within ten years of the passage of the Smith-Lever Act, South Carolina was employing 42 county agents, 14 agricultural specialists, and 36 home-demonstration agents.[12]

South Carolina quickly began to use some of its county agents to give instruction in agriculture in the public schools. This program was broadened in 1917 by the

11. Knapp's work is described in C. Vann Woodward, *Origins of the New South, 1877-1913* (Baton Rouge, La.: Louisiana State University Press, 1951), pp. 409-13.
12. *South Carolina, a Handbook* (1927), p. 119.

Smith-Hughes Act which provided federal funds for vocational training in the public schools. A state survey in 1925 showed that approximately 3900 white and 1750 colored pupils were enrolled in vocational education classes, a majority studying agriculture.[13]

During World War I the American government greatly encouraged increased agricultural production. The farmers soon enjoyed prosperity such as they had never seen before, as the world demand for American agricultural products outdistanced the supply. Cotton prices skyrocketed to 40 cents a pound, while tobacco soared to 30 cents. The value of South Carolina agricultural production rose from $166,000,000 in 1913 to $446,000,000 in 1918. Part of this increase was due to inflation. None the less, the inflated dollar permitted many debt-ridden farmers to pay off their financial obligations and even to purchase additional equipment and farm land.[14]

2. *Two Decades of Agricultural Depression, 1921-1941*

The wartime farm prosperity collapsed in 1921 with the advent of another sharp, though short-lived, depression. The American farmer was hit especially hard because of rapidly expanding agricultural production in Europe and elsewhere. Prices of cotton, tobacco, wheat, livestock, and other farm products plunged downward. Thus began 20 years of farm depression.

To add to the South Carolina farmers' woes, the boll weevil invaded the state during the war. By 1921 this pest was causing havoc in every county. Before measures of control could be instituted, the weevil destroyed almost 50 per cent of the South Carolina cotton crop in some years. Several dry growing seasons in the mid-twenties added

13. *Ibid.*, p. 120.
14. *Fifteenth Annual Report of the Commissioner of Agriculture . . . 1918* (Columbia, S.C.: Gonzales and Bryan, 1919), p. 5; *Sixteenth, 1919*, p. 5.

further to the farmers' hardships. Then in 1929 another general depression began. As times became worse, cotton prices dropped to five cents a pound and tenancy increased until two-thirds of the South Carolina farmers were working on someone else's land. South Carolina farm wages in 1933 were 50 cents per day with board, rivaling Mississippi and Georgia as the lowest in the United States.[15]

The depression of 1929 forced several score of South Carolina banks into bankruptcy. Most of these institutions failed because of heavy loans to farmers and a subsequent decline in agricultural prices. By March, 1933, several South Carolina counties were without the services of a single bank.

At this juncture President Roosevelt inaugurated the "New Deal," which included a number of measures designed to aid the stricken farmers. The federal government set up several agricultural lending agencies; it fostered soil conservation and reforestation; and it sought to eliminate overproduction of crops.

The New Deal farm measures were bolstered by the Clemson College agricultural program and at least one outstanding private research organization, the Coker Pedigreed Seed Company, founded in 1914 by David R. Coker of Hartsville. Coker's work included the development of several dozen varieties and strains of cotton, one of which grew fiber to a length of one and five-sixteenths inches. Meanwhile, to combat the boll weevil Coker devised an effective method of mixing poison with molasses before application to the cotton plants.

David R. Coker's experiments also led to improved varieties of wheat, sweet potatoes, rye, tobacco, asparagus, soybeans, and oats. He and his company received nation-

15. South Carolina Agricultural Experiment Station, *Bulletin No. 312* (October, 1937); Alfred G. Smith, Sr., "Agriculture," *South Carolina: Economic and Social Conditions in 1944*, ed. Wilfred H. Callcott (Columbia, S.C.: University of South Carolina Press, 1945), p. 114.

wide recognition for their agricultural research and educational work. Some 3000 to 4000 persons annually visited the Coker laboratories, and one agriculturist claimed that David R. Coker "did more for the farmers of South Carolina than any other man has ever done."[16]

Slowly the state recovered from the depression, and by 1940 there was a decided improvement in agriculture. South Carolina's crop production was up from a low of $63,000,000 in 1932 to $119,600,000. Rural electrification, begun in 1935, reached one-fourth of the South Carolina farm dwellings by 1940, while tenancy dropped from a high of 65 per cent (1930) to 56 per cent. The 1941 wheat, oat, hay, rye, and peach crops were the largest in the state's history. With the outbreak of the war in Europe the South Carolina farmer appeared to be headed for boom times.[17]

Yet, when measured against the nation's standard, the South Carolina farmer fell pitifully short. Tenancy, although falling in the state, ran about 20 per cent above the national average. Only Mississippi, Georgia, Alabama, and Louisiana had higher tenancy ratios in 1940 than South Carolina. Moreover, in South Carolina the tenant's farm was valued at an average of only $1657 and the owner's at an average of $2461, compared to national averages of $4569 and $5518, respectively. Finally, the average per capita farm income for South Carolina in 1940 was $147; the average for the United States was $318.[18]

16. David R. Coker was one of several prominent sons of Major James L. Coker, who was a pioneer industrialist and successful businessman in the Darlington-Hartsville area. Helen K. Hennig, *Great South Carolinians of a Later Date* (Chapel Hill, N.C.: University of North Carolina Press, 1949), pp. 203-24.

17. *Year Book of the Department of Agriculture . . . 1932-33* (Columbia, S.C.: General Assembly of South Carolina, 1933), p. 12; *1940-41*, pp. 19-25. Also, *Statistical Abstract of the United States, 1942* (Washington: Government Printing Office, 1943), pp. 709, 730.

18. *Ibid., 1943*, pp. 575, 588-89; Smith, in *South Carolina: Economic and Social Conditions in 1944*, p. 103.

There were several reasons for the South Carolina lag behind the states of the Northeast and Midwest. First, the state had very little first-class farm land. USDA studies showed that most of the South Carolina soil was third class or poorer. Low crop yields supported this dismal revelation. For instance, in 1940 the state's corn yield was 14.7 bushels per acre, compared to a national average of 32. South Carolina was compelled to spend a disproportionate amount of money for fertilizer to push yields as high as they were. In 1940 South Carolina purchased 686,000 tons of fertilizer and Iowa 16,000.[19]

Another reason for low agricultural income was the low educational level of many South Carolina citizens, especially the tenant farmers. From the Civil War until 1924, the state attempted to do little more than provide an elementary education for white children and even less for Negroes. Hence, in 1940, 62.3 per cent of the Negroes over twenty-five and 17.9 per cent of the white adults had completed no more than four years of school.[20]

Also, there was a lack of crop diversification in South Carolina. As recently as 1935, three-fourths of the state's cultivated land was planted either in cotton or in corn.[21] Many farm families were buying foodstuffs they could have produced at home. Under the New Deal, the federal government encouraged and aided diversification, but the state had a long way to go. There was less diversification in 1935 than in 1870: rice and Sea Island cotton were no longer grown, and sheep raising had all but disappeared. All three were victims of changing conditions and outside competition.

Autumn storms in 1910 and 1911 administered the

19. *Ibid.*, pp. 106-7; *Statistical Abstract, 1942*, p. 733.
20. *United States Census of Population: 1950* (3 vols.; Washington: [Bureau of Census] Government Printing Office, 1952), II, Part 1, 244-45.
21. South Carolina Agricultural Experiment Station, *Bulletin No. 312*, p. 30.

coup de grâce to the dying rice industry, while the boll weevil in 1919 struck the Sea Island cotton such a devastating blow (90 per cent crop failure) that the planters gave up the crop.[22]

One writer stated in 1941: "Considering that the population of the State is now almost three times what it was in 1850, it is evident that food crops have by no means increased in the same ratio. Tobacco and truck produce have replaced rice as a source of income, but nothing has replaced it as a food crop." And in conclusion: "Whether the South Carolinian likes it or not, the future of agriculture in the State depends on grass, cattle, and legumes. These are matters within the control of the South Carolina farmers themselves."[23]

22. For the history of rice culture in South Carolina, see Duncan C. Heyward, *Seed from Madagascar* (Chapel Hill, N.C.: University of North Carolina Press, 1937). As late as 1905 about 50,000 acres of long staple cotton were cultivated on Sea Islands, producing 12,500 bales. *South Carolina Handbook* (1907), pp. 279-83; *Sixteenth Annual Report, Commissioner of Agriculture, 1919*, p. 36.

23. *South Carolina: a Guide to the Palmetto State* ("WPA Guide Series" [New York: Oxford University Press, 1941]), p. 60.

Chapter Six

Education and Religion, 1865-1941

Table 4 shows a steady decline in illiteracy in South Carolina from 1880 onward. But improvement in educational achievement failed to keep pace with the national average.

A. THE DECLINE IN IGNORANCE

1. The Public Schools

The foundations for the twentieth-century public school system in South Carolina were laid in the Constitution of 1868, which called for free public education without segregation for all children of school age. Yet no attempt was made to integrate whites and blacks in the public schools. Radical Governor Scott and the school commission viewed with disfavor the racial mixing of school children, and Radical Superintendent of Education Justus K. Jillson did not seek integration.

Under the Radical program, public schools were financed by a combination of state appropriations, a poll tax, and local district taxes. Each county was divided into school districts. Uniform textbooks were selected, and the voters chose county superintendents of education and county commissioners to direct the schools.

Besides the state-supported schools there were many private schools and academies for both races established at the close of the war. The greatest number of such schools were those operated briefly by the Freedmen's Bureau of the federal government. Freedmen's Bureau schools and

TABLE 4
EDUCATIONAL ACHIEVEMENT STATISTICS

	Illiterates: persons over ten unable to read or write			Illiterates and semi-literates: adults over twenty-five who completed not over 4 years of school	
	1880*	1910	1930	1940†	1950†
U. S. Average............	17%	7.7%	4.3%	13.5%	10.8%
S. C. Average...........	55.4%	25.7%	14.9%	34.8%‡	27.4%
S. C. Native Whites Av...	21.9%	10.3%	5.1%	17.9%	15.3%
S. C. Negroes Av........	78.5%	38.7%	26.9%	62.3%	51.3%

* Unable to write only.
† Bureau of the Census changed its method of measuring educational achievement.
‡ S. C. ranked forty-seventh of 48 states. Only Louisiana had a higher illiteracy rate.
  Sources: Statistics of the Population of the United States . . . (June 1, 1880) . . ., pp. 919-20, 924; *Thirteenth Census, 1910: Abstract . . . with Supplement for South Carolina*, p. 587; *Census of Population: 1950*, II, Part 1, 244-45, Part 40, 33; *Statistical Abstract of the U. S., 1912*, p. 78, *1932*, p. 33, *1942*, p. 133; *Sixty-third Annual Report of the State Superintendent of Education of the State of South Carolina, 1931*, pp. 78-80.

other private schools received much support from Northern philanthropic agencies, while employing both Northern and Southern teachers. All schools used whatever buildings and equipment were available.[1]

The Radicals' elaborate program attracted thousands of young whites and Negroes to school. Superintendent Jillson tried to carry out the provisions of the law. Still, the results of education during Reconstruction were unsatisfactory. Jillson discovered that the legislature was slow to provide financial support for the schools. In his annual report of 1873, he complained that a school deficiency appropriation of $75,000 for 1871 had not yet been disbursed and that over two-thirds of the $300,000 appropriation for 1873 remained unpaid. He pointed out, moreover, that many school officials were "eminently disqualified" for their positions and that a large majority of the state-employed teachers were "wholly unworthy, either

1. Francis B. Simkins and Robert H. Woody, *South Carolina during Reconstruction* (Chapel Hill, N.C.: University of North Carolina Press, 1932), pp. 416-34.

morally or intellectually," to instruct their charges. As for buildings, Jillson noted that 1129 of 1908 schoolhouses in use were constructed of logs.[2] Under these conditions thousands of school children received, at best, only a smattering of education.

For several years after the Democrats regained control of South Carolina in 1877, there was little noticeable improvement in the school program. Had it not been for the manful efforts of Superintendent of Education Hugh S. Thompson (1877-82), public education might well have suffered serious retrogression. In spite of financial reorganization, increased school attendance, and the appointment of a State Board of Examiners, Thompson encountered much the same difficulties that had beset Jillson: inefficiency of some school commissioners, poorly trained personnel, insufficiency of funds, and indifference to education in "some portions" of the state.[3]

The reduction of the impoverished state's meager school appropriations threw the burden of education largely on the individual school districts. Some of the poorest districts were thus left without schools in the 1880's. This was in keeping with the political philosophy of the dominant Conservative Democrats. When the Abbeville *Press and Banner* asked a number of "leading men" in the state if they favored the two-mill tax for educational purposes, the replies were 35 nays to seven yeas. The same paper, on another occasion, editorially commented: "The great army of teachers, at present, we believe constitute the only organized raiders on the public treasury. . . . We think that it is about time the teachers were working to earn their living."[4]

2. *Fifth Annual Report of the State Superintendent of Education . . . 1873* (Columbia, S.C.: Republican Printing Company, 1873), pp. 7-11, 57-61—hereinafter cited as *Annual Report, Supt. Educ.*
3. *Annual Report, Supt. Educ., 1878* (Columbia, S.C.: Calvo and Patton, 1878), pp. 5, 11.
4. Quoted in Paul Knox, "The Development of Education in Abbe-

Eventually, in 1888, the General Assembly passed a law permitting school districts to increase their taxes for school purposes. Through this step some schools were re-opened. However, during the entire period of Conservative Democratic rule (1877-90), the plight of the public schools was appalling.

During those years, most South Carolina school children attended one-teacher schools in ill-equipped log or frame buildings. The pupils studied the alphabet, reading, writing, arithmetic (mental and written), spelling, geography, English grammar, and American history. Advanced students in a few schools studied the "higher branches." School terms varied from two to three months in the poorer counties to eight or nine in Charleston, while teachers' salaries ranged from $15 to $35 per month, except in Charleston and a few towns.[5]

To attend a typical one-teacher rural school, the pupils first of all had to walk there, sometimes four or five miles for the more distant students. After school "took in," the day was an endless succession of classes being called to the front bench to recite. The time allotted to each recitation varied greatly, perhaps five minutes for spelling for one class, 20 minutes for arithmetic for another, and so on until the end of the school day.

When not reciting, pupils were expected to sit quietly and study. Often the teacher, if a stern disciplinarian, interrupted the recitations to descend upon some unruly pupil in the study group. Besides inflicting corporal punishment, the teacher required some disorderly students to chop wood for the school's pot-bellied stove and clean the building after hours.

A school administrator might be no less busy. The superintendent of the Greenville public schools (1890-

---

ville County, South Carolina" (Master's thesis, University of South Carolina, 1929), pp. 63-65.

5. See *Annual Report, Supt. Educ.,* 1878-1890, *passim.*

1914) was, by his count, "bookkeeper, treasurer, buyer, business manager, secretary, telephone operator, full corps of supervision, band leader, hirer and firer, and wielder of the rod of correction." He visited each school room in the system twice a week and held two teachers' meetings per week, one for whites and one for Negroes.[6]

In 1895 Ben Tillman's Constitutional Convention reorganized the state's public school system. The new Constituition provided for a State Board of Education, to be composed of the governor, the superintendent of education, and an additional number of persons (not to exceed seven) appointed by the governor. The Board was to regulate teachers' examinations for qualifying certificates. The Constitution also provided for free public education for children of both races on a segregated basis. School districts were to be not less than nine nor more than 49 square miles each. To support the schools, the Constitution provided for a poll tax, to go to the respective school districts in which collected. "Surplus" liquor license monies, escheated property, undesignated gifts to the state, and several other minor sources of revenue were to go into the state school fund. In addition, the school districts were empowered to levy property taxes for school purposes. However, any local unit of government was prohibited from increasing its bonded indebtedness above 8 per cent of the assessed value of its taxable property.[7]

With these changes the public schools, especially the white schools, began to improve. By 1923, as shown in Table 5, considerable progress had been achieved.

In 1923 the Negro schools were greatly inferior to the white. With the restoration of Democratic control in South

6. E. L. Hughes, "Recollections of Educational Conditions and Activities in South Carolina, 1890-1914" (MS in South Caroliniana Library, University of South Carolina, Columbia, S.C.).

7. Inez Watson (ed.), *Constitution . . . of the State of South Carolina as Amended, April 2, 1954* (Columbia, S.C.: State Budget and Control Board, 1954), Art. X, Sect. 5; and Art. XI, Sects. 1-7, 11-12.

TABLE 5
SOUTH CAROLINA PUBLIC SCHOOL STATISTICS

	Total Enrollment		Average Daily Attendance		Number of Pupils Enrolled per Teacher	
	White	Negro	White	Negro	White	Negro
1890................	93,024	116,535	67,599	81,004	..	..
1907................	144,668	169,731	103,304	118,885	40	64
1923-24.............	238,909	228,516	169,261	155,561	32	62
1929-30.............	248,200	221,170	192,477	156,005	27	48
1939-40.............	265,845	215,905	222,800	162,195	28	38

	Number of Schools		Number of Teachers		Length of School Term	
	White	Negro	White	Negro	White	Negro
1890................	3,621		2537	1622	70 days	
1907................	2652	2343	3688	2540	116½ days	74 days
1923-24.............	2181	2413	7889	3677	159 days	97 days
1929-30.............	1744	2349	8888	4592	173 days	117 days
1939-40.............	1785	2343	9398	5644	175 days	147 days

	Annual School Expenses		Current Expense per Pupil Enrolled		Classroom Teachers' Average Salaries	
	White	Negro	White	Negro	White	Negro
1890................	$426,250		$2.03			
1907................	$ 1,148,474	$ 267,250	$ 8.00	$ 1.57	$ 267 yr.	$ 95 yr.
1923-24.............	$11,561,850	$1,400,151	$48.39	$ 6.13	$ 885 yr.	$262 yr.
1929-30.............	$14,417,449	$1,769,868	$58.09	$ 8.00	$ 1048 yr.	$320 yr.
1939-40.............	$15,383,186	$2,460,374	$46.80	$11.40	$ 939 yr.	$388 yr.

Sources: Annual Report of the State Superintendent of Education, 1890, 1907, 1923-24, 1929-30, 1939-40 passim.

Carolina in 1877, the state government came under considerable pressure to reduce educational expenses, especially for Negro schools. Many whites disliked the whole educational program because it was begun by the Radicals, it implied racial equality, it might "spoil" good Negro field hands, and it might improve the Negro's political potential. Nevertheless, during Governor Hampton's administration the state's school expenses per school child were increased from $1.85 to $2.70 for members of both races. Beginning with the school year 1879-80, inequalities were apparent. By the time the Constitution of 1895 was written, the state had raised its expenses per white pupil to $3.11, while reducing expenses per Negro pupil to $1.05.[8]

8. George B. Tindall, *South Carolina Negroes, 1877-1900* (Columbia, S.C.: University of South Carolina Press, 1952), pp. 212-16.

For many years this inequality continued. In 1911 W. K. Tate, the state's first elementary rural school supervisor, reported: "The negro school houses are miserable beyond description. . . . Most of the teachers are absolutely untrained and have been given certificates by the County Board not because they have passed the examination, but because it is necessary to have some kind of a negro teacher. Among the negro rural schools I have visited, I have found only one in which the highest class has known the multiplication table."[9]

Only in Charleston did the Negro schools compare at all favorably with white. For years the city operated two grammar schools for Negro children through the fifth grade. Influenced by the Booker T. Washington educational philosophy, the city in 1911 added a colored industrial school to teach horticulture, carpentry, cabinetmaking, shoe cobbling, blacksmithing, and domestic science to advanced students. For teachers the city relied on whites exclusively.

In 1916 the Charleston Colored Ministerial Union petitioned the school commissioners for a third grammar school, a sixth grade for all grammar schools, a regular high school curriculum to be added at the industrial school, and the employment of Negro teachers. Sympathetic to their pleas, the board by 1924 had met all their requests.[10]

In establishing its colored industrial school, Charleston obtained money from the Peabody and Slater funds which, along with the Rosenwald Fund and the General Education Board, rendered financial aid to many other Negro schools in the state. In 1900 South Carolina schools received $130,000 from these four agencies. Through those private

9. *Annual Report, Supt. Educ., 1911* (Columbia, S.C.: Gonzales and Bryan, 1912), p. 115.

10. In replacing white teachers with blacks, the school board was careful not to mix the two races in the same school. B. R. Moore, "A History of the Negro Public Schools of Charleston. S.C., 1868-1942" (Master's thesis, University of South Carolina, 1942), pp. 30-41.

sources and through gradual increases in state aid, a few towns in South Carolina improved their Negro schools, several of which offered some high school instruction (about 20 in 1925). But it was not until 1929 that the first Negro pupils received state high school diplomas (at Columbia, Darlington, and Union).[11]

In 1924 the General Assembly passed a significant school measure, commonly known as the "6-0-1" law. This act was especially intended to aid the poor school districts. In 1923-24, Greenwood County spent only $31.63 per white pupil enrolled, compared to $99.77 spent by Charleston. The same wide variation occurred in the Negro schools. Charleston and Hampton counties spent $18.01 and $2.29, respectively, per Negro pupil. At that time the white school properties were valued at $25,500,000, compared to less than $3,000,000 for the black schools.[12]

By the terms of the "6-0-1" law, the state would pay six months of teachers' salaries if local authorities furnished funds for the seventh. The state also set about consolidating a large number of small schools and establishing more high schools, including the first accredited Negro high schools. But unfortunately, this promising program was halted in 1930 by the depression. For several years thereafter the legislature found it necessary to reduce public school appropriations. It cut salaries, curtailed building programs, and reduced school terms. The lost ground was hardly recovered before 1940. Appropriations were then slightly higher than in 1930 and distributed more equitably between the two races, although still about four to one in favor of white students. The value of the white school property in 1940 was $45,800,000 and that of the Negro $7,100,000. Another particularly glaring discrepancy ex-

11. *Annual Report, Supt. Educ., 1900* (Columbia, S.C.: State Company, 1901), pp. 60, 264; *ibid., 1930* (Columbia, S.C.: General Assembly of South Carolina, 1930), pp. 14, 18.
12. *Ibid., 1924*, pp. 9, 114-15.

isted in the use of buses by school children; there were hardly any for Negro pupils.[13]

Compared to other American states, South Carolina made a poor showing in 1940. The average salary of all American teachers was $1441 per year, of South Carolina teachers, $743. Only Arkansas and Mississippi ranked lower. Current expenses per pupil enrolled for the United States were $81.50, for South Carolina $34.08. Only three states fell below the South Carolina average.[14]

2. Special Phases of Public Education

a. High Schools

Prior to 1907, South Carolina high school students had either to rely on the preparatory departments of the colleges or to attend one of several tuition-charging private high schools widely scattered over the state. That same year the State Department of Education inaugurated a regular state-supported high school program. Within 12 months, 101 high schools were in operation, although they were mainly one-, two-, and three-teacher institutions with less than 100 pupils each.

The state high school inspector until 1919 was Professor William H. Hand, of the University's Department of Education. His lengthy annual reports revealed the fumbling inadequacies of the new program. It was in high school education that the state's educational system was weakest, so Professor Hand believed. He pointed out that the religious groups and philanthropists had long neglected secondary education.[15]

As the program was initiated, every three-teacher grammar school that could possibly find the required minimum

13. *Ibid.*, *1940*, p. 145. In 1941 the state furnished transportation or 82,000 whites and 442 Negroes. *Ibid.*, *1941*, p. 178.

14. *Statistical Abstract of the United States, 1942* (Washington: Government Printing Office, 1943), pp. 136-37.

15. *Annual Report, Supt. Educ., 1910* (Columbia, S.C.: Gonzales and Bryan, 1910), p. 130.

of 15 students for high school grades tried to open a high school. Laurens County serves as an example of the educational waste that followed. In 1910, there were eight two- and three-year high schools in the county. Altogether they employed 14 teachers for 338 pupils. But not a single Laurens County high school offered the fourth year of instruction, nor was there any laboratory equipment for science courses. In fact, all the teaching apparatus "would not equip one good high school." It was such a situation that caused 58 so-called high schools in 26 counties to fail between 1907 and 1917.[16]

The teachers in the small high schools were forced to cut instruction periods to 20, or at most 30, minutes in order to crowd classes for two or three grades into the day's schedule. Hand concluded that a four-year high school with but one course of study could not properly be taught by fewer than three teachers. On that basis he listed only 13 four-year public high schools in 1910.[17] With the exception of Charleston, no college town supported a four-year high school, for college preparatory departments in their eagerness for students discouraged the establishment of state-supported high schools in their vicinity.

The curriculums of the first high schools were severely restricted courses of study, primarily intended to prepare students for college. Of the 101 high schools in 1908, all offered arithmetic, algebra, history, English grammar and literature, and Latin, but only 11 taught French, 10 bookkeeping, 8 German, 6 botany, 5 agriculture, 3 trigonometry, and 2 chemistry. And, as mentioned, many schools were poorly equipped with scientific apparatus.[18]

The teachers of the high schools often attempted to give instruction in courses for which they had little or no preparation. On this subject Hand reported that the "poorest

16. *Ibid., 1908*, pp. 93-103, *1910*, pp. 143-48, *1917*, pp. 64-65.
17. *Ibid., 1910*, p. 147.
18. *Ibid., 1908*, pp. 100-3.

teaching" was in the subject of English, which had "the least definite aim and organized purpose in it." As for Latin, the next poorest taught, men and women who were wholly ignorant of the subject were trying to teach it. While in many schools history was either "a grind of unfamiliar names and meaningless dates" or "a line for line repetition of some text-book." The inspector blamed the situation on the lack of examinations of teacher fitness in the subjects to be taught.[19]

In 1915 Professor Hand noted much improvement in high school instruction but still maintained that many teachers, although having college degrees, were trying to teach subjects for which they were ill prepared. As evidence he noted that the sale of language "ponies" exclusively to teachers was a lucrative business within the state.[20] A new high school law abolished the one-teacher high schools in 1915, and by 1921 the high school program, though still lagging in the teaching of science, showed marked improvement. All of the 148 schools then in operation were either three- or four-year high schools, while 136 ran nine-month terms. All but 17 per cent of the high school teachers held bachelor's degrees.[21]

During the 1920's the high schools also began to expand their extracurricular activities. The South Carolina High School League had been organized as early as 1913 to encourage interscholastic competition in athletics, debating, and scholarship, but such competition was limited until the early twenties. In 1925 there were 123 schools in the League. So intense had become the drive for high school athletics that some people worried about its overemphasis. The South Carolina High School Debating League (or-

19. *Ibid., 1910,* p. 137.
20. *Ibid., 1915,* p. 153.
21. The teaching time was concentrated in mathematics (24.6 per cent), English (18.8 per cent), Latin (14.6 per cent), history (14.4 per cent), natural science (12 per cent), and vocational subjects (11.2 per cent). *Ibid., 1916,* p. 71, *1921,* pp. 116-34.

ganized 1917-18) entered the fray by adopting the following topic for its 1923 state-wide contest: "Resolved, that present tendencies in high school athletics are hurtful."[22]

The question of overemphasis did not get beyond the talking stage. More and more high schools organized interscholastic athletic teams. A query sent to 120 high schools in 1927, to which 84 replied, showed 79 schools engaged in sports: 76 in baseball, 73 in football, 71 in basketball, 45 in field and track, and a handful in tennis, wrestling, boxing, or swimming. Seventy-two schools boasted of "athletic fields," but only 28 had indoor basketball courts. Nearly all the smaller schools played basketball on outdoor courts and their other athletics on whatever level fields were available. At that time all schools competed in either of two categories (A and B), according to size.[23]

In the thirties there seemed to be increased interest in interscholastic athletics, though some schools were forced to curtail their programs because of the depression. By the outbreak of World War II, the program was in full swing again, with even most of the smaller schools then sporting new gymnasiums. The State High School League, in the meantime, divided the competitors into three categories (A, B, and C) instead of two.

Keen rivalry developed between neighboring schools such as Walhalla and Seneca, Dillon and Latta, Laurens and Clinton, and so on. In the smallest towns, the "big game" might be accompanied with much fanfare, the closing of the business houses, and the attraction of a crowd of spectators twice the size of the population of the community. The larger high schools packed in the fans by the thousands. There were few college football games in

22. University of South Carolina Extension Department, *Bulletin No. 117* (February, 1923), p. 7.

23. Samuel F. Burke, "The Status of High School Athletics in South Carolina" (Master's thesis, University of South Carolina, 1927), pp. 6-9, 17, 37.

South Carolina played before larger crowds than attended the Greenville-Parker, Columbia-Sumter, and Spartanburg-Gaffney high school contests.

In the twenties such extracurricular activities as debating, declamation, dramatic productions, literary societies, and glee clubs were likewise emphasized.[24] By 1941 debating, declamation, and literary societies were yielding to bands, drum majorette corps, scout troops, student newspapers, and a multiplicity of clubs.

In 1941 there were 46 Negro high schools in the state. These offered about the same curriculum as the white schools and engaged in the same type of extracurricular activities. However, lack of school buses for the colored schools hampered interscholastic athletic competition, and their athletic fields and gymnasiums were inferior to those furnished the whites. In the classrooms the Negro high schools likewise suffered from inferior equipment and over-crowded conditions, but the quality of instruction in the larger schools was probably fairly good. In Charleston, for instance, nearly all the Negro high school teachers held bachelor's degrees.[25]

As a final note, in 1941 there were nine white private and 14 Negro private institutions which offered 16 units (four years) of high school work.[26]

b. Mill Schools

Before the Civil War, William Gregg set up a school at Graniteville and made attendance compulsory for all

24. *A Study of South Carolina High School Conditions* (Columbia, S.C.: State Department of Education, 1930), p. 30.

25. Of 41 teachers in the Charleston Negro high school in 1942, 37 held bachelor's degrees and one a master's degree. By comparison only 8 of 99 grammar school teachers in Charleston held bachelor's degrees. Moore, "Negro Public Schools of Charleston," pp. 44-49; Janet S. Leake, "Survey of the Negro Public Schools of Columbia, South Carolina" (Master's thesis, University of South Carolina, 1932), pp. 49-65.

26. *Annual Report, Supt. Educ., 1941* (Columbia, S.C.: General Assembly of South Carolina, 1942), pp. 90-91.

village children too young to work in the factory. This idea was generally followed by other textile mill owners elsewhere in the state. For support the companies drew upon the public school fund, but this was usually insufficient to meet their wants. As a consequence, a majority of the mill companies invested their own funds in school property and supplemented the teachers' salaries.

The one-room school was not the rule in the mill village. Rather, a three- or four-room building was common with at least four grades taught. In 1907 August Kohn estimated the companies had investments in school properties amounting to $300,000 or $350,000. And in 1920 W. A. Shealy, state supervisor for mill schools, reported 145 such schools in operation at an annual cost of about $100,000 to the companies in addition to funds supplied through public taxation. He added: "Better salaries and better living conditions are attracting many of our best teachers to the mill schools. . . . The trustees of these schools are demanding the best and willing to pay good salaries for the right teacher." Nevertheless, the supervisor pointed to crowded classrooms, inadequate playgrounds, and the neglect of industrial training at the mill schools.

With the passage of the "6-0-1" law, the mill schools were gradually taken wholly under public control. In 1925, the last year that the superintendent of education included a report of the mill schools, 130 were in operation with almost 30,000 pupils.[27]

c. Special Adult Education Programs

In South Carolina's fight against ignorance, the State Department of Education at the close of World War I embarked upon a broad program to reach illiterate and

27. *Ibid., 1920* (Columbia, S.C.: Gonzales and Bryan, 1921), pp. 162-64; *ibid., 1925* (Columbia, S.C.: General Assembly of South Carolina, 1926), pp. 76-78; August Kohn, *Cotton Mills of South Carolina* (Columbia, S.C.: State Department of Agriculture, Commerce and Immigration, 1907), pp. 133-42.

semi-literate adults. In cooperation with industrial leaders, the Department established a number of special vocational training schools in factory centers for the purpose of teaching young workers carding, weaving, loom fixing, auto-mechanics, spinning, carpentry, arithmetic, elementary electricity, and other practical courses. In 1921 there were 70 such classes with 756 pupils in 14 towns.[28]

At the same time, the State Department appointed Miss Will Lou Gray as Supervisor of Adult Schools. Under Miss Gray's guidance, three general types of adult schools were organized. "Lay-by" schools, mainly for rural people, were set up in 1920 in 24 counties. Each school ran a few weeks in the summer with teachers from regular school systems. "Night" schools, the second type of adult school, were established in 34 counties (mainly in mill communities). These schools, holding evening classes three times per week, were able to operate over a six-month period. Again, the teachers were recruited from the regular school systems. And finally, special schools for adults were maintained in seven mill villages. In these schools the teachers were full-time employees, spending much time in the homes of the students, most of whom were married women. The mill companies paid the larger share of the expenses in maintaining these special schools.

Altogether the adult education program in 1920 reached 11,250 students, about 5000 of whom were Negroes. In many cases the teachers had to perform some real salesmanship to obtain pupils. As one teacher wrote: "Excuses of all kinds, from bad eyes, indigestion and nervous troubles, to protracted meeting, canning [farm produce] and lots of company had to be met."[29]

The adult program was modified from time to time but steadily grew until 1930. In that year 55,000 students

28. *Annual Report, Supt. Educ., 1921* (Columbia, S.C.: Gonzales and Bryan, 1922), pp. 89-95.
    29. *Ibid., 1921*, p. 251.

enrolled, about two-thirds of whom were Negroes. This large number resulted from an unusually vigorous campaign and from a better supply of funds than usual. The 1930 enrollment was equal to that of the previous five years together, and the average attendance was over 70 per cent. Approximately 13,000 to 14,000 Negroes were taught to read and write in this one year. Thereafter, as the depression reduced funds for adult education, the program was cut somewhat. By 1941 the enrollment was down to about 9000. In the meantime, adult schools were established in 24 Civilian Conservation Camps throughout the state, and over 1800 young men were enrolled in off-duty classes.[30]

One other result of the movement against adult illiteracy was the opening of the Opportunity School. It began as an adult vacation school under the leadership of Miss Gray. The first meeting was held in the summer of 1921 at the Daughters of the American Revolution School at Tamassee, in upper Oconee County. The Opportunity School quickly outgrew its quarters and was forced to look elsewhere. In 1930, after several moves, it settled down at Clemson College, where its annual summer sessions attracted 300 or more pupils. The sessions were about a month in length, and the attending students ranged all the way from illiterates learning their ABC's to college graduates working on special hobbies. A similar vacation school was organized for the Negroes. In 1930 it was situated at the colored Seneca Junior College, and its program was practically the same as was offered at the Clemson Opportunity School.[31] Later, it divided and moved to Voorhees Industrial School at Denmark and Benedict College in Columbia.

These various adult education programs helped reduce illiteracy in South Carolina, but in their limited time and

30. *Ibid., 1930* (Columbia, S.C.: General Assembly of South Carolina, 1930), p. 31; *1941*, pp. 236-37.
31. *Ibid., 1941*, pp. 41-47.

way they could do little more than teach their pupils the rudiments of reading, writing, and arithmetic. In 1940 more than one-third of all South Carolinians over 25 years old had not advanced beyond the fourth grade. In the rest of the United States, only Louisiana had a poorer record.

3. Higher Education

The Civil War all but wrecked the South Carolina colleges. Their students marched away to battle, while their administrators invested large portions of their slender resources in Confederate securities. During Reconstruction most of the schools made energetic efforts to raise funds and reopen. Erskine College, for instance, sold tuition certificates ($20 each) to private subscribers. Each certificate was worth one year's tuition whenever presented.[32]

As valiant as their efforts were, it was touch-and-go for the colleges. Their staffs were small, usually no more than five or six professors; their equipment was meager; their plants were antiquated. The historic South Carolina College was reorganized as a university in 1866, and engineering, law, agriculture, and other practical subjects were added to the hitherto exclusively classical curriculum. There was a period of brief progress, but the reaction to the admission of Negro students in 1873 cut it short. Faculty and white students resigned in such numbers that for a time the institution was almost devoid of patronage.[33]

With the end of Reconstruction, the University was closed for three years, and for a time it seemed doubtful that the legislature would reopen it. The appropriation for 1880 was a niggardly $2500. The next year Governor

32. *Semi-Centennial Addresses, Erskine College . . . June 26, 1889* (Charleston, S.C.: Walker, Evans and Cogswell, 1890), pp. 94-99.

33. Daniel W. Hollis, *College to University* (Vol. II of *University of South Carolina;* Columbia, S.C.: University of South Carolina Press, 1956), pp. 3-79. During the years 1865-1960 the University had its name altered several times, but for clarity I shall refer to it as it has been known in recent years: "The University of South Carolina," or simply "Carolina."

Hagood indirectly breathed new life into the University when he advocated a reopening of the Citadel, closed since the latter part of the Civil War. This led to cooperation by supporters of the two state institutions. The Citadel was reopened; the University appropriations were increased to $12,500 and rose steadily for several years thereafter.[34]

However, there was deep-seated antagonism to the University. This latent opposition burst into the open in 1885 as a result of two forces: resentment by supporters of the denominational schools against the free-tuition system at the University, and demand by the farmers for the institution to provide as good an education in agriculture as it did in the liberal arts. The poverty-stricken church colleges were naturally jealous of the University. They could ill afford to pay salaries of $2000 a year to match those of the University. And as they competed strongly for students, they resented seeing prospects wander off to Columbia. In 1885 some of their legislative friends attempted to force the University to charge tuition.[35]

That same year the Tillman movement got under way. Tillman's early program in part called for the establishment of a separate agricultural college and for the abolition of the Citadel, "that military dude factory." But Tillman shortly reconciled himself to the continued existence of the Citadel in return for the support of the editor of *The News and Courier,* Francis Dawson, who agreed to take up the fight for a separate agricultural college.[36]

In December, 1886, as the churchmen and the farmers were about to combine their forces to reduce the University's appropriation, the supporters of the school agreed to compromise. A tuition fee of $40 per year was henceforth

34. *Ibid.,* pp. 99-101, 118-19.
35. *Ibid.,* pp. 128-36.
36. Francis B. Simkins, *Pitchfork Ben Tillman, South Carolinian* (Baton Rouge, La.: Louisiana State University Press, 1944), pp. 96, 104-7.

to be charged, except for "competent and deserving" South Carolina youths unable to pay the same.[37] Having satisfied the churchmen, the University's legislative friends successfully held the agrarians at bay. Tillman, discouraged, retired from active politics, to emerge only after the death of Thomas G. Clemson in April, 1888. Clemson's will paved the way for the chartering of an agricultural and mechanical college the following year. A few months later Tillman was well on his way to the governorship.[38]

As the Edgefield farmer entered the executive mansion in 1890, friends of the University feared its fate would soon be sealed by the establishment of Clemson College and a proposed college for women. Clemson opened its doors to students in 1893 and was an immediate success. The college's financial security was placed beyond the whims of the legislature for annual appropriations when the fertilizer tax was earmarked for its support. Thus Clemson, enrolling some 400 students at its first session, grew and prospered.

The Tillman legislature chartered Winthrop College for girls in 1891. This institution, after temporary operations in Columbia, opened its Rock Hill plant in 1895. It, too, was well patronized from its beginning. Under the guidance of its energetic and resourceful president, David Bancroft Johnson, Winthrop for many years received much greater legislative financial support than did the University.

Meanwhile, Governor Tillman amazed the Citadel and University friends by supporting continued operations of the two "pets of aristocracy." He was quite willing, however, to cut appropriations for the University, especially after the panic of 1893 reduced state revenues. When University partisans protested further cuts in the school's

37. For many years after 1900, less than 50 per cent of the students in the four state-supported white colleges paid tuition, as there was much abuse of the privilege of exemption for those "unable" to pay. In 1933 the legislature abolished free tuition at the state colleges. Hollis, *College to University*, pp. 312-13, 332-33.
38. *Ibid.*, pp. 141-49.

funds, Josh Ashley, an illiterate legislator from Anderson County retorted, "Let 'er die."[39]

Josh Ashley was not without backing, for as Professor Hand later pointed out, the state had "blundered badly" in establishing four white institutions of higher learning. Other states of wider area, more wealth, and greater population maintained but one or two such institutions. Hand added that the four South Carolina colleges paralleled each other in more than one-half of their work and overlapped each other's work in nearly every department, and that at least three of them were "vigorous rivals for patronage."[40]

The University suffered further at the hands of Governor Cole Blease (1911-15). Blease hated the University, at least partly because he had been expelled as a student in earlier years for plagiarizing an essay. As governor he sought to cut the University's annual appropriation, and succeeded in doing so to some extent. Fortunately for the school, its legislative friends were generally stronger than the Governor. In 1913 Blease carried his opposition to the point of attacking University President Samuel C. Mitchell on the charge that Mitchell had signed a petition depriving Winthrop College of $90,000 of Peabody funds in favor of educating Negro teachers in other Southern states. Although a legislative investigation showed the meaning of the petition had been distorted and Winthrop had lost no funds as a result, the irate Blease vowed to drive out Mitchell. Winthrop's President Johnson craftily used the feud to strengthen the position of his college, and the sensitive Mitchell eventually resigned.[41]

In sum, with Winthrop and Clemson riding the crest of a wave of popularity, the 1890-1920 era was filled with "lean years" for the University of South Carolina and for the Citadel, too. The University's historian ruefully ad-

39. *Ibid.*, pp. 168-69.
40. *Annual Report, Supt. Educ., 1910*, pp. 130-31.
41. Hollis, *College to University*, pp. 249-62.

mitted: "One statement is beyond argument: in 1850 the South Carolina College and the University of Virginia were the two most influential institutions of higher learning in the South; in 1906, while Virginia still held much of its former distinction, the University at Columbia was one of the weakest state institutions in the region and not even preeminent in South Carolina."[42]

At the turn of the century, a year's expenses for a college student in South Carolina ranged from about $100 to $150, and admission to college was easily obtained. There were 19 institutions of "recognized college grade" and about half a dozen others with the word "college" pinned to their names. High School Inspector Hand called the college canvasser "as ubiquitous, as persistent, and as ready to drive a bargain for students as the proverbial book canvasser." He reported in 1915 that "any high school pupil with ten units to his credit can get into the freshman class of any college in the State, with hope and expectation of being graduated within four years."[43]

Hand further pointed out that 14 of 19 colleges maintained preparatory departments, but "how many," he asked, "have a *bona fide* four-year high school course resting on even a seven-year elementary course?" The operation and policies of their preparatory schools were clothed in mystery. Nor could one find the information in their catalogs. Hand concluded that there was "more figurative language" in a college catalog of 100 pages "than in the Song of Solomon."[44]

The Inspector's reports lead one to believe that college courses of instruction were not very demanding, no matter how impressive the curriculum appeared in print. The required course of instruction at Newberry College in 1896 for a bachelor's degree included: Latin, Greek, German,

42. *Ibid.,* pp. vii-viii.
43. *Annual Report, Supt. Educ., 1910,* p. 131; *1915,* p. 269.
44. *Ibid., 1912,* p. 188; *1911,* p. 158.

Bible study, ethics, "natural theology," mathematics through calculus, astronomy, geology, mineralogy, history, sociology, psychology, political economy, international law, civil government, physics, chemistry, zoology, essays, debates, orations, logic, English grammar, rhetoric, literature, and composition, and classics. Optional courses were given only in French, Latin, Greek, and calculus, with advanced work in the latter three.[45]

While the curriculum at Newberry was typical of most men's colleges in the state, the girls' schools, also emphasizing the classics and liberal arts, devoted much time to music and fine arts. A few even experimented with "secretarial science" about 1900.[46]

At best the South Carolina colleges had one- and two-member departments, poor libraries, and few teachers of renown. There was an occasional scholar of note, such as Professor Edwin S. Joynes at the University of South Carolina, and an administrator who developed high academic standards, such as President Harrison Randolph of the College of Charleston. But most of the professors and administrators who left their mark on the state were remembered more for their high moral principles and integrity than for their research, scholarship, or maintenance of high academic standards. They sought to mold character rather than to develop scholars.[47]

As a result of academic weakness, the South Carolina colleges were largely excluded from the Southern Association of Colleges and Secondary Schools until the second

45. J. H. Bedenbaugh, "A History of Newberry College" (Master's thesis, University of South Carolina, 1930), pp. 71-77.
46. W. C. Taylor, *History of Limestone College* (Gaffney, S.C.: privately printed, 1937), pp. 74-77.
47. In 1908, of 37 white and colored institutions of "higher learning" listed in South Carolina, 21 had properties valued at $100,000 or less. The University of South Carolina had 40,000 volumes in its library; eight other colleges claimed to have between 8,000 and 17,000 each; the remainder had less. *Annual Report, Supt. Educ., 1908,* chart opposite p. 206.

decade of the twentieth century. And until the same decade many South Carolina college graduates were forced to take additional undergraduate work before being admitted to the graduate schools of renowned Eastern universities.[48]

The 1920's added considerable strength to South Carolina institutions of higher learning. The improvement of the state's public school system enabled the colleges to raise entrance requirements to 15 units in 1921, to abandon their preparatory departments (Negro colleges excepted), to maintain higher scholastic standards, and to broaden their curriculums. The colleges also became "Ph.D. conscious," and with teaching salaries up to $3000 per year in several institutions, a few prominent teachers and scholars were lured into the state.

For advanced study, the state supported at the University a law school (accredited by the American Association in 1924) and a school of pharmacy (established as a school in 1925), and offered the Ph.D. degree (first awarded in 1925) in limited fields. In 1913 the state also took over support of the well-established Charleston Medical College.[49] Otherwise, as recently as 1941 students found only limited opportunities for graduate study at any college in South Carolina. This was due to a lack of interest, a lack of funds, and, as already mentioned, too many schools. When the General Assembly passed the "6-0-1" law for public schools, the voters at the same time turned down a proposed bond issue of $10,000,000 to provide permanent improvements at state-supported colleges. President William D. Melton of the University attributed the defeat of the bond issue to the "ignorance, lack of information, and lack of vision" among the voters. He sadly pointed out that the University of North Carolina at Chapel Hill annually received more than all the South Carolina state-supported institutions of higher learning put together.[50]

48. Hollis, *College to University*, pp. 179, 270.
49. *Ibid.*, pp. 277, 306.
50. *Annual Report, Supt. Educ., 1925*, p. 36.

The accompanying table lists the institutions of higher learning in the state with some pertinent information about each. Not included are the junior colleges and several special schools such as business colleges, Bible colleges, and the South Carolina Medical College.

A detailed discussion of college life cannot be included in a general study of this sort. However, a few generalizations are in order. In the last half of the nineteenth century students lived under a much sterner code of discipline than in 1941. They were usually required to wear uniforms, participate in physical training, and attend daily chapel exercises. College authorities frowned on unauthorized absence from class or leaving town without permission. In some cases, however, students could rejoice in a relative absence of restraint. An Erskine professor cryptically noted in 1889, "The practice of patrolling students' rooms at night, and the general systems of espionage once somewhat common in colleges, have long since been abandoned in Erskine."[51]

Notwithstanding rules, college boys were great pranksters. It was not uncommon for them to place a pig in the dean's office, a cow in the chapel, or a wagon atop the administration building. Professor D. D. Wallace at Wofford told of his embarrassment trying to get one of his cows down the chapel steps after some students had sneaked the poor creature into the building: "I quietly went to church at the 11 o'clock hour, and left during the first hymn to assist, without any students observing, two colored men get the cow down. . . . To my surprise, half the student body beat me to the college and shouted advice on how to do it."[52]

By the 1930's practical jokes against faculty members had largely died out, but the hazing of freshmen was still

51. *Semi-Centennial Addresses, Erskine College,* p. 109.
52. D. D. Wallace, *A History of Wofford College* (Nashville: Vanderbilt University Press, 1951), p. 122.

TABLE 6
SOUTH CAROLINA COLLEGES

	Year Estab.	Location	Controller in 1941	1904 T	1904 S	1930 T	1930 S	1941 T	1941 S	1958 ‖ T	1958 ‖ S
White Degree-Conferring Colleges											
South Carolina Univ.	1805	Columbia	State Owned	16	214	103	1710	116	2000	287	4600
The Citadel	1842	Charleston	"	9	134	52	671	80	1348	138	2106
Clemson	1893	Clemson	"	43	605	122	1238	155	2381	283	3398
Winthrop	1895	Rock Hill	"	39	429	132	1770	84	1741	85	1133
Erskine	1839	Due West	Assoc. Ref. Pres.	8	156	33‡	334‡	25	359	39	446
Col. of Charleston	1785	Charleston	City	8	61	34‡	251‡	21	385	19	303
Furman Univ.	1851	Greenville	Baptist	12	167	33	479	72	1030	93	1266
Wofford	1854	Spartanburg	Methodist	13	334	33	463	23	483	46	685
Converse	1890	Spartanburg	Independent	21	308	54	418	43	370	52	396
Columbia	1854	Columbia	Methodist	14	180	39	358	31§	347§	40	578
Coker	1908	Hartsville	Baptist			24	234	28	245	30	340
Limestone	1845	Gaffney	Baptist	14	141	26	344	26	344	27	310
Newberry	1856	Newberry	Lutheran	8	164	15	327	35	384	35	608
Presbyterian	1880	Clinton	Presbyterian	5	58	22	240	22	324	41	501
Lander	1872	Greenwood	Methodist	10	127	38	401	35	367	29	319
Bob Jones Univ.	1927	Greenville								164	2236
Chicora	1894	Greenville and Columbia		13*	142*	30	185	47	500		
Greenville Col. for Women	1894	Greenville		7	100						
Leesville	1881	Leesville		8	109						
Clifford Seminary	1881	Union		8	61						
Presbyterian Col. for Women	1890	Columbia		24	256						
Due West Female	1854	Due West		15	101						
Greenville Female	1857	Greenville		17	262	32	405				
Reidville Female	1857	Reidville		6†	75†						
S. C. Coeducational Inst.	1891	Edgefield		12*	211*						
Negro Degree-Conferring Colleges											
State A&M	1896	Orangeburg	State Owned	23	711	71	1691	55	1064	107	1488
Benedict	1871	Columbia	Baptist	20	449	31	426	30§	499§	31	750
Claflin	1869	Orangeburg	Methodist	20	481	30‡	394‡	24	279	25	365
Allen Univ.	1880	Columbia	AMEC	14	401	28	587	24	382	55	805
Morris	1908	Sumter	Baptist			18	352	45	250	40	532

* 1905.   † 1908.   ‡ 1929.   § 1942.   ‖ Spring Term.   T—Teachers.   S—Students.

Sources: *Annual Report of the State Superintendent of Education*, 1904, pp. 227-29, 1905, p. 260, 1908, p. 206, 1929, pp. 120-21, 1930, pp. 118-19; *World Almanac and Book of Facts*, 1942, pp. 535-43, 1943, pp. 542-44, 1959, pp. 461-71.

quite commonly practiced in nearly all men's schools. This long-standing sophomore prerogative consisted of paddling the new boys, shaving their heads, and requiring them to perform absurd tricks.

For extracurricular activities, the men's schools devoted much time to literary societies, debating, and literary journals. The State Oratorical Association, organized in 1898, soon had nine colleges participating in its annual oratorical contest. In the early years of the Association, the contests attracted much state-wide attention, but by the thirties student interest in forensic activities was on the wane. World War II brought a halt to the contest, and it was not revived afterwards. In the 45 years that the Association held its annual forensic battle, Wofford and Erskine each won ten times.[53]

Also, in the realm of extracurricular activities, the students of all the men's colleges showed a lively interest in intercollegiate athletics, especially baseball and football, and in later years in a variety of other sports.

The first intercollegiate football game in the state was played in 1889 between Wofford and Furman. The Methodists won by five goals to one; whereupon *The Baptist Courier* rationalized Furman's defeat by crediting the Baptist students with paying more attention to their heads and less to the training of their feet. The following year Wofford again won. This victory *The Wofford Journal* attributed to a Yale coach and a heavier team.[54]

The University of South Carolina, a late comer in the field of intercollegiate athletics, hastily assembled a football team in 1892 for a Christmas Eve battle against Furman at the Charleston baseball park. The "Mountain Boys" from Furman with their "razzle-dazzle" swamped the "College Boys" from Carolina 44 to 0. Two years later the

53. *Ibid.,* pp. 188-90.
54. *Ibid.,* p. 108.

University began regularly scheduled football contests, the first against the University of Georgia at the fairgrounds race course. Admission was 25 cents, and the public was informed that rain would not interfere with the game.[55]

In 1896 the Carolina faculty minutes contained this brief entry: "The football team was allowed to play a match game with Clemson College on Thursday, November 12." This was the only official Carolina reference to what was to become the annual "Big Thursday" game, the greatest football spectacle in the state.[56]

The early football contests were rough. Fights were not uncommon, and occasionally a contest was stopped by one team in protest against some referee's decision. There were also endless disputes over the eligibility of players. A near tragedy occurred in 1902 at Columbia due to frayed tempers and several melees between Carolina and Clemson students. Several hundred Clemson boys, armed with bayonets and swords, threatened to storm the Carolina campus in search of a rival banner showing a proud gamecock crowing over a dejected tiger. A small band of armed Carolina students stationed behind a low wall held off the would-be attackers until police and faculty arrived to cool tempers.

The brutality of the early football contests aroused severe criticism in some circles. Wofford from 1896 to 1914, Furman from 1897 to 1913, and the University of South Carolina in 1906 dropped football from their intercollegiate programs. However, public pressure was too strong to permit the college officials to maintain such positions. There was one exception: the College of Charleston, after "tragic defeats" by Stetson and Florida University in 1912, abolished football permanently.[57]

55. Hollis, *College to University*, pp. 189-90.
56. *Ibid.*, p. 192.
57. *Ibid.*, pp. 227-30; Wallace, *History of Wofford College*, p. 109; R. N. Daniel, *Furman University: a History* (Greenville, S.C.: Furman University, 1951), pp. 107, 131-33; J. H. Easterby, *A History of the*

In the pre-1920 era, though the public took a fervid interest in intercollegiate athletics, a high degree of skill was evidently lacking in most college contests. Newberry, for instance, boasted of state championship teams in both basketball and tennis during the 1911-12 season, the first year the school competed in these two sports.[58]

By 1920 college football was subsidized at several institutions and well established throughout the state. The Clemson-Furman and the Clemson-Carolina games, already traditional, annually drew stadium-packing crowds of 12,000 to 15,000 spectators during the roaring twenties. With the advent of the depression, some of the colleges were hard pressed to meet normal operation costs, much less the expenses of large athletic programs. There followed a severe curtailment of intercollegiate competition, especially in so-called minor sports such as tennis, track, and boxing. Even intercollegiate baseball almost expired. But as the depression came to an end, strong competition was renewed in all sports. Some of the smaller colleges, however, did not again try to keep up with the larger schools on the gridiron. Instead, they concentrated on other sports: Newberry on baseball, Charleston on basketball, and Presbyterian on track and tennis.

At the girls' colleges there was no intercollegiate competition in athletics. Rather, the girls participated in a host of intramural sports. Before World War I college girls were customarily arrayed in none-too-flattering uniforms, were expected to attend meals and classes punctually, to respect the afternoon quiet hour and the "lights off" signal at night, to conduct themselves in a lady-like manner at all times, to attend church services regularly, and to leave the campus only in the company of college-approved chaperones. Whenever a group of girl students left the campus

College of Charleston: Founded 1770 (Charleston, S.C.: College of Charleston, 1935), p. 208.
58. Bedenbaugh, "History of Newberry College," pp. 156-57.

to attend a meeting or a church service, they were usually marched in a quasi-military formation. And to spend the night away from the school premises was strictly forbidden.

Some restrictions seemed more severe. Girls at Limestone in 1885 were not permitted to correspond with boys "without the written permission of parents and guardians"; neither were they allowed to receive visitors except on the same condition. This rule applied at several other girls' colleges. Clifford Seminary (1881-1917) at Union went a step further and forbade its girls to engage in "excessive" letter writing, while at Summerland College (1912-26) in Batesburg, girls could not make telephone calls without special permission.[59]

Women were first permitted to enroll at the University of South Carolina in 1895. From the beginning these students enjoyed greater freedom of social activity than did girls in other schools. On the other hand, the male students resented their intrusion into the University and largely excluded them from the numerous campus organizations until after World War I.[60] Elsewhere in the state, most girls' colleges as recently as 1930 retained close supervision over their students off campus, and several (including Winthrop) prohibited dancing, smoking, and card playing on campus.

With regard to student life at the University in the thirties, Carolina's historian has painted the following picture:

Apart from dances, which were as lavish as festooned crepe paper, the music of local bands, home-made evening dresses, and ill-fitting borrowed tuxedoes could make them, the amusements of the day were simple. Smokers bought the ten-cents-

59. Taylor, *History of Limestone College*, pp. 63-64; Pearle McKenzie, "A History of Summerland College" (Master's thesis, University of South Carolina, 1929), pp. 50-51; E. S. Bennett, "The History of Clifford Seminary . . ." (Master's thesis, University of South Carolina, 1931), p. 67.

60. Hollis, *College to University*, pp. 170-73.

a-pack brands, and when the dime was unavailable, were not above shouting "ducks on that cigarette!" whenever a momentarily more opulent companion lighted up. The few automobiles in student possession were of the rattletrap variety; but these in transit were always crowded with boys and girls, three and four to the seat, plus those poised on fenders and running boards. City girls who could guarantee the use of father's car for the evening had a distinct advantage over the temporarily fatherless and carless out-of-town coeds resident on the campus. Boys and girls walked uptown at night to the Main Street movie houses, went bowling, shared a milk-shake at Burnett's Drug Store, played the piano in the Woman's building lounge, or simply sat, talked, and held hands on campus benches.[61]

If the students seemed little inclined to serious study in the 1930's and more in favor of gaiety, this view is misleading, for there were always those who struggled diligently to perfect their educations. It is probably true that in each generation the critics regarded the college students as frivolous. William E. Woodward, a Citadel cadet from 1889 to 1893, wrote in later years that among the 200 students in college with him were a large crowd of "gay boys" who "thought all the time, night and day, of having fun." They focused their attention on the next social event, baseball game, prize fight, or gossip party. To these cadets the required course of study was merely a "necessary nuisance." They gave their books just enough attention to get by. But Woodward admitted there were also some studious boys who "acted as if every problem that they were destined to encounter in life might be solved by what they learned at the Citadel." And in 1915 President William Currell of the University of South Carolina remarked that "the average student takes his collegiate vocation too lightly and his collegiate avocations too seriously."[62]

61. *Ibid.,* pp. 335-36.
62. *Ibid.,* pp. 270-71; William E. Woodward, *The Gift of Life: an Autobiography* (New York: E. P. Dutton and Company, 1947), pp. 95-96.

The Negro colleges, by and large, tried to emulate their white counterparts.[63] Their curriculums were modeled on those of the white schools, and on paper their programs appeared impressive. In 1914 Benedict offered B.A. and B.S. degrees from nine "college" departments. It supported a theological school, a high school, and a grammar school, and offered courses in commerce, music, domestic science, and nursing. But up to that time few Negro students were enrolled in regular college courses. For instance, of 956 Claflin graduates between 1880 and 1913, only 93 were listed in the school's catalog as "college" graduates.[64]

Moreover, the academic standards of the college departments were generally weak—in course content, library and laboratory facilities, and qualification of teachers. In 1927 the Arthur J. Klein Committee recommended that Allen discontinue its college department and that Morris discontinue its "liberal arts college and theological department."[65]

The rules of conduct in the Negro colleges were similar to those imposed upon students in white institutions. In 1892 Benedict students were expected to attend daily prayer meetings, were forbidden to receive visitors or leave the campus on Sundays, or use tobacco, alcohol, or profane language. They were to desist from "disgusting and injurious" habits and to waste no food at the table. Strangers to the college president "must not expect to call upon young women at any time without presenting letters from the

63. For a brief history of the Negro senior colleges up to 1900, see Tindall, *South Carolina Negroes,* pp. 226-32.

64. *Annual Catalog of Claflin University, 1912-1913* (Orangeburg, S.C.), p. 68; *Annual Catalog of Benedict College, 1914-1915* (Columbia, S.C.), *passim.* Questionable figures from *Annual Report, Supt. Educ., 1904* (Columbia, S.C.: Gonzales and Bryan, 1905), pp. 227-28, show that of 1561 students enrolled currently at Allen, Benedict, and State A&M, only 75 were classified as taking "regular" courses. Reports for succeeding years indicate discrepancies in those figures.

65. Cited in Lewis K. McMillan, *Negro Higher Education in the State of South Carolina* (privately printed, 1952), pp. 94, 161.

parents of the young women." Later the college began the practice of marching the student body to church on Sundays. These rules varied little until the 1920's, when the ban on tobacco was replaced by restrictions on card playing and dancing.[66]

Benedict and Claflin were organized primarily through the efforts of Northern missionaries, and these institutions remained largely under white control until the twenties, retaining many white faculty members until that time. Morris was founded in 1908 because the white Baptists who controlled Benedict refused to permit the Negroes a share in the policy-making of the latter institution.

Quite commonly instructors in the sub-collegiate departments of Negro colleges held no college degrees, while holders of master's degrees from reputable institutions were rare even in the college departments as recently as 1941. A genuine Ph.D. was unknown to some of the Negro schools.[67]

Claflin's and Benedict's staffs seemed to be poorer in 1930, after the white teachers had left, than in the earlier years. The white teachers worked with some purpose, while their Negro successors struggled rather aimlessly along opportunistic lines. Of Benedict's leadership since 1930, a Negro historian concludes: "It is a sad fact that the two Negro presidents have not come up to the standards of white presidents."[68]

The Negro college teachers were also plagued with low pay, insecurity in their jobs, and no voice in the control of the institutions, and were subjected to whims of autocratic

66. *Annual Catalog of Benedict College, 1892-93, 1909-10, 1921-22,* passim.

67. At Claflin in 1913 only one of 14 instructors in the "Manual Training" department held a bachelor's degree. *Annual Catalog of Claflin University, 1912-1913,* pp. 7, 9. In 1949-1951 McMillan found no teaching member of the Allen, Benedict, Claflin, or Morris staffs with a Ph.D. McMillan, *Negro Higher Education,* pp. 91, 113, 128, 149.

68. *Ibid.,* p. 114.

executives, many of whom had little or no background for their positions. The staff members found desirable living quarters almost nonexistent, and many single members at all five senior colleges lived in overcrowded and squalid student dormitories.

At State A&M the teaching staff was badly inbred with many of the school's own graduates, and political interference from the white board of trustees was not infrequent. Negro President Thomas E. Miller was forced from his position in 1911 by Governor Cole L. Blease. Miller, a former United States congressman, had actively worked against Blease's election because, as he stated, "I feel that your announced policy against the Negro was not founded upon justice and the best interest of the State."[69]

The Negro colleges participated as freely as the white schools in extracurricular activities insofar as their finances would permit. As early as 1907, Allen had a small band and a baseball team, neither with uniforms. Five years later the Claflin catalog proclaimed that "Football, Baseball, Tennis and other sports" were carried on by students on fenced-in "Dunton Field."[70]

Benedict, which in 1892 had frowned on sports as "a most wicked waste of time," by World War I boasted of an Athletic Association supporting both football and baseball teams. By that time, most Negro colleges supported glee clubs, bands, literary societies, YMCA's, YWCA's, and a few other student organizations. All Negro colleges were coeducational from the start.[71]

Attendance expenses at Negro schools were low. Tuition for non-boarding students at Benedict in 1900 was

69. For a reprint of Miller's entire reply to Blease see *ibid.*, p. 245. McMillan, former professor of history at State A&M, paints a dismal picture of the South Carolina Negro colleges.

70. *Annual Catalog of Claflin University, 1912-1913*, pp. 60-61; *Views and Facts, Allen University* (Columbia, S.C.: privately printed, 1907), pages unnumbered.

71. State A&M College, *Bulletin*, V (Orangeburg, S.C.: April, 1917), 16-18; *Catalog of Benedict College, 1914-1915*, pp. 55-59.

$1.50 per month (four weeks). Boarding students apparently were expected to work a minimum of one hour per day for the college. They paid $8.25 every four weeks, or $66 per school year of eight months.[72] Most white colleges charged from $100 to $150 per year at that time.

With fees such as these, the Negro schools had to look for much outside support. All the private senior colleges relied partly on white donations, but to a greater degree on various fund-raising rallies among the Negroes themselves. During most of their history, these colleges have had a hand-to-mouth existence. And at the outbreak of World War II they failed to equal the white colleges in South Carolina by most standards. Whatever their faults, however, in some measure they broadened the horizons of thousands of Negro young people.[73]

B. SOUTH CAROLINA CHURCHES

The Civil War left the South Carolina churches grievously wounded. They suffered from material losses, scattered and broken congregations, a dearth of ministers, and restless Negro communicants, soon to withdraw. In May, 1865, the Presbyterian *Narrative* deplored the spirit of worldliness prevalent in the state: "The Lord's Day was desecrated by worldly pursuits, profane swearing and drunkenness had become much more common. As these vices were to be seen on the increase in the army, during the last year of the war, so the evil lessons then learned are but too boldly practiced at home. . . . A spirit of unbelief prevails to an alarming extent."[74]

1. Revival and Growth of the White Churches

At the end of the war, Northern churches sent missionaries South to help their destitute Southern brethren and to

72. *Ibid.,* 1899-1900, p. 13.
73. McMillan, *Higher Negro Education, passim.*
74. Quoted in F. D. Jones and W. H. Mills (eds.), *History of the Presbyterian Church in South Carolina since 1850* (Columbia, S.C.: R. L. Bryan Company, 1926), pp. 128-29.

win converts for their respective Northern denominations. In view of the bitterness engendered by the war, it is small wonder that the Yankee missionary efforts met a cool response. The Southern denominations, the Episcopalians excepted, were in no mood for immediate re-union with their erstwhile enemies.

Whatever accomplishments were achieved came about largely as a result of Southern efforts. Religious leaders, laboring against depressed spirits, slowly rallied their scattered charges. By April, 1866, the Presbyterian *Narrative* noted a "transition from a state of despondency to one of hope" and "a slow but steady increase of the membership."[75]

The most active denominations in the post-war revival were the Methodists and the Baptists, the strongest antebellum sects. The growth of the Baptist Church and the broadening of its program may be followed through the work and reports of its annual state convention.

In 1870 the Baptist Convention embarked upon an optimistic program of raising $200,000 for Furman University's endowment. Between 1880 and 1890 the Baptists established Connie Maxwell Orphanage, devoted money and attention to home and foreign missions, and gained many converts in the new textile communities. Their churches increased in number from 639 in 1880 to 909 in 1900, with 97,000 members enrolled.

In 1913 the Baptist Convention set up a "Board of Education," opened a hospital in Columbia in 1914, and adopted the weekly *Baptist Courier* as the official church organ in 1920. That same year the Baptists accepted Limestone College as a church-governed institution.[76]

The Methodists' expansion was along similar lines.

75. *Ibid.*, p. 129.
76. Charles M. Griffin, *The Story of the South Carolina Baptists, 1683-1933* (Greenwood, S.C.: Connie Maxwell Orphanage, 1934), pp. 57-79.

In 1870 they established a state-wide conference which grew steadily in strength until it boasted of 98,000 members in 1914. The church then divided it into two conferences. By that time the Methodists operated Columbia, Lander, and Wofford Colleges, the Epworth Orphanage (established in 1896), Textile Industrial Institute (established in 1911 and later renamed Spartanburg Junior College), Cokesbury School near Greenwood, and Carlisle Fitting School at Bamberg, and supported missions in seven foreign countries. The official Methodist organ was *The Southern Christian Advocate,* published since 1836.[77]

The increased Baptist and Methodist support of education, orphanages, and missions was common to all denominations whose membership was large enough to afford such efforts. Surveying the religious picture in South Carolina, Dr. D. D. Wallace proudly proclaimed in 1916: "The influence of the church on society at large is more powerful today than ever before. The disrespect with which she and her ministry were frequently treated a century ago by public men would today retire such men to private life. In some parts of our country she lacks unfortunately any strong hold upon the masses; but the question is, did she ever have it?"[78]

In the early post-Civil War period, the Methodists and the Baptists continued to lay great stress on emotionalism. Week-long revivals during the "lay-by" season or after the fall harvest were held by most congregations. A favorite type of revival was the camp meeting. To these religious gatherings people came from miles around. They brought their tents, bedding, and cooking equipment and remained

77. E. O. Watson, "Methodism in South Carolina—A Sketch," *The Sesqui-Centennial of Methodism in South Carolina, 1785-1935 . . .* (Columbia, S. C.: State Company, 1936), pp. 25-39; W. V. Dibble, "Methodism's World Parish," *ibid.,* p. 101.

78. D. D. Wallace, *Historical Background of Religion in South Carolina: Annual Address before the Upper South Carolina Conference Historical Society . . .November 14, 1916* (privately printed, n.d.), p. 32.

for several days. A few churches had elaborate camp grounds with cabins for their people.

Much singing, shouting, preaching, praying, and baptising accompanied the camp meetings. Nearly all accounts agree that the ministers spoke with great fire and emotion. One person wrote: "The altar was crowded with weeping penitents, and the 'grand old woods' rang with shouts of the new born souls." Another said: "There was a rush for the altar of many who were heard earnestly crying aloud for mercy." Another witness related: "The Holy Spirit was there in mighty power. The old people and preachers say that they had never seen the like. . . . One afternoon the services continued from the three o'clock sermon until midnight."[79]

From time to time, disputes or outright schisms over doctrine developed among some of the Protestant sects. The Presbyterian Synod of the state was almost split apart in the 1880's over the question of evolution. The controversy raged around Professor James Woodrow of the Theological Seminary. Woodrow admitted that evolution "was probably true" but denied that he taught it to his students as his attackers accused. Although ousted as a teacher at the Seminary in the five-year hassle, Woodrow was eventually vindicated and remained a pastor in good standing in the Presbyterian Church.[80] Later he served as president of the University of South Carolina.

Also in the 1880's a "holiness" heresy developed in some of the Protestant churches. According to one theologian, the holiness adherents held that regeneration left much of the old sin in a person's heart, so a "second work of grace" was necessary for a full and victorious Christian life. This meant that the member had to be "sanctified" by a special act of the Holy Spirit subsequent to conversion.

79. For these and other examples see Simkins and Woody, *South Carolina during Reconstruction*, pp. 399-402.
80. Jones and Mills, *Presbyterian Church*, pp. 169-92.

The second blessing was much preached and discussed in South Carolina until the end of the century. Some of the holiness preachers claimed a monopoly of the experience, practice, and advocacy of holiness, while the more conventional ministers took exception to such teachings.[81]

Religious controversies such as the one just described led to the founding of the Pentecostal Holiness Church (1898), the Church of God (1907), and several other small denominations. Some of the new sects were labeled "Holy Rollers" or "Primitivists." They were in revolt against the growing liberalism of the theological leaders in the older churches. They would not accept scientific teachings that seemed to contradict the literal word of the Gospel. Instead, they believed in a close relationship between man and God and in direct Divine intervention to help the sick and weary. The Holy Rollers, furthermore, disliked the toned-down rituals of the older churches.

The Holy Roller revolt was but part of a larger conflict between fundamentalism and religious liberalism that cut across denominational lines. Many loyal Baptists and Methodists, like the primitivists, interpreted the Bible literally. From 1914 to 1930, the fundamentalists made heavy attacks on academic freedom in the colleges and public schools. In some states they succeeded in pushing bills through the legislature to outlaw the teaching of evolution in public institutions. Such a proposal failed in the South Carolina legislature in 1921.[82]

The fundamentalists upheld a rigid code of moral conduct. From their strongholds in small-town, rural, and mill churches they frowned on dancing, gambling, card

81. This controversy is discussed in Albert D. Betts, *History of South Carolina Methodism* (Columbia, S.C.: Advocate Press, 1952), pp. 412-14.
82. Religious trends in the New South are briefly described in Francis B. Simkins, *A History of the South* (New York: Alfred A. Knopf, 1953), pp. 416-25.

playing, drinking, and in some instances smoking and theatre-going.

The Episcopal Church led in appeal to the upper classes, with the Presbyterian running a close second. Geographically, Episcopal strength lay in the lowcountry, where the church had become entrenched in colonial times, and to a lesser degree in the middle and upper South Carolina towns. The Presbyterian strength was state-wide, but it was primarily urban. The sophistication of these two denominations was partly due to their early emphasis on an educated and well-trained clergy. The larger Baptist and Methodist denominations, on the other hand, were not particular so long as their ministers had "the call."

The Lutherans and Associate Reformed Presbyterians likewise emphasized a well-educated clergy.[83] Both of these denominations dated back to the eighteenth century. The Lutherans' most numerous supporters lived in the Saluda-Lexington-Newberry area. This sect was greatly strengthened in 1922 when an ante-bellum schism was healed. Nineteen South Carolina congregations which were members of the North Carolina Synod reunited with the South Carolina Synod, thus increasing the latter's membership from 13,695 to 17,445.[84] The ARP's were strongest in Abbeville, York, and Chester counties.

The 1920's were an era of prosperity for the religious sects as well as for other institutions. Nearly all the denominations embarked upon fund-raising programs to improve their colleges and orphanages, to expand their mis-

83. A statistical study of 84 rural South Carolina ministers in 1921-1922 showed 10 of 29 Methodists having bachelor's degrees, 9 of 20 Baptists, 12 of 13 Lutherans, 9 of 9 Presbyterians, 6 of 6 ARPs, and 5 of 5 Episcopalians. Only 12 of 49 Baptists and Methodists had completed the three-year seminary course. By contrast 29 of the other 33 had finished the same study. Q. O. Lyerly, "The Country Church Problem" (Master's thesis, University of South Carolina, 1922), pp. 3-5.

84. S. T. Hallman (ed.), *History of the Evangelical Lutheran Synod of South Carolina, 1824-1924* (Columbia, S.C.: Farrell Printing Company, 1925), pp. 29-31.

sionary activities and auxiliary services, and to repair and build churches.

With the depression of the thirties, many of the activities had to be curtailed in face of mounting financial difficulties. For instance, the Presbyterian Synod in 1937 faced a lawsuit from the creditors of Chicora College, whose Columbia campus had been closed when the school united with Queens College in Charlotte. Presbyterian College at Clinton had an accumulated deficit of over $70,000, of which $10,000 was owed to teachers in back salaries. The College needed $500,000 for improvements to place it back on the accredited list of the Southern Association. Of $3150 voted by the Synod for work among Presbyterian students at the state colleges for the previous year, only $300 had reached the treasurer. Thornwell Orphanage, with 300 boys and girls, was running "in the red," and so on.[85] Other denominations had similar troubles.

Traditionally, the smallest and weakest congregations were the country churches. The vast majority of these were either Baptist or Methodist, and seldom could afford full-time pastors. Of 639 Baptist churches in South Carolina in 1880, only 21 held services every Sunday in the month. This situation improved but little in the intervening years. In 1937 only 10 of 32 churches in the Orangeburg Baptist Association (mainly rural) held meetings four times per month.[86]

Prior to World War I, the rural pastor traveled from church to church on horseback. Only infrequently did he become well acquainted with his parishioners. They showed their "confidence" in him by keeping his salary low. Moreover, they paid a portion of his salary in "showers" of

85. *Minutes of the [Presbyterian] Synod of South Carolina, 1937* (privately printed, n.d.), pp. 31-68.

86. Griffin, *South Carolina Baptists*, p. 58; *Minutes of the 68th Annual Session of the Orangeburg Baptist Association . . . Oct. 13-14, 1937* (privately printed, n.d.), pages unnumbered.

TABLE 7
SOUTH CAROLINA CHURCH STATISTICS

	1916		1936			
	Number of Churches	Number of Members	Number of Churches	Number of Members	Average Value per Church	Sunday School Members
Total..................	5679	794,126	4263	710,163	$ 7313	387,491
Negro Total.................	3136	447,084	2158	330,479	3223	142,665
Leading Negro Churches:						
Baptist..................	1353	255,479	1351	238,217	$ 3061	103,197
African Meth. Episc........	645	90,469	188	25,956	3811	10,521
African Meth. Episc. Ch.,						
Zion..................	192	23,169	179	19,547	3900	9786
Colored Meth. Episc.......	81	7341	54	5065	4018	1775
[Northern] Methodist Episc.	407	52,568	227	28,527	3453	12,258
Leading White Churches:						
Southern Baptist Conv.....	1096	158,151	673	159,887	$10,201	109,746
Meth. Episc. Church, South	851	105,306	418	91,514	13,192	57,791
Presbyterian, U. S........	288	30,041	261	37,709	18,996	26,781
Presbyterian, U. S. A......	108	8320	59	5112	4968	3063
Lutheran.................	103	14,788	104	27,166	14,323	14,008
Episcopal.................	133	11,000	120	18,163	17,249	5419
Roman Catholic...........	49	9514	76	11,543	18,291	1516
Assoc. Reformed Presbyt....	47	4923	48	7064	14,122	4515
Jewish..................	9	570	19	4408	14,667	381
Church of God...........	..	..	53	3289	3003	4949

Annual Expenses	1916	1936
All Churches..................	$3,701,000	$5,100,000
Negro Churches................	1,129,000	1,320,000

▶ *Sources:* Census of *Religious Bodies, 1916,* I, 218-20, 306, 572-74; Census of *Religious Bodies, 1936,* I, 284-85, 894-95.

home-grown products, although "showers" were sometimes extra. Many rural ministers supplemented their pastoral pay by farming, teaching, or by working at other part-time jobs.[87]

Despite its financial weakness, the country church was a center of social as well as spiritual activity until the

87. C. Vann Woodward, *Origins of the New South, 1877-1913* (Baton Rouge, La.: Louisiana State University Press, 1951), pp. 444-50; Lyerly, "The Country Church Problem," pp. 11-13, 18-19. The 84 ministers Lyerly questioned in 1921-1922 averaged 2.78 churches each. These ministers also held an average of 7.7 services per month.

1930's. At that time the depression, coupled with the coming of good roads, dealt the country church a heavy blow. As Table 7 shows, hundreds of churches literally disappeared between 1916 and 1936, the Baptists and the Methodists suffering most of all.

2. Development of Negro Churches

Before 1865 Negro slaves had been encouraged by their masters to attend white churches, and numerous lowcountry congregations had as many Negro as white communicants. But in these ante-bellum churches the whites carefully directed all religious affairs. They assigned the Negro worshippers to seats in the galleries and permitted them no voice in the church government.

After the war the whites still refused to permit the blacks to share in the management of church affairs. Most of the freedmen were no longer willing to accept white dictation in religious matters. Therefore, the Negroes began to drift away from white churches.

At the same time a number of Northern missionaries began working among both white and black Southerners. Although largely rebuffed in their overtures to the South Carolina whites, the missionaries, especially those of the [Northern] Methodist Episcopal Church, met with some success among the Negroes. These missionaries encouraged the blacks to organize independent congregations. They gave financial aid and set up Claflin University in 1869 to help train Negro leaders.

Except in the Episcopal and the Presbyterian churches, few white congregations sought to prevent Negro withdrawals. Instead, they frequently permitted their Negro brethren to continue to use the white church until the Negroes had a structure of their own.[88] By the end of Reconstruction, only a handful of Negroes remained with

88. For early Negro church development, see Simkins and Woody, *South Carolina during Reconstruction*, Chap. XIV.

white congregations. The following examples show various ways in which Negro churches were formed. At St. Helena Negroes in 1865 simply took possession of the "Old Brick Church," built in 1855 by white Baptists. From this congregation several others were formed, usually as a result of disputes over ministers. At Sumter the Mt. Pisgah Methodist Church was formed in 1866 largely as a result of Negro missionary efforts from Charleston. Union Baptist Church near Bamberg was established by four former slaveowners in behalf of their ex-slaves. During the next 77 years seven other churches were organized from its membership. In some cases Negroes worshipped informally in private cabins until they could organize and erect church buildings.[89]

The two most popular denominations among the Negroes were the Methodist and the Baptist. Of the Methodist groups, the most important was the African Methodist Episcopal Church. By 1871 the AMEC counted 33,000 members, heavily concentrated in the Columbia, Georgetown, and Charleston areas. The most successful early minister of the AMEC was the gifted Negro Congressman Richard H. Cain. He organized and preached at the Emanuel Church (Charleston), whose 2570 members in 1871 made it by far the largest AMEC congregation in the state.[90]

Throughout the South the AMEC was under the guidance of Bishop Daniel A. Payne, who earnestly worked toward a well-educated ministry. Partly for that purpose, the African Methodists established Allen University in Columbia in 1881.

Another Negro Methodist group, the African Methodist

89. S. C. Smith, "The Development and History of Some Negro Churches in South Carolina" (Master's thesis, University of South Carolina, 1942), pp. 13-15, 18-19.

90. *Minutes of the Seventh Annual Session of the South Carolina Conference of the African Methodist Episcopal Church* . . . (Columbia, S.C.: John W. Denny, 1871), pp. 39-60.

Episcopal Church, Zion, was strong in the eastern South Carolina counties bordering North Carolina. However, this denomination was better known in the latter state, where it supported a college. The other large Methodist organization for Negroes in South Carolina—the [Northern] Methodist Episcopal Church—has already been mentioned. In addition, three smaller Negro Methodist groups were established.

Negro Baptist churches quickly sprang up over most of the state at the close of the Civil War. Each congregation was a law unto itself. The members simply selected someone to preach and secured his ordination as a minister. An outstanding Negro Baptist leader was Alexander Bettis, a former slave. He established more than 40 churches, two Baptist associations, and an industrial school at Denmark. At one time Bettis served as pastor of ten churches he had organized.[91]

After the establishment of numerous Baptist churches, a state-wide convention was organized in 1876 under the leadership of the Reverend E. M. Brawley. Within seven years' time, the convention had 550 affiliated churches and about 100,000 members.

In the first decade or two following the Civil War, the Negro ministers were highly influential, probably more so then than later, for they were almost the only Negroes who had gained experience as leaders during slavery times. While some were capable and devoted men, others took advantage of their ignorant followers. In general, the ministers became the rulers of their neighborhoods. Besides preaching, they farmed, ran shops, taught school, followed various trades, and entered politics. They prided themselves on their oratory, which was often quite effective.[92]

91. Tindall, *South Carolina Negroes*, pp. 188-89; Simkins and Woody *South Carolina during Reconstruction*, p. 390.
92. *Ibid.*, pp. 412-13; Tindall, *South Carolina Negroes*, pp. 203-4.

By and large, in Negro meetings singing and shouting accompanied the minister's fiery sermon. The "shout" was known among Negroes throughout the state, but it was most commonly practiced in "pray's houses" among the Sea Islanders. Benches were pushed back, while in one corner singers furnished lively music mingled with loud hand-clapping. In the middle of the room the remainder of the congregation shuffled, jerked, and danced with the rhythm of the music and the clapping. Quite often the shout lasted far into the night.[93]

The Negro churches also had camp meetings and singing conventions. Such meetings were attended by choirs and ministers from neighboring churches. After World War I the larger Negro congregations frequently secured singers and brass bands from Buffalo, Philadelphia, Detroit, and other Northern cities.

Regular church meetings, camp meetings, funerals, weddings, and baptism ceremonies were social as well as religious events. The Negroes observed many of these with great feeling and much ceremony. Religion thus furnished emotional release for this race that had known so much pain, hard work, and sorrow. It is interesting to note that the Negroes' religious practices were copied from the more emotional white groups. A Negro camp meeting of 1920 was conducted much like a white Methodist one of 1870.

By the 1930's there was a decline in emotionalism in some Negro congregations, especially among the higher economic groups in the towns and cities. The rural camp meetings likewise declined in importance. Moreover, the more sophisticated churches were beginning to manifest considerable interest in the religious aspects of national and world affairs.[94]

93. Simkins and Woody, *South Carolina during Reconstruction*, pp. 141-45.
94. For example, see the annual report of an African Methodist committee on "The State of the Country" in 1937. The committee was

In contrast, the rural congregations of the poorer classes of Negroes retained their highly emotional worship services, and in some instances the more illiterate groups continued to practice superstitious rites, especially at funerals.[95]

Church organization among the Negro denominations was similar to that of the white denominations. The Negro Methodists were strongly centralized, whereas the Negro State Baptist Convention was a loose-knit order. All Negro groups apparently placed great emphasis on a church hierarchy, and, like their white brethren, some of the Negro clergy spent much of their time at conventions currying the favor of the bishops. Occasionally a strong leader could dominate a sect. Such a man was the late Dr. J. J. Starks, president of Morris College (1921-30) and Benedict College (1930-44). According to a Negro historian,

Starks always had cash money on hand; the leaders among the Negro Baptist preachers were always "broke." Dr. Starks tied all of these men to him through little insignificant emergency loans. All of the Baptist big shots owed Starks money or were obligated to him for some moneys they had owed to him at various times. The good "Doctor" exploited this situation for all that it was worth. He handily manipulated the

---

concerned over Italy's "rape" of Ethiopia, Japan's invasion of China, America's unemployment problem in which Negroes were "last hired and first fired," the needs of the Negro sharecropper, the rising death rate from automobile accidents, the progress of the "New Deal," and so on. *Minutes of the . . . Columbia Conference of the African Methodist Episcopal Church . . . Oct. 27th to 31st, 1937* (Columbia, S.C.: Allen University Press, 1937), pp. 31-33.

95. After an extended stay in South Carolina, author Ruby F. Johnston reported that as recently as 1947-48 clergymen at some isolated rural churches in Beaufort, Orangeburg, Chesterfield, and Kershaw counties observed "sporadic occurrences" of ancient practices in connection with burial ceremonies. A baby would be thrown across the grave of the deceased to prevent the departed spirit from returning to claim the child or some other member of the family. Spoons, plates, or medicine bottles were placed in the grave with the body to prevent the spread of disease in the community. *The Development of Negro Religion* (New York: Philosophical Library, 1954), pp. 63-68, 135.

debt ties to his own personal ends. He literally held South Carolina's Negro Baptists in his hands!

Dr. Starks was the "bishop" among the Negro Baptists of the entire state. He always knew where a church was vacant, when and where one was to be vacant, who the key men in that church were, and how they could be reached. The filling of these vacancies was one of his main concerns. Here again there was a large group of young preachers and old preachers, ignorant preachers and fairly intelligent preachers who owed (and paid) allegiance to J. J. Starks.[96]

With the passing of time, some Negro church leaders became better educated and more concerned about the moral conduct of the members of their race. During slavery times, white masters frequently cared little about slave morality so long as the Negroes performed their plantation chores and committed no serious offenses. In the early days of freedom, then, most ex-slaves maintained a lax moral code in keeping with this ante-bellum philosophy. Even as recently as the 1930's, the Negroes' moral code was still relatively lax. Progress was hampered by the continued low educational and moral status of some Negro ministers and by continued white indifference toward Negro morality so long as Negro deviations affected members of their own race only.[97]

Finally, many Negro churches of the 1930's seemed to be losing their hold on their members. As in the case of the white churches, Negro membership declined greatly between 1916 and 1936, especially among rural congregations.

96. McMillan, *Negro Higher Education,* pp. 152-53.
97. Traditionally, Southern courts have dealt more leniently with Negroes found guilty of crimes against other Negroes than with whites guilty of similar offenses against other whites. With nearly all law-enforcement agencies in white hands, Negro crimes of petty theft, bigamy, bastardy, simple assault, and disorderly conduct, unless involving whites in some way, are frequently overlooked or given only a cursory investigation.

Chapter Seven

Political Developments and Problems, 1941-1960

From 1877 to 1914 South Carolina was a steadfast supporter of the Democratic party. Centered in the heart of "the Solid South," the state even polled a 91.4 per cent vote for the Democratic presidential nominee in 1928, the one election year when a Republican candidate penetrated the South in appreciable strength.

After 1941 the Democratic hold on the South began to weaken, and by 1948 many Southern Democrats were in outright rebellion against the party's national leadership. This opposition, very strong in South Carolina, stemmed mainly from two grievances—President Roosevelt's support of a civil rights program, and the Supreme Court's decree outlawing the white primary.

A. NEW TRENDS IN SOUTH CAROLINA POLITICS

1. United States Courts and the White Primary, 1944-1948

The Democratic party's white primary for nominating officials had double significance in South Carolina. Not only were Negroes excluded from participating in the primary, but the party's nominees faced no real Republican opposition in the general elections. In consequence, between 1900 and 1944 only white Democrats were elected to state offices in South Carolina.

The fight over the legality of the white primary began in the 1920's in Texas. After a series of decisions on this issue, the Supreme Court in 1935 (Grovey v. Townsend) declared the Texas primary valid. Nine years later the Court reversed itself (Smith v. Allwright). In the latter case the Court ruled that the State of Texas had violated the Fifteenth Amendment by denying its Negro citizens the right to vote in the primary.[1]

The Allwright decision drew immediate hostile comment from South Carolina political leaders. Senator Ellison D. Smith declared that the Court's decision might be considered by some as the law of the land but that did not mean it would "rule the spirit and destiny of South Carolina." He urged the advocates of white supremacy in "this hour of Gethsemane" to save South Carolina from a "disastrous fate." Meanwhile, the state junior senator, Burnet R. Maybank, warned that regardless of Court or congressional action the South would maintain the political and social institutions "we believe to be in the best interest of our people."[2]

Anticipating a judicial attack on the South Carolina primary, Governor Olin D. Johnston[3] sought to forestall it through special legislative action. On April 14 he called the General Assembly into an extra session and recommended repeal of all primary election laws. Control of the primary would thereafter lie in the hands of the state Democratic party, a private organization. The Governor's determination to thwart the Court was seen in his address to the legislature. He said: "White supremacy will be maintained in our primaries. Let the chips fall where they may." If his proposed legislation proved inadequate, the Governor promised that "we South Carolinians will use the necessary methods to retain white supremacy in our primaries."[4]

1. For the entire struggle over the white primary, see V. O. Key, Jr., *Southern Politics in State and Nation* (New York: Alfred A. Knopf, 1949), Chap. XXIX. The Fifteenth Amendment states that "The right of citizens of the United States to vote shall not be denied or abridged by the United States or by any State on account of race, color, or previous condition of servitude."

2. *The State* (Columbia, S.C.), April 7, 14, 1944.

3. Johnston was elected in 1942, defeating Wyndham Manning in the Democratic primary.

4. *The State*, April 15, 1944.

Within a week's time the legislature enacted 147 laws separating party primaries from state government control.[5] The voters soon afterward approved an amendment erasing all mention of the Democratic primary from the South Carolina Constitution. Then the state Democratic convention met and adopted a new set of rules for the conduct of primaries. Negroes were excluded from voting.

The April session of the legislature redounded to Governor Johnston's benefit in his contest for the United States Senate against "Cotton Ed" Smith in July, 1944. At the special legislative session, state Senator Richard M. Jefferies, a party regular, publicly charged that the elderly Senator Smith was "largely responsible" for the Negro issue. He declared "Cotton Ed's" race-baiting speeches were "enough to picture South Carolina and the people of the South as an uncivilized race."

Senator Smith tried to dismiss the seriousness of Johnston's candidacy with a "pshaw, he has adopted my platform." Moreover, he shifted the blame for the race issue to the loyal Democrats, ardently contending there would have been no such issue if "Jefferies and his fellow travelers had followed me out of the Philadelphia Convention in 1936." And he acidly noted that the National Association for the Advancement of Colored People (NAACP) "also denounced me and demanded my defeat."

Continually during the campaign "Cotton Ed" heaped invective upon the Governor, who in turn stressed his deeds as chief executive, his loyalty to the Roosevelt administration, his belief in white supremacy, and his promise to cooperate wholeheartedly with the war effort. In the end Johnston won by a stunning 45,000-vote majority.

As *The State* editorialized, "Cotton Ed" had neglected

5. *Ibid.*, April 21, 1944. At the same time, Negro doctors attending their medical association meeting in Columbia unanimously endorsed a resolution condemning the Governor's action. There were more than 100 signatures.

to keep his political fences mended at home, and many voters felt his constant opposition to Roosevelt had nullified his usefulness in Washington.   In contrast, Johnston had campaigned hard and long to build up a machine of loyal supporters throughout the state.[6]   However, the grand old man of South Carolina politics was spared the pain of seeing Johnston take his seat in the Senate, for "Cotton Ed" died a few weeks after the primary.   At the time of his death, he had served in the Senate for a term of almost 36 years—a national record.

There was no Supreme Court interference in the South Carolina primary before the 1946 election, and the race issue remained relatively quiet during the hectic struggle among 11 candidates for the governor's office.   From this battle royal, J. Strom Thurmond of Edgefield emerged victorious, defeating Dr. James McLeod of Florence in a runoff primary.

The following year a Negro citizens' committee in Richland County brought suit in the federal courts for the right to participate in the Democratic primary.   Backed by the NAACP, these Richland Negroes claimed that the primary, whether supported by state law or by party rules, controlled the choice of office holders in South Carolina.

The resulting case (Rice v. Elmore) was tried before federal district court Judge J. Waties Waring, of a well-known Charleston family.   In keeping with the philosophy of the Allwright decision, Judge Waring decided in favor of the Negro plaintiffs.   He said that under the law of the land all citizens were entitled to a voice in the selection of such officers as congressmen and the president.   He called the repeal of the state primary laws a mere subterfuge, and he added that he did not think the skies would fall if South Carolina were put in the same class as other states.

6. The campaign and results are covered in *ibid.,* April 21, May 26, June 28, July 27, 1944.

Although Judge Waring's decision was loudly denounced in South Carolina as unconstitutional, his property molested, and he himself cast out of Charleston society, his decree was upheld by the United States Circuit Court of Appeals. The Supreme Court refused to review the case.

Immediately the Democrats looked for some way to subvert the Court's decision. The state Democratic committee decided not to enroll Negroes in the party, but to permit qualified Negro electors to vote in the primary, provided they would subscribe to an oath which included the following phrase: "I believe in and will support the social and educational separation of the races."

Not all party leaders endorsed the committee's oath and the rule that Negroes be excluded from party rolls. Some were prepared to comply with the Court's order. In support of this view, Columbia attorney R. Beverly Herbert told the graduating class at the University of South Carolina, June 2, 1948, that "common impulses of humanity demand that we cease to humiliate a large part of our population." And at least six county committees balked at the new rules.

In the midst of this confusion, a Beaufort County Negro brought suit against the party because 34 names had been stricken from its roll in that county. Again Judge Waring interceded. At a hearing on July 16, the Judge listened to arguments from both sides, had senatorial candidate Alan Johnstone bodily ejected from the court room for insisting on filing "a paper," and then ordered the Democratic party to enroll Negroes and grant them full participation in party affairs. He warned that further violations of "the letter and spirit" of his ruling would be met with punishment by imprisonment. Turning to the Negro plaintiff, he exclaimed: "It is a disgrace and shame when you must come into a court and ask a judge to tell you you are an American."

Several Democratic leaders breathed defiance. Alan Johnstone declared Waring had "gone beserk"; Congressman Bryan Dorn introduced resolutions of impeachment in the House of Representatives; and staid Senator Maybank believed the Judge had "exceeded his authority." But upon the counsel of party lawyers, Democratic Chairman W. P. Baskin on July 23 advised county chairmen to enroll all electors constitutionally qualified. Within a few days, some 35,000 Negroes were registered to vote in the August primary.[7]

As Judge Waring predicted, the skies did not fall in South Carolina. Negroes have voted in every primary since 1948, but to date (January, 1960) no Negro has been elected to public office in the state. With the re-registration of the voters in the spring of 1958, about 500,000 whites and 50,000 Negroes enrolled in time to participate in the June primary. A number of Negroes have run for legislative or city-council posts, and two have tried to win congressional seats.[8] Invariably they have trailed badly on the ticket.

As far as Negro support of white candidates is concerned, the colored vote overwhelmingly went to regular Democratic nominees in the November elections until 1956. At that time the Negro vote seemed to be about evenly divided between Republican candidate Eisenhower and Democratic candidate Stevenson. Within the Democratic primary, the Negro vote is sometimes divided. At other times it is cast largely as a bloc, depending more on the personalities and actions of the candidates than on what they preach from the stump. Wherever the Negroes vote

7. *The State,* June 3, 18, July 9, 17, 24, 29, August 8, 1948.
8. Negro candidate A. J. Clement of Charleston ran for Congress as a Democrat in 1950 but failed to secure the party's nomination; I. S. Leevy, a Columbia Negro, tried to win a congressional seat as a Republican candidate in 1954.

as a bloc, the candidates they support lose more often than they win.[9]

2. The Dixiecrat Movement of 1948

The Northern Democratic leaders supported the Court's decision invalidating the white primary. This attitude naturally angered the South Carolina Democrats. But the action which drove the state Democratic leaders into open revolt was the national administration's espousal of a civil rights program.

As early as 1944, a number of disgruntled South Carolina Democrats were ready to desert the Roosevelt leadership. Judge Eugene Blease, brother of the late Cole L., summed up their view when he stated: "I do not see how any one of the Roosevelt men can follow the President and at the same time stand for white supremacy in South Carolina." Further bitterness was created at the national convention when Roosevelt "pitched Jimmy Byrnes in the creek" in favor of Harry Truman as the party's vice-presidential candidate. The editor of *The State* asked: "Speaking of minorities, do you know of any that is more neglected than the Democratic Party in the South?" There was no outright rebellion at this time, although 7800 South Caro-

9. Ward Nine of Columbia is a bellwether of the Negro vote. In the following results of Ward Nine voting, only the two highest candidates are recorded: the 1948 primary for United States Senate: Bennett—744, Maybank (winner)—149; primary for governor in 1950: Bates (a Columbia resident)—1,176, Byrnes (winner)—108; primary for governor in 1954: Bates—932, Timmerman (winner)—84; primary for state Senate in 1954: Joe Berry—766, Fletcher Spigner, Jr. (winner)—172; Columbia mayoralty race in 1958: Bates (winner by 14 votes)—690, J. T. Campbell—45; second primary of state Senate race in 1958: Claude Sapp—706, Walter Bristow, Jr. (winner)—170; first primary for governor in 1958: Johnston—515, Russell—385; second primary for governor in 1958: Russell—757, Hollings (winner)—147. But in many county and state-wide contests no significant bloc voting is discernible from the returns. *The State,* August 11, November 3, 1948, July 9, November 5, 1952, June 9, 1954, November 8, 1956, June 25, 1958; *The Greenville News* (S.C.), March 12, 1958; *The Columbia Record* (S.C.), June 11, 1958.

lina "Southern Democrats" voted for Virginia Senator Harry Byrd for president in the November election.[10]

After President Roosevelt's death in April, 1945, President Truman continued to support a civil rights program. In October, 1947, a special committee on civil rights proposed the following program: (1) a joint Congressional Committee on Civil Rights, (2) a federal antilynching law, (3) protection of citizens' right to vote, (4) elimination of racial segregation on interstate buses and trains, (5) the establishment of a Fair Employment Practices Commission (FEPC). The FEPC would have opened all types of work, including textile jobs, to persons of all races. In February, 1948, President Truman submitted the committee's recommendations to Congress.

A few days later the governors of the Southern states held a conference to discuss the civil rights proposals. At first they tried to persuade the Northern Democrats to withdraw or change the committee's recommendations. Meeting with no success on that proposal, the Southern governors suggested that the Southern Democrats try to block President Truman's nomination for re-election.

At the Philadelphia convention in the summer of 1948, nearly every Southern delegate voted for Senator Richard Russell of Georgia as the Democratic nominee for president. But in spite of these efforts, President Truman was renominated by the preponderant Northern and Western majority.

Immediately following the Philadelphia convention, a number of Southern malcontents met in Birmingham, Alabama. Deciding not to support Truman in the November election against Republican candidate Thomas E. Dewey, the rebellious Southerners endorsed South Carolina's Governor J. Strom Thurmond for president and Mississippi's

10. *The State*, April 20, July 22, 1944. For more complete coverage of the Dixiecrat revolt, see Key, *Southern Politics*, Chap. XV; and Alexander Heard, *A Two-Party South?* (Chapel Hill, N.C.: University of North Carolina Press, 1952), Chap. II.

Governor Fielding Wright for vice-president. At the same time the Birmingham delegates adopted a resolution condemning the civil rights program. The dissenters called themselves States' Rights Democrats, but their Party soon carried the label "Dixiecrat." A few weeks later, a regular Dixiecrat convention in Houston, Texas, gave formal assent to the actions of the Birmingham group.

Strom Thurmond himself was on hand for the Birmingham meeting and addressed the conclave. He accused President Truman of stabbing the Southern Democrats in the back with an "unconstitutional and misleading" civil rights program. "I am going to stand for an end to rule by minority blocs in the United States," he told his audience. And he manifested that "there are not enough laws on the books of the nation, nor can there be enough laws, to break down segregation in the South."[11]

Thurmond's Birmingham speech set the tone for the campaign. For the remainder of the summer and into the fall, the Governor worked tirelessly on his program of states' rights and white supremacy. He called Truman, Dewey, and Henry Wallace, the Progressive party candidate, "birds of a feather." The Dixiecrats' openly avowed strategy was to prevent a winner in November, thus throwing the election into the House of Representatives where the Southerners' bargaining power could at least gain concessions and at best defeat both Truman and Dewey.[12]

On election eve Thurmond glowingly broadcast via radio that "we will have brought recognition for the South in the political affairs of the nation which it has not fully enjoyed since the War Between the States." And again he blasted Truman's civil rights message as "a cold-blooded proposal . . . to barter away the sovereign rights of 48 sovereign states to win an election."[13]

11. *The State*, July 18, 1948.
12. *Ibid.*, August 1, 1948.
13. *Ibid.*, November 2, 1948.

The Dixiecrat revolt was strongest in South Carolina and Mississippi, the states with the highest proportion of Negroes among the population. The movement was strong elsewhere in the "black belt," from Virginia to Texas. Some of the Texas oilmen, with an eye on the offshore fields, apparently favored the states' rights appeal of the party for reasons not arising from the civil rights question. In the November election, Thurmond won four states—South Carolina, Mississippi, Alabama, and Louisiana. Within his home state, the Governor encountered feeble resistance from the regular Truman Democrats, who carried only two counties. The popular vote was three to one for Thurmond.[14]

Although the Dixiecrat revolt failed in its purpose to defeat President Truman, it worried the national Democratic leaders, who previously had generally ignored the wishes of the South. The 1952 convention witnessed the Democratic choice of a vice-presidential candidate from the deep South for the first time since the Civil War. In addition, the Dixiecrat revolt probably caused the race issue to become sharper in Southern politics. Nonetheless, regardless of the long-range effects, the immediate result was the kindling of a Southern fire that continued to smolder after the election.

3. Lingering Political Discontent

After its defeat in 1948, the Dixiecrat party fell apart as a separate political group. The dissenters once more sought to solve their problems within the framework of the regular Democratic organization. The election of 1950 clearly revealed the extent to which the old antagonisms still existed.

14. *Ibid.*, November 4, 1948. South Carolina Senators Johnston and Maybank remained quiet during the canvas. According to a report appearing in *The State*, November 11, 1948, Johnston even failed to vote, explaining that a rainstorm on election day had delayed his arrival at his home precinct until a few minutes after the polls had closed.

In the governor's race, James F. Byrnes came out of retirement to run. He did so, he said, because "the people of this state have been good to me, and I have decided to be a candidate in the hope, if elected, I can be of service to them." He also hoped to secure cooperation of other governors, North and South, "in resisting further encroachment by the federal government upon the states."[15] Resting on his laurels as former congressman, senator, Supreme Court justice, war mobilizer, and secretary of state, Byrnes hardly needed to campaign to swamp his three opponents.

The senatorial contest was quite different. It quickly developed into a demagogic free-for-all between Democratic regular Olin D. Johnston, the incumbent, and Dixiecrat Governor Strom Thurmond. In the canvass both candidates' tempers frequently flared, and a personal collision almost took place at Newberry when Johnston interrupted a Thurmond accusation with a vehement "You are a liar!" Thereafter the crowds grew in size, reaching a peak of 4200 at the campaign finale in Columbia.

Hecklers were numerous in the audience at several places and almost prevented Thurmond from being heard at Anderson, a Johnston stronghold. The contestants, especially Thurmond, lashed back at the hecklers, and both men exhibited superb showmanship on occasion. Johnston ridiculed Thurmond for standing on his head for a *Life* magazine photographer. Thurmond retorted: "Even when I stand on my head when I am exercising you can tell which side of the fence my feet are on." To a Thurmond attack on his pardon record while governor, Johnston accused Thurmond of appointing some of those pardoned as "colonels" on his staff. Thurmond countered: "He turned 'em out by the thousands and I may have gotten one by mistake."

During the campaign both men repeatedly vowed un-

15. *Ibid.*, July 12, 1950.

swerving loyalty to racial segregation, and each tried to detect inconsistencies in the other's stand. Johnston, for instance, scored Thurmond for appointing Negro physician Dr. T. C. McFall to the hospital advisory council of the South Carolina Medical Association. When the Governor defended his action as being directed by law and that he "had no other choice," the Senator loudly proclaimed that he would have suffered his right arm to be severed from his body before signing the commission.[16]

Thurmond in turn intimated that Johnston was not to be trusted on segregation. He declared at Conway that the CIO and NAACP were "working against Strom Thurmond." Johnston thereupon shouted that "any man that says I am for mixing of the races is an unmitigated liar . . . a low-down, contemptible liar."

Another issue in the contest, and probably the most significant, was Johnston's loyalty to the Truman administration. Thurmond averred that, if elected, he would not be "one kind of Democrat in South Carolina and another kind in Washington." Johnston replied that only through party loyalty and consequent control of committee chairmanships did the South stand its best chance to block civil rights programs in Washington. He repeatedly reminded his listeners that he had labored manfully to thwart the civil rights program in the Senate. In reality, however, the only clear-cut issue in the campaign was President Truman's foreign aid program: Thurmond favored it, Johnston opposed it. In the end Senator Johnston was renominated by a 25,000-vote majority. The industrial workers of the piedmont seemed to have furnished the margin of victory.[17]

The civil rights issue remained very much alive in the

16. Dr. McFall was still on the commission in 1958. Inez Watson (ed.), *South Carolina Legislative Manual, 1958* (Columbia, S.C.: House of Representatives, 1958), p. 274.

17. For the campaign speeches, see *The State*, June 20, 23, 27, July 2, 5, 8, 1950.

1952 presidential election. The Democratic convention endorsed another civil rights program, and its nominee, Governor Adlai Stevenson of Illinois, supported the proposals. In South Carolina the former Dixiecrats organized a "Democrats-for-Eisenhower" movement to back the Republican candidate, General Dwight D. Eisenhower. The regular South Carolina Republicans, under the leadership of J. Bates Gerald, refused to cooperate with the Democrats-for-Eisenhower. Consequently, there were two separate slates of presidential electors for the General. As it turned out, Stevenson won the state's electoral vote by a slender popular margin over the combined vote for both lists of Eisenhower electors.

Stevenson's greatest strength came from the piedmont, where the Dixiecrats had been weakest in 1948. Eisenhower's vote was by far the strongest showing made by a Republican candidate in South Carolina since 1876. Some observers believed that closer liaison between the Republican regulars and the Democratic irregulars would have produced an Eisenhower victory.[18] By the time of the next election, the Democrats-for-Eisenhower had disbanded their organization.

In the Democratic primary of June, 1954, the chief interest was centered on the governor's race between Lieutenant Governor George Bell Timmerman, Jr., of Edgefield, and Lester Bates, a Columbia insurance executive. Bates, unsuccessful against Byrnes in 1950, keyed his platform to "more business in government in less government

18. *Ibid.*, November 5, 1952. The 1952 vote was Democrats—172,957, Democrats-for-Eisenhower—158,250, Republicans—9,793, according to a recapitulation in *ibid.*, November 7, 1956. The South Carolina Republicans, always weak, were split by factional strife in the post-war period. The J. Bates Gerald group finally received state recognition under the 1950 election law. *Ibid.*, November 3, 1954. Heard in *A Two-Party South?*, Chap. VII, explains that Republican leaders in South Carolina and some other Southern states have not tried to win elections for several decades. They have preferred to be "big fish in little ponds" in control of Republican patronage.

in business." However, Timmerman quoted State Insurance Department reports which criticized Bates's business practices. Timmerman likewise intimated that the NAACP and the CIO supported Bates. In reply Bates charged that a "desperate attack" had been launched on his family, his friends, his business, and his policyholders. He said he would fight to preserve constitutional rights, free enterprise, the gains labor had made, and racial segregation, and to rid the state of the professional politicians. Furthermore, he defended his right to divide his profits as he saw fit.[19]

Bates's chief support came from the Democratic regulars, while Timmerman drew heavily from the former Dixiecrats. The insurance executive was undoubtedly injured by the charges of mismanagement of his company, and Timmerman won by an astounding 60,000 popular majority.

On September 1 the state was startled by the news of Senator Maybank's sudden death from a heart attack. Maybank had faced no opposition in his race for renomination at the June primary. His death, so close to the November election, threw the Democratic leaders into temporary confusion. Only hours after the Senator's funeral, the state Democratic executive committee met in a hurry-up conclave to consider a party nominee for the November election. Without calling a special primary, the executive committee decided to replace the deceased nominee with state Senator Edgar A. Brown of Barnwell. Brown was also a member of the executive committee, as well as chairman of the Senate Committee on Finance. Long a powerful political leader in South Carolina, Brown had tried unsuccessfully for the United States Senate twice previously, losing one contest by a narrow margin to "Cotton Ed" Smith in 1926.

Publicly the executive committee contended that it had not called a special primary because of insufficient time be-

19. *The State*, June 5, 1954.

fore the November election. The committee explained that the state law required all party nominees to be certified two months before the general election. Nevertheless, the explanation was unsatisfactory to many persons. They denounced the action of the executive committee as high-handed and undemocratic. Many newspapers followed the lead of *The Greenville News,* whose editorial, "Let the People Vote," appeared two days after Senator Maybank's death.

At this juncture, Strom Thurmond decided to enter the contest as a write-in candidate. He and his backers argued that the executive committee had had several legal alternatives to outright appointment of state Senator Brown.[20] Furthermore, Thurmond stoutly declared that if elected he would resign in 1956 to permit the voters to choose a candidate in the regular primary for the remaining four years of his Senate term.

Thurmond was supported by many of his Dixiecrat followers of 1948 and by Governor Byrnes. Brown had the backing of Senator Johnston and most of the members of the state Democratic executive committee. Thurmond was especially helped by the fact that the campaign became a "moral" issue: democracy versus committee rule. All the daily newspapers, except those in Anderson, either aided Thurmond openly or remained neutral. The results produced a Thurmond victory with a 60,000-vote majority. The ex-Dixiecrat swept the state, except for nine scattered counties, to become the first write-in candidate in American history to be elected to the United States Senate.[21]

True to his promise, Senator Thurmond resigned in

20. Governor Byrnes proposed that a preference primary be held, and that in the November election "all the votes cast for the name printed on the ticket would be counted for the candidate who received a majority of votes in the Democratic primary and whose name was thereupon certified to the secretary of state as the nominee of the Democratic Party." *Ibid.,* September 16, 1954.

21. *Ibid.,* November 3, 1954.

1956 and faced the voters again. But no opponent offered to run against him. South Carolina's other senator, Olin D. Johnston, likewise had no opposition in the primary race for renomination. There seemed to be a tacit understanding between the party regulars and the ex-Dixiecrats that neither faction would put up a candidate to challenge either incumbent.

In the presidential contest of 1956, Eisenhower again faced Stevenson, the Democratic nominee. As in 1948 and in 1952, discontent over civil rights loomed large in South Carolina. Since both presidential candidates were pledged to support civil rights legislation and integration in state-supported schools, the majority of the South Carolina whites seemed inclined toward neither. At the last minute an "Independent" ticket running Virginia Senator Harry Byrd for president was placed before the voters.

On election eve, the Independents declared that a vote for Stevenson, "The Great Integrator," was a vote for federal control of education, world government, destruction of states' rights, destruction of America's national defense, and a new America "built on Socialistic and Communistic theories." Their attack on President Eisenhower was limited to the simple statement that "everyone knows it is utterly impossible for the Republican party to carry South Carolina," so a vote for Eisenhower would merely aid in Stevenson's victory.[22]

Stevenson carried the state with approximately 45 per cent of the popular vote; the Independents won 30 per cent; and the President trailed with 25 per cent. Former Governor Byrnes, noting Stevenson's victory with less than a majority, predicted, "It means that four years hence the candidates of both parties will give more consideration to the views of South Carolina on important issues."[23]

22. *Ibid.*, November 4, 1956.
23. *Ibid.*, November 8, 1956. Stevenson carried the upstate and the lowcountry counties bordering North Carolina; the President carried only Aiken and Beaufort counties.

In the 1958 South Carolina Democratic primary, only one congressman faced opposition and there was no senatorial race. As in 1954, public interest was centered on the gubernatorial contest. Even here excitement was lacking, for the party modified the 46 county-by-county debates in favor of 14 meetings, one in each judicial district. Furthermore, the race was conducted in a listless, gentlemanly fashion by three candidates, none of whom stood for anything much except a desire to be governor.

In the contest were William C. Johnston, Anderson mayor and brother of Senator Olin D. Johnston; Donald Russell, former law partner of James F. Byrnes and former president of the University of South Carolina; and Ernest F. ("Fritz") Hollings, the young lieutenant governor from Charleston. All three candidates were on the "safe" side of the controversial issues of the day, but Mayor Johnston stood off slightly from the other two in his appeals to the farmers and mill workers. Hollings led the first primary with 158,000 votes to Russell's 132,000 and Johnston's 87,000.[24]

Bidding desperately for votes, Russell livened up the runoff by a dramatic and unexpected attack on the "Barnwell Ring," alleged supporters of the lieutenant governor. He pleaded for the selection of delegates to the national Democratic convention by primary vote, he attacked Hollings' unwillingness to push "local option" on whisky, and he declared that the "liquor interests" were behind the Charlestonian. Russell generally bored in hard wherever he thought he detected a weakness in the Hollings armor. The lieutenant governor effectively countered the blasts, however, pointing out inconsistencies in Russell's own attitude toward the "Barnwell Ring." Hollings stated as well that Russell's stand on segregation was not clear, a charge which led to numerous verbal blows on the race

24. *The State,* June 19, 1958.

issue in the closing days of the campaign.[25]   The expected Hollings victory, by a popular majority of 45,000, seemed to prove, if anything, that an able and experienced politician can defeat a capable amateur.

Regardless of the issues involved, post-1945 political campaigns did not create the interest of the pre-war contests.   The public increasingly turned to other recreational outlets or followed the political battles via radio and television.   Where the old spellbinders, "Pitchfork Ben," "Coley," and "Cotton Ed," attracted thousands to their rallies, Strom Thurmond and Olin D. Johnston drew hundreds.   With rare exceptions, recent campaigns have been relatively mild, and devoid of the color and bitter partisanship of yesteryear.   The best example of the decline of public enthusiasm for politics is to be noted in the state's congressional elections.   Of 48 potential regular primary races in six districts from 1944 through 1958, only 16 took place, and only four incumbents were defeated: Butler Hare (1946), John Riley (1948), James Hare (1950), and Hugo Sims, Jr. (1950).

B.   THE ORGANIZATION AND OPERATION OF THE SOUTH CAROLINA GOVERNMENT

1.   Constitutional Framework of the South Carolina Government

The present South Carolina constitution was written in 1895 under the guidance of Ben Tillman and his farmer friends.   The constitution contains a preamble and 17 articles.   These articles, varying greatly in length, were amended 227 times before 1958.[26]   The Constitution establishes three departments—legislative, executive, and judicial.[27]

25. For a summary of most of the campaign issues, see *ibid.*, June 18, 1958.
26. W. D. Workman, Jr., in *The News and Courier* (Charleston, S.C.), July 30, 1958.
27. For a more detailed discussion of the constitutional framework,

(a) The legislative department: The lawmaking power in South Carolina rests with the "General Assembly of South Carolina," which is divided into the "Senate" and the "House of Representatives."[28] The General Assembly has 46 senators and 124 representatives. There is one senator from each county, but the representatives are apportioned among the counties according to population. In 1958 Greenville and Charleston counties each had 10 representatives, Spartanburg had 9, Richland had 8, and the 13 smallest counties had one each.[29]

The terms of representatives are two years; terms of senators are four years. Thus, one-half the senators and all the representatives face re-election every two years. Senators and representatives must be residents of the county that elects them. A senator must be at least twenty-five years old, a representative at least twenty-one. Pay for members of both houses is $1000 each, per session.[30]

The General Assembly begins its regular annual session the second Tuesday in January. In recent years its sessions have tended to be lengthy, usually from three to five months, and sometimes longer. The number of acts the legislature has ratified per regular session has not been less than 300 since 1918, and the number reached 766 in 1936.[31] The lawmaking procedure in South Carolina is about the same as in most states. Bills may be introduced in one of three ways: by a member of either house, by one of the standing committees, or by a county legislative delegation. The

see George R. Sherrill, "State Governmental Organization," *South Carolina: Economic and Social Conditions in 1944,* ed. Wilfred H. Callcott (Columbia, S.C.: University of South Carolina Press, 1945), pp. 141-76.

28. Inez Watson (ed.), *Constitution . . . of the State of South Carolina as Amended, April 2, 1954* (Columbia, S.C.: State Budget and Control Board, 1954), Art. III, Sect. 1.

29. *Ibid.,* Sect. 3; *Legislative Manual, 1958,* pp. 128-33.

30. *Constitution, South Carolina,* Art. III, Sects. 2, 6-8.

31. *Legislative Manual, 1958,* p. 327; *Constitution, South Carolina,* Art. III, Sect. 9.

county delegation consists of the senator and the representatives of that county.

In the House a bill is drawn up, signed, and dropped in the speaker's box. When the clerk removes the bill from the box, he reads the title of the bill and turns it over to a standing committee, unless the House unanimously agrees, without debate, to "dispense" with it.[32] The success or failure of a bill usually depends on the action of the committee. There are eight standing committees in the House, and their chairmen are influential legislators. Favorable or unfavorable committee action is usually followed by similar House action.

After a bill has successfully passed through the committee, it is printed and copies furnished each representative. The bill is read for a second time, now word for word, and debated. When finally approved, with or without amendments, the bill is read for the third and last time. The last reading is usually a formality. The bill is read by title only and little or no debate follows. After acceptance of the bill by the House, the speaker sends it to the Senate.[33]

In the Senate the bill goes through almost the same procedure as in the House. If the Senate approves the bill without change, a day is appointed for ratification. Amid ceremony and in the presence of members of both houses, the speaker of the House and the president of the Senate sign the act.[34]

When the two houses cannot agree separately on parts of the bill, the house proposing an amendment or amendments may ask for a conference committee. Such a committee is limited to ironing out existing differences in the two versions of the bill, nothing more. However, by a two-thirds vote of each house the bill may be sent to a committee on free conference, which has the power to introduce new

32. *Legislative Manual, 1958*, p. 173.
33. *Ibid.*, pp. 173-75.
34. *Ibid.*, pp. 186-87.

matter into the measure.[35] In actual practice, many appropriation bills wind up before a committee on free conference.

After a bill has passed both houses of the General Assembly, it is sent to the governor. The governor may approve the bill, veto it, or take no action. If he vetoes the bill, it is killed unless both houses of the legislature decide to override him. To override a veto requires a two-thirds vote in each house. Should the governor take no action at all, the bill automatically becomes a law after three days (Sundays excepted), unless the General Assembly by adjournment prevents return of the bill. In the latter case, the bill becomes law unless the governor returns it within two days after the next meeting of the legislature. The governor can also veto separate items in appropriation bills.[36]

(b) The executive department: "The supreme executive authority of the state shall be invested in a Chief Magistrate who shall be styled the Governor of the State of South Carolina."[37] The governor is not the only executive officer, but is chief among a host of executive officers. Among them are the lieutenant governor, the secretary of state, the treasurer, the comptroller general, the attorney general, the adjutant general, the commissioner of agriculture, and the superintendent of education. These officials are elected for four-year terms of office by popular vote[38] and are largely independent of the governor's control.

The governor is elected by popular vote every four years but is ineligible for re-election. His salary is $12,000 per year (1958). The governor must be at least thirty years old, a citizen of the United States, and a citizen and resident

35. *Ibid.*, pp. 185-86.
36. *Constitution, South Carolina,* Art. IV, Sect. 23.
37. *Ibid.*, Art. IV, Sect. 1.
38. *Ibid.*, Art. IV, Sect. 24.

of South Carolina for at least five years before the day of his election.   If the governor's office becomes vacant, the lieutenant governor will succeed to the governorship.[39]

The governor has numerous constitutional powers.   Acts of the legislature have conferred upon him a great number of additional powers and duties.   He has the right to call the General Assembly into special session, to adjourn the General Assembly if both houses cannot agree on a time of adjournment, to send recommendations and information to the General Assembly, and, as noted, to veto bills of the legislature.

The governor is also commander-in-chief of the state's militia, except when the militia is called into active service of the United States.   He commissions all officers of the state and is directed to suspend from active service any officer indicted for misuse of public funds.   The governor may grant reprieves and commute death sentences to life imprisonment.   Furthermore, the governor is to take care that all laws of the state be "faithfully executed in mercy."

The governor is empowered to require written reports from all other executive officers and from boards of public institutions on management and financial matters.[40]   In 1958 there were upwards of 90 boards, commissions, educational institutions, penal institutions, and independent governmental agencies in South Carolina.[41]   Noting this situation, a political scientist remarked critically a few years earlier, "The sprawling, clumsy, irresponsible administrative structure of the government of South Carolina stands in strange contrast with an industrial corporation."   He pointed out that most of these agencies were added one at a

39. *Ibid.,* Art. IV, Sects. 2, 3, 9.
40. For the governor's many duties, see *ibid.,* Art. IV, Sects. 10-17, 22.
41. *Legislative Manual, 1958,* pp. 228-309.

time with "little or no attention" given to the administrative structure as a whole.[42]

(c) The judicial department: This department consists of the supreme court, the circuit courts, five special county courts, the civil and criminal court of Charleston, the probate courts, the recorders' courts in cities and towns, the magistrates' courts, several special children's courts, and several special juvenile-domestic relations courts.

The South Carolina constitution provides specifically for the supreme court, the circuit courts, the probate courts, and the magistrates' courts. These seem to be more important than the numerous tribunals created by the legislature.

The supreme court consists of the chief justice and four associate justices. All five are selected by the legislature for staggered terms of ten years each. The court meets at least twice yearly, with the chief justice presiding. Justices of the supreme court must be citizens of the United States, citizens and residents of South Carolina for five years "next preceding . . . election," and at least twenty-six years old, and must have been licensed attorneys for five years. The supreme court has power "to issue writs or orders of injunction, mandamus, quo warranto, prohibition, certiorari, habeas corpus and other original and remedial writs." Additionally, it has appellate jurisdiction "only in cases of chancery."[43] Serving on the supreme court in 1959 were Chief Justice Taylor H. Stukes (Manning) and Associate Justices Claude A. Taylor (Spartanburg), George D. Oxner (Greenville), Lionel K. Legge (Charleston), and Joseph R. Moss (York).[44]

The circuit courts are the best known of South Carolina's judicial bodies. The General Assembly has divided

42. Sherrill in *South Carolina: Economic and Social Conditions in 1944*, pp. 163-64.
43. *Constitution, South Carolina*, Art. V, Sects. 2, 4-5.
44. *Legislative Manual, 1959*, pp. 208-10.

the state into 14 judicial circuits (each having two to five counties) and has assigned one judge to each circuit. The legislature selects circuit judges for four-year terms and provides that judges shall rotate circuits.[45]

The circuit judge presides over two types of court sessions: the court of common pleas and the court of general sessions. The former has jurisdiction over civil cases, the latter over criminal cases. Any person charged with an offense has the right to demand and obtain a trial by jury. In the circuit courts the jury consists of 12 men, "all of whom must agree to a verdict in order to render same." Common pleas and general sessions courts are held in each county at least twice a year. Both courts have original jurisdiction in most cases of importance and hear appeals from inferior tribunals.[46]

The magistrates' courts are the most numerous in the state, there being several in each county. The governor with the consent of the Senate appoints magistrates (justices of the peace) for two-year terms, except in six counties where their terms are four years. Magistrates hear civil cases involving property valued not above $100 and criminal cases in which fines do not exceed $100 or imprisonment more than 30 days. There are, however, four counties in which magistrates have jurisdiction over more important cases. A magistrate's jury, when used, is composed of six persons.[47]

Probate courts meet in each county once a month and are primarily concerned with the administration of business relating to minors and mentally incompetent persons. In several counties the probate judge presides over a children's court to handle cases of juvenile delinquency. Probate

45. *Ibid.*, pp. 212-13; *Constitution, South Carolina*, Art. V, Sects. 13-14.
46. *Ibid.*, Art. V, Sects. 15-18, 22.
47. *Ibid.*, Art. V, Sects. 20-22.

judges are elected by popular vote for four-year terms of office.[48]

2. *The Location of Political Power in South Carolina*

Constitutional framework aside, this question often arises: Where is the real political power in South Carolina? No one person or small group of persons control the state. It is true that there are a number of small political rings, but no politician has a well-knit, state-wide organization that can assure victory at the polls. The late Senator Ellison D. Smith had no political machine, although he was re-elected numerous times. Most of the political rings in South Carolina are small courthouse cliques. These rings are strong in some counties but weak in others. Their members are seldom tied closely together. The courthouse rings come together, break up, reorganize, break up again, and so on.

One of the best-known political groups in South Carolina is the so-called "Barnwell Ring," headed by state Senator Edgar A. Brown (chairman of the Senate Finance Committee) and Solomon Blatt (speaker of the House of Representatives). Both men have come into their positions through seniority and above-average political ability. They exert great influence on legislative matters, but they do not possess the dictatorial powers some of their enemies attribute to them. Senator Brown is hardly the "prime minister" with the governor merely a "ceremonial chief of state" as claimed by one political scientist.[49] Instead, on state-wide matters Brown and Blatt are leaders of like-minded conservative legislators from central and lower South Carolina. On national issues the "Barnwell Ring," more consistently loyal to the Democratic administration than the ex-Dixiecrats, is frequently out-voted in the state.

Regardless of clique, party, or ring, the chief political

48. *Ibid.,* Art. V, Sect. 19; Sherrill in *South Carolina: Economic and Social Conditions in 1944,* pp. 172-73.
49. Key, *Southern Politics,* pp. 153-55.

power in South Carolina lies with the legislature. It controls appropriations, appoints numerous executive officials, dominates the county governments, appoints the judiciary primarily from its own ranks, and frequently thwarts the governor.[50] Professor George R. Sherrill concluded in 1941 that the legislature had "enormous powers—powers that no legislative body should ever have. Such concentration in one department violates the principle of separation of powers, hamstrings the other departments, impairs the efficient operation of government, and blocks progress."[51]

Within the legislature itself, the key men are the state senators, usually older and more experienced than the members of the House. In fact, a majority of the senators serve one or more terms in the House before moving up to the Senate. Whenever House and Senate bills are ironed out in conference committees, the senators usually carry the most weight. Furthermore, the state senator is the head of his county's legislative delegation. The House members of the delegation can secure no legislation for their county without the senator's consent.

In addition, it may be noted that the senators from the less populous counties below the fall line are more powerful than those from other counties. This is because since World War II the smaller counties have re-elected the same men more often than the more populous counties. In turn, the small-county senators control most of the committee chairmanships. In 1954 there were 33 Senate standing committees, and 25 of these were headed by lowcountry senators: J. D. Parler (Dorchester) was chairman of five committees; J. C. Kearse (Bamberg) headed four; and Rembert Dennis (Berkeley) and J. P. Mozingo (Darling-

50. In 1958 all five supreme court justices and all 14 circuit court judges were former members of the legislature, and all but one were members at the time they were elevated to the judiciary. *Legislative Manual, 1958*, pp. 205-16.

51. George R. Sherrill, "Legislative Domination in South Carolina," *Proceedings* of the South Carolina Historical Association, 1941, p. 31.

ton) each headed three. At the same time the senators from the populous counties of Greenville, Charleston, Spartanburg, Richland, and Anderson held no committee chairmanships.[52]

In 1958 there was practically the same alignment of power in the Senate. Twenty-seven of 35 committees were chaired by lowcountry senators: Parler and Mozingo headed four each; Dennis, Brown, J. H. McFaddin (Clarendon), and Wilbur Grant (Chester) headed three each. The only senators above the fall line to hold committee chairmanships were Grant, L. L. Hester (McCormick), W. B. Williams (Lancaster), and J. D. Long (Union). As was true four years earlier, the senators from Greenville, Charleston, Spartanburg, Richland, and Anderson held no chairmanships.[53]

All politicians and political groups of significance in South Carolina are Democratic. In spite of the Dixiecrat rebellion in 1948 and that of the Democrats-for-Eisenhower in 1952, the Democratic party controls state, county, and city governments in the state. The Republican party is simply too weak in local politics to offer serious opposition. The Radical Reconstruction era gave the party a bad name in South Carolina from which it has never recovered. When the Republican candidate for president in 1952 almost carried South Carolina, some observers believed that the Republicans were making a comeback. The poor Republican showing in the 1954 congressional elections dispelled any such illusion.

In 1956, however, the Republican party was slightly rejuvenated under the chairmanship of David S. Dows of Bradley. At considerable personal expense, Dows built up sufficient interest in the party to swing 49,000 votes to

52. *Legislative Manual, 1954*, pp. 39-43.
53. *Ibid., 1958*, pp. 41-45. In 1959 Mozingo headed seven committees, Parler five, and Dennis and Grant four each. *Ibid., 1959*, pp. 42-46.

Clemson Mayor Leon P. Crawford in his contest against Senator Johnston in the November election of that year.[54] In the presidential race at the same time, the regular Republican vote was 25 per cent.

Republican prospects fell again when President Eisenhower sent troops into Little Rock, Arkansas, in September, 1957, to enforce a federal court school integration order. One Republican bigwig in South Carolina privately admitted that the President's action, extremely unpopular in the South, had greatly damaged the party in the state. Nevertheless, at the biennial state Republican convention in March, 1958, almost 300 delegates showed up, the largest number in recent years. The convention chose Gregory D. Shorey, Jr., 34-year-old Greenville manufacturer, as its chairman. The group then proceeded to bicker over a states' rights plank (adopted) and the seating of several delegations.

In an appeal to the Negro voters (several Negro delegates were present), outgoing Chairman Dows reminded the convention that the Negro vote would increase in time, so it behooved the party to "make every effort" to see that Negroes' civil rights were "amply protected" under the law.[55] Obviously, the white delegates were of divided opinions as to what course to follow concerning Negroes' civil rights. Should the majority in the near future endorse Dows's policy, factionalism will undoubtedly arise once more in the party. As matters stood in January, 1960, the Republican party seemed destined to play a minor role in South Carolina politics for some years to come.

C. Recent Political Problems in South Carolina

A point of departure for a discussion of recent political problems in South Carolina is the election of 1946. The 11

54. *The State,* November 3, 1954; *The Greenville News,* March 26, 1958.
55. *Ibid.,* March 27, 1958.

gubernatorial candidates in this feverish and somewhat humorous race dredged up about every issue imaginable. Candidate Roger W. Scott ran simply on his opponents' demerits and enjoyed lambasting each in turn. At the campaign windup in Columbia, Scott proclaimed that the state needed a cave man for governor and proposed himself to fill that need.[56]

The control of alcohol has been and is a significant issue in South Carolina. A state-wide referendum in 1940 resulted in a majority vote for prohibition. But the legislature failed to take action, the "wets" contending that the wording of the referendum confused many voters. In the 1946 primary, Strom Thurmond, personally a non-drinker, apparently had the support of the "drys." Incumbent Ransome Williams sought state-operated stores modeled on Virginia's Alcoholic Beverage Control system. Williams criticized the "domination of the State government by liquor interests." The favorite of the "wets" was Del O'Neal, who campaigned for open bars: a legal "one-ounce drink rather than a 32-ounce drunk." After the election Thurmond, the winner, promised to clean up the "liquor mess."[57]

The new governor brought no revolution in alcohol control, and the issue remained very much alive. With greater determination the "drys" began to work hard for local option on prohibition. They very nearly succeeded in pushing such a measure through the legislature in 1955. The "wets" blocked it and subsequent moves mainly through political trickery. Whether the "wets" can forestall a showdown much longer is doubtful, for in the 1958 gubernatorial primary all three candidates, when pressed, publicly committed themselves to local option.

The 1946 campaign also featured Strom Thurmond's onslaught against the "Barnwell Ring," notwithstanding the

---

56. *The State,* August 9, 1946.
57. *Ibid.,* July 9, 12, 17, September 5, 1946.

fact that he had previously been on friendly terms with both Brown and Blatt, and with their support had secured a circuit judgeship before World War II.   In his fight against the government "of the Barnwell Ring, for the Barnwell Ring, and by the Barnwell Ring," Thurmond was seconded by gubernatorial hopeful Dr. Carl Epps, who called Brown, Blatt, and state Senator Richard Jefferies "three political devils."[58]

After his victory over Dr. James McLeod in the second primary, Thurmond jubilantly trumpeted: "A new day has dawned.   The people are aroused.   They are determined that a clique of self-serving politicians who have so long held power of life and death over our political life be driven from control of the State House."[59]

Nevertheless, whatever power the "Barnwell Ring" held remained intact, except for Blatt's temporary resignation as speaker of the House.   In 1954 Thurmond again clashed with the "Barnwell Ring" as he defeated Brown's bid for a United States Senate seat.   Contrariwise, Donald Russell's attack on the Brown-Blatt forces after the first primary in the 1958 governor's race availed him nothing.   The old cry of "ring rule," a favorite vote-getting device, evoked little response, and Russell may have lost more votes than he gained by denouncing the "Barnwell Ring."[60]

Closely allied to the question of "ring rule" is one of "reform" in the state government and the demand for a constitutional convention.   In 1946 at least five of the gubernatorial candidates stood for reform in the state government.   A sixth, Dr. McLeod, called for a new constitution.[61]

Once in office, Governor Thurmond also recommended

58. *Ibid.,* July 12, 1946.
59. *Ibid.,* September 5, 1946.
60. Russell too had enjoyed "Barnwell" support when chosen as president of the University of South Carolina.
61. *The State,* July 9, 12, 1946.

calling a constitutional convention, as did his successors Byrnes and Timmerman. The 1895 Constitution was badly in need of modernizing in some particulars and was encumbered with 227 amendments by 1958. A number of younger legislators fought hard in 1956 to persuade the General Assembly to call a convention, but the old-timers, led by several lowcountry senators, refused to budge.[62] Their opposition was clearly understandable: a new constitution might shear away some of the power of the legislature and of the Senate in particular.

The campaign of 1946 renewed the long-standing fight of business against organized labor. The strongest of five "businessmen's candidates" in the governor's race was the moderate Dr. McLeod. He advocated "industrial progress" while at the same time favoring labor's right to organize and bargain collectively. Then, four days before the second primary, he charged Thurmond with having CIO support. McLeod boldly asserted: "Endorsement of my opponent by the CIO has made the issue clear—your choice is between James McLeod and the CIO."[63] Four years later, Thurmond, classed as somewhat of a liberal in 1946, vilified Olin D. Johnston with the same charge—CIO support. During the 1950's the politicians shied away from the CIO or any organized labor backing like the plague. To admit such support was tantamount to political suicide in South Carolina.

In reality labor unions have been so weak in the state since 1945 that business versus organized labor has been no real issue. In 1954 there was a little political flurry when the legislature enacted a "right-to-work" law. The measure, aimed at "busting" unions, outlawed the union shop throughout the state. A few upcountry legislators protested

---

62. W. D. Workman, Jr., in *The News and Courier*, July 30, 1958.

63. *The State*, August 31, 1946. Defeated candidate John C. Taylor had earlier decried "dictatorial labor leadership." *Ibid.*, July 9, 1946.

but were overwhelmed by the proponents of the law. However, it is quite common to hear candidates from the stump lash out at "big business" without furnishing any particulars.[64]

Since World War II several significant issues have been settled. Under Strom Thurmond's guidance, the voters in 1948 eliminated the "pardon racket" by amending the constitution to limit the governor's clemency powers to reprieve and to commutation of death sentences to life imprisonment. In the same election the voters, by means of another constitutional amendment, empowered the legislature to legalize divorce on four grounds: adultery, physical cruelty, desertion, and habitual drunkenness.[65] The following year the General Assembly complied. South Carolina therefore became the last state in the Union to grant divorces.

A once-prominent issue in South Carolina politics that is rapidly fading away is the lowcountry-upcountry antagonism, which arose in colonial times primarily because of lowcountry control of the colonial assembly. This sectionalism continued into the twentieth century due partly to tradition but also to genuine differences in geography, climate, economy, and race. The lessening of antagonism was quite noticeable, for instance, in 1950 when Burnet

64. In the 1946 campaign John D. Long warned that big business was "on the prowl." *Ibid.,* July 17, 1946.

65. *Ibid.,* November 4, 1948. In November, 1959, M. S. Stackhouse, a member of the State Probation, Pardon and Parole Board, blasted penitentiary officials with the charge of an "unofficial parole system" which permitted dangerous felons to work at state jobs outside the prison walls. Although the charges seemed to be exaggerated, they brought to light friction between Wyndham Manning, penitentiary superintendent, and Parole Board officials. Manning favored a reorganization of the Board and a more lenient parole system, primarily because of overcrowded conditions within the prison. J. C. Todd, director of the Board, admitted following a "tough" policy but opposed placing prisoners on parole just to relieve an overcrowded penitentiary *The Greenville News,* November 10, 1959.

Maybank of Charleston carried many upstate counties in winning renomination to the Senate. In 1958 "Fritz" Hollings, also of Charleston, likewise carried much of the upcountry by a wide margin in his successful bid for the gubernatorial nomination.

Strangely, in the 1946 election little attention was focused on the race issue. Only John D. Long of the 11 gubernatorial hopefuls vigorously expressed an extreme racist viewpoint, and he polled only 16,503 votes to run sixth.[66] Long, however, did voice the dominating issue in South Carolina politics. Race has been, is, and will be in the foreseeable future the issue that dwarfs all others in the state. It is responsible for the absence of genuine two-party politics in the state. Moreover, the race issue has become intensified since 1941 due to Supreme Court anti-segregation decisions and civil rights battles in Congress.

In the congressional struggle, Southern leaders have repeatedly blocked most features of the civil rights bills, but the South has no way to check the Court. As matters stood, South Carolina whites grumblingly accepted the federal judiciary's doctrine of equality until May, 1954. At that time the Supreme Court handed down its South-shaking Clarendon County decision. In this significant case, several Negro plaintiffs brought suit against school officials in Clarendon to force the admission of Negro children into white schools on an unsegregated basis. The Court declared enforced segregation in state-supported schools to be in violation of the Fourteenth Amendment. The Court did not, however, order immediate enforcement of its decree.

After the stunning decision some religious and civic leaders urged caution and moderation. Several newspapers followed the same line, intimating that eventual integration might be achieved. But to date (January, 1960) no promi-

66. *The State,* August 20, 1946.

nent politician in the state has hinted at compliance, token or otherwise, even in the distant future.

The few South Carolinians who openly favored compliance with the Court's decree pointed out that, moral considerations aside, the decision would eventually be enforced. Therefore, they favored gradual preparation for the inevitable. This view was unacceptable to the vast majority of the whites, who bitterly opposed integration at any level. The Negroes, except for a few leaders, remained silent on the issue, but there was little doubt that the Negroes hailed the Court's ruling as a great victory in their long march toward racial equality.

Meanwhile, the General Assembly sought ways to thwart the Court's decision. Anticipating the decree well ahead of time, the legislature had submitted to the voters in 1952 a constitutional amendment empowering the lawmakers to close the public schools if necessary to prevent integration. By a slightly more than two-to-one majority the voters approved the amendment.[67]

In 1956 the General Assembly tackled the segregation problem in dead earnest. In fact, W. D. Workman, Jr., journalist for *The News and Courier* and *The Greenville News,* called the 1956 legislative session the "Segregation Session."[68]

Acts passed by the legislature provided for closing public schools and colleges if necessary to prevent integration. Sheriffs were empowered to transfer pupils from one school to another whenever any responsible school official thought the transfer necessary to prevent riots or trouble. The legislature closed Edisto State Park in the face of a lawsuit to open the park to all races. And the legislature made it unlawful for any state employee to join the NAACP.

67. Governor Byrnes had suggested the amendment to the legislature. *Ibid.,* November 5, 1952.
68. *The Greenville News,* April 5, 1956.

Other legislative actions included resolutions defending segregation and condemning the Supreme Court's decision in the Clarendon case.

The state legislature was not alone in trying to uphold segregation. Throughout South Carolina white people organized a number of "citizens' councils." These councils disclaimed any intention of violence. Their leaders declared that the councils would use only legal means to maintain segregation in the public schools.

In some cases, however, the citizens' councils used means of doubtful legality, all of which gave encouragement to the more radical Ku Klux Klan. Threats, intimidation, and outright violence broke out occasionally. In 1955, Negro minister Joseph A. DeLaine, whose home and whose church had been mysteriously burned, fired on a carload of white men and then fled the state rather than face arrest.[69]

Jack O'Dowd, editor of *The Florence Morning News,* was subjected to threats and attempts to force his car off the road. Two members of his staff were likewise mistreated, all because O'Dowd advocated compliance with the Supreme Court's decision. As the newspaper's circulation dropped and complaints mounted, O'Dowd finally admitted defeat in an editorial "Retreat from Reason," March 11, 1956. A few months later he moved outside the state.[70] Several white ministers, also under pressure, relinquished their pulpits.

Other incidents included the beating of a Greenville Negro, for which confessed Klansmen were sentenced to prison, and the bombing of a Gaffney physician's home, apparently because his wife spoke openly for moderation.

69. Governor Timmerman made no attempt to extradite DeLaine. He expressed the opinion that the state was "well rid of this professional agitator." *The State,* October 18, 1957.

70. Idus A. Newby, "South Carolina and the Desegregation Issue, 1954-1956" (Master's thesis, University of South Carolina, 1957), pp. 270-75.

There were indictments but no convictions in the latter case.[71]

In spite of these isolated incidents, the race issue became relatively quiet in early 1957. The legislature and the politicians made no new moves to strengthen segregation. The integrationists brought no new cases before the courts. This illusory calm was shattered by events in Little Rock, Arkansas, in September. In the face of a federal district court order to admit nine Negro students to Central High School in Little Rock, Governor Orval Faubus first used the national guard to obstruct the Negroes' entry. Later he refused to use the guard to protect the Negroes once they had entered the school. When several Negroes were beaten and mob rule threatened, President Eisenhower sent in federal troops against the wishes of the Governor.

The use of troops produced a great wave of resentment among Southern segregationists, and even some of the moderates deplored the President's action. In South Carolina former Congressman James P. Richards stated: "It's about time they realize an issue like this in the South can't be handled by the Federal government." Senator Johnston opined that "Eisenhower acted unconstitutionally."[72]

Probably the gravest charges hurled at the President came from Governor Timmerman. As he learned that Eisenhower was preparing to use troops in Little Rock, he reacted as follows: "I think that if the President has directed the people of Arkansas to mix the children of Arkan-

71. Mrs. Claudia T. Sanders, the physician's wife, was one of 12 contributors to a pamphlet entitled: *South Carolinians Speak: A Moderate Approach to Race Relations.* Reverend John B. Morris, one of five ministers connected with the project, reported that 9,000 copies were distributed free and 10,000 sold for 50 cents each. Morris further reported seven negative and 18 favorable editorials in South Carolina newspapers. William Peters, *The Southern Temper* (New York: Doubleday and Company, 1959), pp. 95-96. Conviction in the bombing case was thwarted when the prosecution's chief witness, a self-confessed participant, was accidentally killed before the trial.

72. *The State,* October 27, 1957.

sas against their will, he is attempting to set himself up as a dictator and this action may be taken as further evidence of an effort to communize America." A few days later the Governor resigned his commission as a lieutenant in the United States Naval Reserve "because of the recent change in official attitude on the federal level toward the personal and property rights of American citizens."[73] Immediately, pressure developed on some of the higher ranking reserve officer politicians to resign also. But with one or two exceptions, the reservists remained silent on that score.

Undoubtedly the Little Rock incident hardened the determination of the segregationists to yield no ground. The word "never" was increasingly heard from political leaders in late 1957 and early 1958. Most South Carolina newspapers editorialized against Eisenhower's use of troops and were gleeful when in July, 1958, Governor Faubus was re-elected to a third term by a two-to-one majority over two opponents.

Where was the end? One perceptive student of the Clarendon County controversy expressed this conclusion in early 1957: "After almost three years, the desegregation decision of the Supreme Court meant little to the Negro in South Carolina except improved but still segregated school facilities. And apparently many school terms would come and go before South Carolina would 'make a prompt and reasonable start toward full compliance' with the Court's directive."[74]

Nevertheless, the Clarendon Negroes kept up their fight. In August, 1959, they filed petitions with school board authorities for reassignment of 76 Negro pupils to white schools. Although again denied the right to integrate their children with whites, the Clarendon Negro leaders promised further legal action. Meanwhile, at the annual meeting of

73. *Ibid.*, September 24, 29, 1957.
74. Newby, "South Carolina and the Desegregation Issue," p. 286.

the South Carolina branch of the NAACP, Negro speakers hinted at early action elsewhere in the state to break down racial barriers.[75]   Events in Virginia, Arkansas, and Georgia in 1959 indicated that South Carolina whites might soon face the prospect of limited desegregation or no public schools.

75. *The Greenville News,* October 14, 25, 1959.

Chapter Eight

South Carolina Today: Some Economic and Cultural Aspects

A. SOUTH CAROLINA AND WORLD WAR II

1. In the Service

Shortly after the Japanese bombed Pearl Harbor, South Carolinians found themselves closer to total war than they had been since 1865. There was hardly an able-bodied unmarried man in the state who did not enter military service. Many married men also answered the call to colors. Approximately 170,000 South Carolina men served either in the army, the navy, or the marines, and 2500 South Carolina women served as volunteers in the women's corps of the three branches.

The men who entered service included reservists with previous military training, members of the national guard, volunteers, and selectees. The Selective Service Act made all males between the ages of eighteen and forty-five eligible for military service. A local three-man selective service ("draft") board was established in each county. As in World War I, a lottery system was used to determine the number assigned to each male registered. Thus, mere chance decided when a man would be selected for military duty. Only the physically unfit and those employed in essential war work were deferred from active military service.

During the course of the conflict, South Carolina combat troops served in every theater of war, while others in the Air Transport Command and Service of Supply were stationed in out-of-the-way places all over the globe: Iran, India, Iceland, Australia, and so on. Needless to say, South Carolina naval personnel sailed the seven seas, performing their most notable work against the Japanese in the Pacific.

As in World War I, only a few Negro troops were used in combat outfits. Most of the battle honors were therefore won by white soldiers. Five South Carolinians won the nation's highest military award. the Congressional Medal of Honor. They were Private First Class Thomas E. Atkins of Campobello, Private First Class William A. McWhorter of Liberty, Private Furman L. Smith of Central, Lieutenant Colonel George L. Mabry, Jr., of Sumter, and Sergeant Robert A. Owens of Greenville.[1]

Sergeant Owens, a marine, won his Medal in the Solomon Islands. According to his citation, he "charged into the mouth of the steadily firing cannon and entered the emplacement through the fire port, driving the gun crew out of the rear door and insuring their destruction before he himself was wounded."

The other four Medal winners were members of army infantry divisions. Privates First Class McWhorter and Atkins won their Medals in the Philippines. Atkins, single-handed, held up the advance of a Japanese platoon for four hours, killing 13 of the enemy. After Atkins went to an aid station because of wounds, he arose from his stretcher to kill an enemy soldier who had infiltrated into the hospital area. McWhorter lost his life in earning his Medal. With his own body he shielded his friends from an enemy hand grenade.

Lieutenant Colonel Mabry was awarded his Medal of

1. Department of the Army, *The Medal of Honor of the United States Army* (Washington: Government Printing Office, 1948), pp. 319, 327, 340, 365; and U. S. Bureau of Naval Personnel, *Medal of Honor, 1861-1949* (Washington: [Government Printing Office, 1950]), p. 234.

Honor for superior leadership of his battalion in the Hurt-gen Forest in Germany. He led the assault against several fortified enemy bunkers. In the fight Mabry personally captured several of the enemy after a hand-to-hand bayonet encounter.

Private Smith won his Medal of Honor in Italy for valor displayed while defending two wounded comrades against an overwhelming enemy attack. Rather than retreat to safety, Smith chose to remain with his comrades, and he thereby laid down his life for them.

2. The Home Front

Within the space of a few months, drastic changes oc-curred in home life. The United States Navy Yard at Charleston mushroomed into a city, where thousands worked feverishly day and night. Some workers daily commuted to the Navy Yard from homes 50 to 60 miles away. Teen-agers, women, and elderly men became welders, riveters, machinists, metal workers, carpenters, electricians, and mechanics of all types.

Most of the state's textile mills turned to war work. They made tents, army clothing, and the like. The mills operated three work shifts daily and extra hours on the week ends. Here again teen-agers, old men, and housewives had to replace those who had been called into military service.

In the meantime, South Carolina became an armed camp. Everywhere were airfields under construction, con-voys moving along highways, and military maneuvers in the pinelands. Besides numerous airbases, there were two large infantry training camps in South Carolina: Fort Jack-son at Columbia and Camp Croft at Spartanburg. Each of these infantry bases trained from 50,000 to 60,000 soldiers at a time. Several of the most famous infantry di-visions of World War II were trained at Camp Croft or

Fort Jackson. Some navy personnel were trained at Charleston, and the marine corps base at Parris Island was the center of great activity.

Very soon after the Pearl Harbor bombing, the federal government began to ration scarce articles of food and other essentials. Rationing boards were set up in every county, and all citizens registered to receive the ration books. These books contained stamps that entitled the holder to buy limited amounts of meat, sugar, gasoline, and shoes. Only one and one-half gallons of gasoline per week were allotted to each automobile for pleasure driving. Rationing boards made tires and tire recaps available only in cases of real necessity.

As a further aid in saving tires and conserving gasoline, the federal government established a national speed limit of 40 miles per hour. The government also conducted drives to collect scrap metal and paper. Boy scouts and church organizations frequently took charge of these drives. Also to save metal, dry cleaning companies began to use cardboard coat hangers, and retail stores required buyers of toothpaste to turn in an empty tube for each new one purchased.

Some unrationed items such as Coca-Cola's, fountain pens, pocket knives, and golf and tennis balls became scarce. Other items such as nylon hosiery, radios, and heavy metal goods all but completely disappeared from the market.

Early in the war a blackout was established along the coast to prevent shore lights from inadvertently aiding Nazi submarines. Even so, the subs sank a number of American ships off the Carolina coast.

Volunteers on the home front performed many types of work. In every town and community, some people served as air raid wardens and aircraft spotters, while others rolled bandages for the Red Cross or studied first aid to help the injured in case of an enemy air attack. Civic leaders in all the larger towns set up and supported United Service Organization (USO) clubs.

The USO clubs did much to furnish recreation for the servicemen. Local ladies took turns acting as hostesses and chaperones in the clubs. Here the servicemen could find food, music, card games, dancing, or quiet reading if they preferred. Since South Carolina had an unusually high proportion of servicemen training within its borders, USO recreational facilities were pushed to the limit to furnish entertainment for the young men. To relieve the crowded USO clubs, many families invited servicemen into their homes for Sunday dinners and for other week-end entertainment.

While maintaining the home front, South Carolinians followed the progress of the war with great interest, from the Pearl Harbor attack until the final surrenders of Germany and Japan.

B. INDUSTRY AND TRANSPORTATION

1. Industrial Growth, 1939-1960

Among the significant results of World War II was the accelerated growth of industry in South Carolina. Immediately following the conflict, new mills began to spring up throughout the state. As one journalist exclaimed after having seen a new Celanese Corporation factory on the Catawba River: "Rock Hill, South Carolina, will never be the same again."[2] This rapid pace continued through 1955. Thereafter, the speed of industrial development slowed somewhat, and South Carolina did not overtake its neighbors. In 1957, for example, expenditures for new plants, expansion of existing plants, and equipment totaled $114,-700,000 for the state and over $195,000,000 each for

2. W. H. Nicholas, "Dixie Spins the Wheels of Industry," *The National Geographic Magazine*, XCV (March, 1949), 281.

TABLE 8
SOUTH CAROLINA INDUSTRY

	1939	1954	1957
	(in millions)		
Value of Mfg. Production in U. S.........	$ 56,843	$262,273	$324,022
Value of Mfg. Production in 16 Southern States.............................	9803	53,133	68,009
Value of Mfg. Production in S. C........	398	2607	3119
Value of Business Volume in S. C........	$ 1446	$ 7258	$ 8837
Value of S. C. Production			
Textiles............................	$ 263	$ 1624	$ 1850
Chemicals..........................	20	230	296
Apparel............................	8	130	190
Food...............................	31	151	176
Pulp-paper.........................	20	145	172
Lumber............................	25	122	129
Stone-Clay-Glass...................	5	38	58
Tobacco............................	4	43	55
	(in thousands)		
Number of S. C. Industrial Workers......	126.8	190.1	230
Textiles...........................	94.8	122.0	131
Chemicals..........................	2.6	7.9	14
Apparel............................	2.8	18.5	25
Food...............................	3.2	5.2	9
Pulp-paper.........................	2.4	5.2	7
Lumber............................	13.0	16.7	18
Stone-Clay-Glass...................	1.9	3.5	6
Tobacco............................	...	1.5	3

S. C. ranked twelfth of 16 Southern states in 1939 and eleventh in 1957.
Sources: Bluebook of Southern Progress, 1958, pp. 17, 73; *U. S. Census of Manufactures: 1947*, III, **556**; *U. S. Census of Manufactures: 1954*, III, 138-40.

North Carolina and Georgia. Of the Southern states, only Mississippi and Arkansas fell behind South Carolina.[3]

Within the state's largest industry, textiles, there was much expansion of plant facilities, consolidation of holdings, and diversification of output. By 1955 a majority of the textile mills had come under the control of a few large corporations—J. P. Stevens, Deering-Milliken, Lowenstein, Abney, and Amerotron. A few large "independents" such

3. By comparison Massachusetts in 1957 spent $243,900,000 for new plants, expansion of existing plants, and equipment, and Connecticut $224,500,000. *Statistical Abstract of the United States, 1959* (Washington: Government Printing Office, 1959), p. 797.

as the Self interests at Greenwood and the Springs group at Lancaster continued to operate, but the day of the small independent cotton mill had passed.

Outstanding examples of large-scale expansion and diversification were Celanese's $60,000,000 synthetic fiber plant at Rock Hill, DuPont's $75,000,000 orlon establishment at Camden, and Deering-Milliken's three modern textile mills in the Clemson-Pendleton area.[4]

In the mid-fifties, the textile industry, always highly competitive, dipped into a slump. Some spokesmen for the industry blamed increasing Japanese competition and asked Congress for a higher tariff on textile imports. Theirs was a dubious argument, for a Department of Commerce report showed that Japanese cotton fabric exports to the United States dropped from $30,400,000 in 1956 to $18,-100,000 in 1957. In the latter year, the Japanese purchased $217,300,000 of raw cotton from the United States. It was more likely that the industry's chief difficulties arose from the increased production of long-wearing synthetics, competition from other industries, changes in Americans' habit of dress, and the government's "two-price" system for raw cotton. By 1959 the slump was over. Business reports in November anticipated the highest profit margins for textiles since 1951. Most companies had orders for goods backlogged into the second quarter of 1960.[5]

Aside from textiles, there has been much expansion and diversification of other industries in the post-war period. In 1955 alone, 25 new factories were begun, each of whose investment was $1,000,000 or greater or whose working force was 100 or more.[6] Several of these plants are listed in Table 9.

4. *Manufacturers Record,* CXXI (April, 1952), 73-74. This particular issue featured South Carolina, pp. 69-108.
5. *The Greenville News* (S.C.), April 1, 1958; *The Wall Street Journal,* November 5, 9, 10, 20, 1959.
6. *Manufacturers Record,* CXXV (January, 1956), 70-72.

TABLE 9

NEW FACTORIES IN 1955

Location	Company	Size and Type of Factory
Easley	Saco-Lowell	Multi-million dollar textile machinery plant
Barnwell	Amerotron	$8,000,000 woolen mill
Bethune	Kendall	$5,000,000 textile finishing plant
Irmo	General Electric	$6,400,000 electrolytic capacitor plant
Mauldin	Sauer	$1,500,000 mayonnaise factory
Simpsonville	Dewey and Almy Chemical	$1,000,000 plastic bag factory
Spartanburg	Kohler	$5,000,000 pottery plant
Charleston	Bird	$2,500,000 roofing factory
Landrum	Bigelow-Sanford	Carpet factory
Pickens	Pickens Electric	$1,000,000 electrical equipment plant

Source: *Manufacturers Record*, CXXV (January, 1956), 70-72.

By 1960 South Carolina also had factories producing fiberglas (Anderson), vermiculite (Traveler's Rest), bathing suits (Seneca), plywood (Orangeburg), cement (Holly Hill), woolens (Johnsonville), portable generators and pumps (Greer), charcoal (Conway), aluminum ladders (Florence), machine tools (Clemson, Columbia, Spartanburg), paper products (Hartsville, Charleston, Spartanburg, Georgetown), chemicals and metals (Charleston). Dwarfing all else was the Atomic Energy Commission's gigantic plant at Aiken. This enterprise alone cost over $1.4 billion. In 1956 it was employing 8500 workers and among its other projects was irradiating cobalt for use in treatment of cancer.[7] Post-war industry, moreover, was broadly scattered over the state, not just concentrated in the piedmont. Nearly every county could boast of one or more new factories.

2. *Encouragement of Industrial Growth*

Why did industry pour into South Carolina at such a rapid rate between 1940 and 1960? The textile industry originally developed primarily because of a friendly recep-

7. *Ibid.*, p. 12.

tion by state and local governments and because of a plentiful supply of cheap labor. These conditions still existed after 1940. There are, as well, new factors. A survey reveals five major inducements between 1940 and 1960, some old and some new.

(1) A friendly reception was promised to new industries. Governors Thurmond, Byrnes, Timmerman, and Hollings were outspoken in their desire to attract industry to the state. In fall, 1959, Governor Hollings and about 100 state business leaders took a three-day "safari" to New York City to hunt for industry.[8] Furthermore, the General Assembly has been favorable to industry. In 1933 it established the forerunner of the present South Carolina Research, Planning and Development Board. This organization is largely a propaganda agency to encourage new industries to locate within the state and to encourage existing companies to expand their South Carolina operations. Its staff of technicians prepares and furnishes data for industrialists.

State and county taxes have been low enough to encourage industrial expansion. Manufacturing machinery and materials used in processing finished goods are exempted from the state's 3 per cent sales tax, while new plants receive reduced tax assessments on their property.[9] Although there is some question concerning tax advantages in South Carolina relative to other states, on April 8, 1958, the State Development Board ran a full-page advertisement in *The Wall Street Journal* headed with this statement: "South Carolina passes law reducing taxes on industry: new flexible tax law offers optional methods of income tax

8. *The Greenville News,* September 25, 1959. Charles E. Daniel, millionaire contractor and super-salesman of South Carolina as a place for industry, supported Thurmond, Byrnes, and Timmerman in their respective races for governor. Freeman Lincoln, "The Northerners Surrender to Charlie Daniel," *Fortune,* L (October, 1954), 145-56. Daniel also supported "Fritz" Hollings, the 1958 winner.

9. *Ibid.,* pp. 147-48.

computation to meet varying requirements of today's diverse industry."

Examples of official cooperation with industry occurred in 1954 when the legislature passed an anti-union "right-to-work" law and in 1956 when the legislature, in special session, repealed an old law forbidding a foreign corporation from owning more than 500 acres of land in South Carolina. The latter action cleared the way for the British-owned Bowaters Southern Paper Corporation to purchase a large tract in York County. The company then announced plans to build a large paper mill.[10]

(2) Resources were factors in attracting new industry. South Carolina has ample supplies of timber, stone, clay, gravel, and water. As resources for industry are becoming increasingly scarce in some states, South Carolina's are becoming relatively more valuable. This is particularly true of the state's water supply. Especially noteworthy is the Bushy Park Authority, a 4000-acre, state-owned water district in Berkeley County. Conceived in 1951 by the late Arthur M. Field, Bushy Park was developed at a cost of $3,700,000. It now consists of the huge Back River Reservoir, into which 2.5 billion gallons of water may be daily diverted from the Santee watershed via Lakes Marion and Moultrie. Situated only a few miles from Charleston, Bushy Park can supply industry in that area with an almost unlimited amount of water.[11]

(3) A plentiful supply of cheap labor played a part. An indication of the labor supply in South Carolina may be seen by comparing wages in the state with the national average. In early 1959 the average weekly wage for production workers in manufacturing was $90.32 for the

10. *The State* (Columbia, S.C.), June 4, 1956. The new plant, known as Bowaters Carolina Corporation and costing $37,000,000, was formally opened October 9, 1959. *The Greenville News,* October 1, 1959.

11. *Manufacturers Record,* CXXVII (March, 1958), 31.

United States and $62.02 for South Carolina. Only North Carolina ($60.75), Mississippi ($60.35), and Arkansas ($61.25) ranked lower. At the top were Michigan ($111.62) and Ohio ($102.13).[12]

Traditionally, South Carolina factory wages were higher than farm wages, but the entire wage scale was conditioned by a normally high birth rate and an unprofitable one-crop economy. This situation was carried over into the post-1940 era. With cotton acreage reductions, increased mechanization, and other changes in the state's agricultural system, fewer farm workers were needed in the fifties than in 1940. Some thousands of rural South Carolinians, in search of better economic opportunities, annually moved to the North and West. Others remained to work at depressed farm wages but were ever ready to flock to any new mill that might arise in their vicinity.

Little need be added to what has been said earlier about labor unions. Since the failure of the big textile strike in 1934, organized labor has been relatively weak in South Carolina textiles. The CIO's "Operation Dixie," begun in 1946 to organize Southern mills, was by 1950 an admitted failure. At the beginning of 1960, probably no more than 6 to 8 per cent of the South Carolina textile workers were unionized. Other industries in the state likewise employ few union workers.

In general, public opinion in South Carolina has been and is strongly anti-union, and labor organizers not infrequently have suffered violations of their civil rights. The workers themselves apparently have been distrustful and suspicious of outside union leaders since the 1934 strike. Yet, as low as wages were in non-union South Carolina, the once widespread differential between Northern and

12. U. S. average is for May, the state averages for March. *Monthly Labor Review,* LXXXII (June, 1959), 720-27; LXXXII (August, 1959), 938.

Southern textile wages had largely disappeared by 1957.[13]

(4) An adequate supply of power also won industries for the state. By 1957 South Carolina could boast of 25 hydroelectric plants and nine steam-generating electric plants. The steam plants are run either with coal or with oil.

Some of these power plants are publicly owned. The Clark Hill hydroelectric project on the Savannah River is owned by the federal government. Clark Hill cost about $85,000,000 to construct and has a capacity of 280,000 kilowatts. In 1955 the Federal government began work on the $100,000,000 Hartwell Dam on the Savannah near Anderson. When Hartwell is completed, however, it will have a smaller power capacity than Clark Hill. The South Carolina government owns the Santee-Cooper project, which is located near Charleston and generates power with both steam and hydroelectric plants.

In the fall of 1959 United States army engineers proposed two more dams in the Savannah valley between the Clark Hill and Hartwell reservoirs. Almost simultaneously Duke Power Company offered as an alternative to construct a $200,000,000 steam power plant in the area. At a hearing in Anderson on November 19 before the United States Study Commission on Southeast River Basins, only one of 30 witnesses expressed unqualified support for the proposed federal project. Some Savannah valley citizens who had earlier supported Clark Hill and Hartwell declared they had been "brainwashed" about the expected benefits. Governor Hollings and Senator Thurmond publicly opposed the army engineers' proposal, but to date (January, 1960) many politicians who had previously been staunch advocates of federal power projects are still sitting quietly on the fence.[14]

13. In 1957 both Northern and Southern hosiery workers received $1.55 per hour; Northern cotton, silk, and synthetic-fiber workers received $1.53 per hour, Southern $1.42. *Ibid.*, LXXXI (March, 1958), 329.

14. *The Greenville News,* November 20, 1959.

The largest electric power producers in South Carolina are three privately-owned companies: Duke Power (in the piedmont), South Carolina Electric and Gas (in central and southern South Carolina), and Carolina Power and Light (in the Pee Dee). Some of the older facilities of these companies are hydroelectric plants. The most notable of such projects is the Saluda Dam, owned by South Carolina E&G, near Columbia. Most of the new power facilities are steam plants.

The major steam plants of the South Carolina E&G Company are Plant Hagood in Charleston and Plant Urquhart at Aiken. Plant Hagood cost $11,000,000 to build and has a power capacity of 100,000 kilowatts. Plant Urquhart cost $45,000,000 and has a capacity of 300,000 kilowatts. In 1956 at the Saluda Dam, the South Carolina E&G Company began construction of a 275,000-kilowatt steam electric plant.[15]

In 1947 Duke Power Company completed near Williamston a $20,000,000 steam plant with a generating capacity of 180,000 kilowatts, and in 1956-1957 added a 165,000-kilowatt unit to it. Duke also in 1956 announced a million-kilowatt steam plant expansion for the Charlotte area. Much of this power will be transmitted to South Carolina.[16]

In early 1958 the Carolina Power and Light Company announced plans to build a $25,000,000 steam plant at Hartsville. About the same time the Carolinas-Virginia Nuclear Power Associates, Inc., was organized to construct a $20,000,000 nuclear power plant at Parr Shoals. The three large private power companies operating in South Carolina in combination with the Virginia Electric and

15. *Manufacturers Record*, CXXI (April, 1952), 92-93; and *Year Book of the Department of Agriculture . . . 1956-1957* (Columbia, S.C.: State Budget and Control Board, 1957), p. 41.
16. *Ibid.*

Power Company are associated in this venture, which is to be completed in 1962.[17]

Between 1938 and 1958, the increase in electric power production in South Carolina was almost six-fold. Specifically, the state produced 1568 million kilowatt hours in 1939 and 9212 million in 1957. South Carolina ranked twelfth of 16 Southern states in kilowatt-hour output in 1939 and again in 1957.[18]

Much of the electric power in small towns and rural areas is retailed by 23 organizations set up under the state Rural Electric Cooperatives Act. These co-ops buy power at wholesale prices from Santee-Cooper, Duke, and other producers. In 1941 the co-ops in South Carolina had about 8500 miles of lines serving 26,000 customers. By the end of 1956 they were operating 31,000 miles of line that reached 123,000 customers. At that time both industrial and residential electric power rates in South Carolina were slightly cheaper than the national average.[19]

(5) A good system of transportation and communication was the final major inducement. The state's railway system, headed by three large companies, is more than adequate to give the services demanded by shippers. The state highway system is likewise in excellent condition to handle the traffic that uses it. Since 1941 the State Highway Department has erected by-passes around many towns, resurfaced thousands of miles of worn-out roads, straightened dangerous curves, constructed new and wider bridges, and built a number of four-lane highways where traffic is

17. *Manufacturers Record,* CXXVII (March, 1958), 12; CXXVII (May, 1958), 20.

18. *Blue Book of Southern Progress, 1958* (Baltimore: Manufacturers Record, 1958), p. 20.

19. Commercial and industrial rates in South Carolina were 1.280 cents per KWH, in the United States as a whole 1.402 cents per KWH; "average rate" paid to privately owned utilities for residential service was 2.16 cents per KWH in South Carolina, 2.60 cents in the United States as a whole. *Year Book of the Department of Agriculture . . . 1956-1957,* pp. 44-48.

unusually heavy. In addition, the roads are well policed by the State Highway Patrol.

In 1958 Chief Highway Commissioner Claude R. Mc-Millan announced that an estimated $340,000,000 would be spent on four interstate highways to cross South Carolina. These roads, each to consist of four or more lanes, are to be part of a federal system of interstate and defense highways. After completion these roads (678 miles) will be kept up and patrolled by the South Carolina Highway Department.[20]

An incidental result of the good highway system has been the demise of factory-owned villages. Companies establishing mills since World War II, whether in town or country, have not constructed homes for their workers, and many of the older firms have sold their villages. By and large, these companies sold the houses to the existing occupants at reasonable prices, requiring small down-payments and giving six or eight years to pay the balances.[21]

For ocean-going commerce, the natural harbor at Charleston is one of the nation's finest. The major shipping facilities, developed during World War II by the army, came under the South Carolina State Ports Authority in 1947. This non-profit state agency also has charge of developing harbor facilities at Georgetown and Beaufort.

Besides the $20,000,000 terminals acquired from the army, the State Ports Authority received two other major terminals and other waterfront facilities from the city of Charleston, also in 1947. Four years later, the state spent an additional $6,000,000 at Charleston on new waterfront equipment. Altogether the port operated 55 piers and docks at that time. In 1957 the State Ports Authority began a $21,000,000 improvement and expansion program,

20. *The State,* July 21, 1958.
21. See Harriett Herring, *Passing of the Mill Village* . . . (Chapel Hill, N.C.: University of North Carolina Press, 1949), *passim.*

$3,000,000 of which was earmarked for Georgetown and Beaufort.

From 1946 through 1952, the value of both exports and imports passing through Charleston expanded from $27,000,000 to $151,000,000. Charleston's commerce includes bananas and other tropical products from Latin America, tractors and machinery from the Midwest, and long staple cotton from Peru and Egypt.[22]

During and after World War II, South Carolina improved its airports, and by 1955 five commercial airlines were serving South Carolina cities—Anderson, Greenville, Spartanburg, Rock Hill, Columbia, Greenwood, Florence, Myrtle Beach, and Charleston.[23] As far as other systems of communications are concerned, South Carolina has ample telephone and telegraph service, and a sufficient number of radio and television stations and daily newspapers.

Besides these five major factors, other recent inducements to industry have been South Carolina's comparatively mild climate, the lack of crowded conditions (70 persons per square mile in 1950), relatively low construction costs, and the increase in banking resources. In 1957 South Carolina's 146 banks had almost $900,000,000 in total assets.[24]

C. Recent Trends in Agriculture

Table 10 shows several significant changes in South Carolina agriculture. The number of farms has decreased, tenancy has declined, but total acreage has remained almost stationary since 1940. In striking contrast, the average South Carolina farm in 1954 was worth about one-third the value of the average American farm.

Table 11 shows the extent to which mechanization has

22. *The State,* January 26, 1958; *Resources of South Carolina . . .* (Columbia, S.C.: State Development Board, 1955), pp. 25-29; *Manufacturers Record,* CXXVI (May, 1957), 13.
23. *Ibid.,* CXXI (April, 1952), 100.
24. *Blue Book of Southern Progress, 1958,* p. 20.

TABLE 10
SOUTH CAROLINA FARM STATISTICS

	1930	1940	1954
Total Number S. C. Farms............	157,931	137,558	124,203
Av. Size S. C. Farms (in acres).......	65.8	81.7	89.1
Percentage of S. C. Farmers Working as Tenants......................	65.1%	56.1%	39.3%
Percentage of U. S. Farmers Working as Tenants......................	42.4%	38.7%	24.0%
Av. Value S. C. Farms..............	$ 2401	$ 2461	$ 7769
Av. Value U. S. Farms..............	$ 7614	$ 5518	$20,405
Number of S. C. White Farm Operators	....	76,251	69,704
Number of S. C. Colored Farm Operators	....	61,307	54,499
Total S. C. Farm Acreage............	....	11,239,000	11,069,000

Sources: Agriculture Yearbook, 1957, pp. 226, 231; Statistical Abstract of the United States, 1943, pp. 575-91, 1957, pp. 619-31.

taken place in South Carolina since 1940. By 1954 a majority of the farms had automobiles and electricity but not tractors and trucks. Despite the decline in horse and mule population, a majority of the South Carolina farmers at that time still had to rely on animal power to some extent for plowing and other heavy work.

TABLE 11
SOUTH CAROLINA FARM EQUIPMENT

	1940	1950	1954
Automobiles on S. C. Farms................	63,653	81,579	89,135
Tractors on S. C. Farms....................	4791	30,329	46,551
Motor trucks on S. C. Farms..............	8242	29,757	40,374
S. C. Farms with Electricity..............	28,764	95,025	109,100
Home Freezers on S. C. Farms.............	....	9170	26,177
Grain Combines on S. C. Farms............	....	6760	7564
Horses and Mules on S. C. Farms..........	201,000	174,000	132,000

Sources: Agriculture Yearbook, 1957, pp. 231, 325; Statistical Abstract of the United States, 1943, pp. 608-09, 628.

Table 12 includes every crop the value of which was above $1,000,000 either in 1940 or in 1958. Not listed therefore are several crops of importance whose annual value generally ranged between $100,000 and $1,000,000 during the 1940-58 period. In this group were rye, lespe-

TABLE 12
SOUTH CAROLINA CROP PRODUCTION

	YIELD PER ACRE		TOTAL PRODUCTION (in thousands)				
	Yearly Av. 1930-39	Yearly Av. 1946-55	Yearly Av. 1930-39	Yearly Av. 1946-55	Value of Prod., 1940	Total Prod. 1958	Value of Prod., 1958
Cotton Lint	265 lbs.	305 lbs.	824 bales	647 bales	$48,654	300 bales	$51,900
Cottonseed	—	—	366 tons	270 tons	$ 9383	125 tons	$ 6012
Tobacco	836 lbs.	1316 lbs.	85,656 lbs.	162,280 bus.	$12,300	131,000 lbs.	$78,529
Corn	13.5 bus.	19.2 bus.	22,831 bus.	25,089 bus.	$17,088	28,954 bus.	$39,088
Oats	21.4 bus.	27.8 bus.	9238 bus.	14,100 bus.	$ 5584	13,101 bus.	$10,874
Hay	.74 tons	.85 tons	412 tons	517 tons	$ 5888	579 tons	$17,949
Peaches	—	—	1236 bus.	3122 bus.	$ 2482	4900 bus.	$11,515
Wheat	10.0 bus.	16.8 bus.	1364 bus.	2847 bus.	$ 2452	3124 bus.	$ 6092
Soybeans for Beans	6.4 bus.	11.2 bus.	65 bus.	987 bus.	$ 99	5611 bus.	$11,222
Sweet Potatoes	85 bus.	49 cwt.	5401 bus.	1522 cwt.	$ 3245	689 cwt.	$ 3169
Cowpeas for Peas	5.8 bus.	4.8 bus.	1052 bus.	361 bus.	$ 1640	168 bus.	$ 756
Peanuts	678 lbs.	716 lbs.	9041 lbs.	11,898 lbs.	$ 774	12,600 lbs.	$ 1373
Irish Potatoes	115 bus.	79 cwt.	2875 bus.	922 cwt.	$ 2472	488 cwt.	$ 1078
Barley	16.9 bus.	24.0 bus.	52 bus.	475 bus.	—	1064 bus.	$ 1170
Commercial Truck	—	—	$ 4944	$ 9915	$ 5303	—	$ 7383

	1940	1955	1958
Total Value of All South Carolina Crops	$119,628,000	$316,574,000	$253,268,000
Total Acreage of All South Carolina Crops	4,972,000	3,825,000	3,069,500

Sources: Agriculture Yearbook, 1968, pp. 134-35, 1957, pp. 103, 106, 109, 1965-1966, p. 35, 1940-42, p. 50, 1940-1941, pp. 24-25, 52.

deza, tall fescue seed, sorghum grain, sorghum syrup, sorghum forage, velvet beans, pecans, grapes, lupine seed, and crimson clover seed.

The table shows that the value of the state's tobacco crop in 1958 was greater than that of the cotton crop. The first time in the state's history that the tobacco crop topped the value of cotton was in 1955. South Carolina farmers had a cotton planting allotment of 740,000 acres in 1958, but many failed to use their full quotas, choosing instead to place their land in the federal Soil Bank program. Thus, the 1958 crop for South Carolina was the smallest since Reconstruction years.

It appears that after reigning for approximately 150 years "King Cotton" is in his death throes, an event foreseen by some persons several decades ago. In the post-World-War-II era, few South Carolina farmers could compete successfully with the planters on the rich Mississippi River delta lands or on the irrigated plains of the Far West. In California, Arizona, and New Mexico the average cotton yield per acre is usually two or three times as great as in South Carolina.

With the demise of cotton, the production of several other crops has been increased in South Carolina. Furthermore, the per-acre yield for nearly all South Carolina crops was greater in the 1946-55 years than in the 1930-39 period. This was due partly to improved methods of farming and partly to a reduction of total crop acreage, the poorer lands being taken out of cultivation. One crop, sweet potatoes, that showed a large per-acre decline suffered from increasing attacks from nematodes, a parasitic scourge that attacks only certain types of plants.

What has happened to the 1,902,500 acres taken out of crops from 1940 through 1958? Most have been diverted to forests or pasture. In 1865 the timber resources of South Carolina were great, but for many years sawmills cut trees faster than the forests naturally replaced them. The timber-cutting peak was reached in 1929 when lumbermen took over one billion board feet from South Carolina forests. Thereafter, production declined, and lumbermen cut only two-thirds as much in 1939 as in 1929. At about that time an important change occurred.

Dr. Charles Herty, a Georgia chemist, in the thirties discovered a cheap method of making newsprint from pine saplings. As a result, paper manufacturing became a new and important industry in the South. Immediately the demand for young pines increased. Several millions had recently been planted by the Civilian Conservation Corps, but this work was halted during the war. After the war the State Commission of Forestry took up the task of reforesting the state's cut-over timberlands. In 1947 the Commission began operation of the Tilghman Nursery at Wedgefield. Within five years, the nursery was annually producing 30 to 40 million pine seedlings for distribution throughout South Carolina. This amount was insufficient to meet the popular demand, which significantly came largely from small landowners.

In 1956-58, the Commission, with the aid of federal Soil Bank funds, established the Piedmont Nursery near Jocassee (Pickens County) and the Coastal Nursery near St. George. Anticipated 1958-59 production was 110,-000,000 seedlings. By comparison, 1933-34 was the first season in which more than a million pine seedlings were planted in South Carolina.[25]

The State Commission of Forestry also encourages farmers to follow good forestry practices. In cooperation with several commercial users of forest products, the Com-

25. *Report of the State Commission of Forestry, 1956-57* (Columbia, S.C.: State Budget and Control Board, 1957), pp. 20-22, 35-37; and *The Greenville News,* December 1, 1957. I have not seen the final report for 1958-59 production.

mission established the State Tree Farm Committee to "certify" tree farms. To qualify for certification a landowner must adopt practices approved by the Tree Farm Committee and demonstrate the ability to protect his trees from "fire, insects, disease, and destructive grazing." By June, 1957, the Committee had certified 206 tree farms comprising 1,425,000 acres.[26]

Conservation, the reforestation which began in the thirties, and the increased demand for forest products have resulted in greater timber cutting since World War II. In 1952 production reached 1.4 billion board feet, an amount well above the 1929 peak.[27] At a meeting of the South Carolina Forestry Study Committee in July, 1958, state Senator John D. Long, a member of the Committee, announced that forestry, directly employing 30,000 persons, ranked next to textiles in importance in the state. Admitting that the cotton economy was a "thing of the past," Senator Long predicted that the "future economy of the state will be pitched on the pine tree in about 18 years."[28]

The increase in South Carolina pasture land is indicated by Table 13, which shows that the state's beef herd increased by approximately 300,000 head between 1950 and 1959.

Another post-war agricultural enterprise in South Carolina is the growing of broilers for commercial markets. From 1937 to 1952, the yearly production of broilers increased ten-fold. The number of birds raised in 1953 was 11,300,000. In the face of severe competition from producers in Georgia and other states, South Carolina growers

26. *Report of the State Commission of Forestry, 1956-57*, pp. 82-83.
27. *Statistical Abstract of the United States, 1958*, p. 689. The Forestry Commission also had under its control four state forests, numerous fire towers and fire stations, and 20 recreational parks for whites and five for Negroes. *Year Book of the Department of Agriculture . . . 1956-1957*, pp. 33-36.
28. *The State*, July 24, 1958.

TABLE 13

LIVESTOCK AND POULTRY ON SOUTH CAROLINA FARMS

	1930-1939 Av.	1940	1950	1959
All Cattle and Calves....	350,000	359,000	353,000	613,000
Milk Cows (2 yrs. & older)	177,000	176,000	146,000	159,000
All Swine...............	540,000	688,000	631,000	550,000
Sheep.................	13,000	10,000	3000	13,000
Horses and Mules.......	207,000	201,000	174,000	84,000
Turkeys on Farms.......	55,000	70,000	90,000	81,000*
Chickens on Farms (not including commercial broilers)............	4,202,000	5,206,000	5,217,000	4,106,000*

* 1958.

Sources: *Agriculture Yearbook, 1939-1940*, pp. 90-91, *1957*, pp. 323-25, *1958*, pp. 168-71; *Statistical Abstract of the United States, 1945*, p. 628, *1959*, p. 679.

thereafter reduced output to about 10,000,000 broilers per season.[29]

In sum, South Carolina agriculture in the mid-fifties was more mechanized than in 1940, and produced greater yields per acre on fewer but larger farms. There was less tenancy, a large reduction in cotton production, more pasture land, more timber and pulp wood, and greater agricultural diversification. Frequently, South Carolina ranks second to California in the production of peaches, and third to North Carolina and Kentucky in tobacco. In truck crops for fresh markets, the state usually ranks from fourth to tenth in such crops as lima beans, snap beans, green peas, cucumbers, and watermelons.[30]

D. EDUCATION AND RELIGION

1. *The Public School Revolution*

Between 1940 and 1958 the South Carolina schools underwent a phenomenal reorganization. Whereas in the

29. *Year Book of the Department of Agriculture . . . 1956-1957,* p. 120. South Carolina's production reached 17,000,000 in 1958. *Statistical Abstract, 1959,* p. 687.

30. *General Statistics on South Carolina* (Pamphlet No. 12; Columbia, S.C.: State Development Board, 1950), pp. 2-3.

1939-40 school year, the state spent $17,800,000 on the public schools, or $46.80 per white pupil enrolled and $11.40 per Negro, in 1957-58 the current expenditures reached $90,600,000, or $176 per pupil.[31]

In 1945 the state introduced a new certification program for teachers. Thereafter, regardless of race, a teacher's salary depended on three factors: (1) educational training, (2) score made on the teachers' examination, and (3) number of years of experience in the profession. By 1956 teachers' salaries in the state reached an annual average of $3005.[32] During the post-war years the state also established a retirement program for all state employees. In 1955 state employees came under the federal Social Security System, which provided additional retirement benefits.

The state expanded its school bus operations to furnish transportation for large numbers of Negro school children for the first time. The state improved and broadened its school lunch and health programs. Pre-school health clinics were held in the spring for children expected to enter the first grade the following autumn. Many schools were provided with special nurses, while others made use of county health department services.

The school curriculum was broadened to include a twelfth grade and a variety of elective courses, especially in the field of vocational training. And in 1954 the state inaugurated a special education program for physically and mentally handicapped children, some of whom were stay-at-home students. In its second year this program reached 1477 pupils in 34 counties.[33]

31. *Ninetieth Annual Report of the State Superintendent of Education . . . 1957-1958* (Columbia, S.C.: State Budget and Control Board, 1958), pp. 133, 148. In 1956 the average yearly expenditure per pupil in daily attendance was $294.22 for the United States, $425.61 for New York (the highest state), and $188.09 for South Carolina, which ranked forty-fourth of 48 states. *Statistical Abstract, 1959*, p. 120.

32. The United States average was $4156. South Carolina ranked forty-second of 48 states. *Ibid.*, p. 119.

33. *Annual Report, Supt. Educ., 1955-1956*, pp. 36-38.

South Carolina streamlined its school administration. By 1958 the number of school districts had been reduced to 109, and several hundred small schools had been consolidated with larger ones. Only eight white and 13 Negro one-teacher schools remained in operation. In scores of places new buildings had been constructed at an unprecedented pace. Between June, 1951, and August, 1954, the state allotted over $100,000,000 for the construction of 200 new Negro and 70 new white schools and for improvements on 70 Negro and 175 white schools. School properties were worth $333,700,000 by 1958. Meanwhile, the school population continued to grow, reaching an all-time high of 584,283 in 1957-58, not counting the 12,368 students in private schools.[34]

Governor James F. Byrnes (1951-55) was largely responsible for the building program. He did much to arouse public opinion in its behalf, and he persuaded the legislature to adopt a 3 per cent sales tax to finance it. Governor Byrnes considered it the duty of the state government to eliminate remaining inequalities between white and colored schools. With the Clarendon County case then pending, the Governor apparently hoped that separate but *genuinely* equal facilities would satisfy the Supreme Court and save segregation. The high tribunal in May, 1954, decided otherwise.

2. Problems Facing South Carolina Schools in 1960

Although no racial integration had taken place in the South Carolina public schools by January, 1960, unquestionably this poses as the gravest problem facing the South Carolina educational system. All available evidence clearly indicates that the majority of whites are opposed to mixing white and colored children in the public schools. On the other hand, there appears to be little likelihood that the

34. *Ibid., 1957-1958,* pp. 14, 141-48, 192. Ned Ramseur in *The Greenville News,* August 15, 1954.

Supreme Court will reverse its position in the foreseeable future. It would seem, therefore, that continued segregation in South Carolina will be maintained, if at all, only through some form of intimidation of the Negroes or by some evasive legal trick. As an alternative the legislature in 1956 provided for the closing of the public schools and state-supported colleges.

Two other grave educational problems are the shortage of well-qualified teachers and the overcrowding of classes.[35] Many of the best brains have been lured to "greener pastures" in nearby states or into more lucrative professions, leaving behind teachers strong on educational methods but weak on subject matter.[36] The Fiscal Survey Commission took note of this latter problem in its recommendations to the legislature in 1956.

Specifically, the Commission recommended that the General Assembly "give serious consideration" to a "substantial increase" in the state schedule of teachers' pay, and that the increase be effected by "rewriting" the salary schedule instead of giving a percentage increase based on

35. The class enrollment average per teacher in 1955-56 was 30 pupils. *Annual Report, Supt. Educ., 1955-1956*, p. 159.

36. I believe the State Board of Education is largely to blame for the emphasis on courses that teach "how to teach" rather than "what to teach." Under the present salary schedule, a teacher receives no more pay (and sometimes less) for earning a difficult master's degree in a subject field than for receiving one in professional education, most frequently considered a "crip." Upon examining several dozen masters' theses in professional education at Clemson and Carolina, I noted in the overwhelming majority careless research techniques. Some few would hardly have qualified as respectable freshman term papers. I do not believe this situation will be measurably improved until public opinion forces the Board of Education to lower the number of hours of methods courses required for a teacher's certificate, and until the legislature redraws the teachers' salary schedule. The extra pay for earning a master's in chemistry or English, for instance, must be greater than that for one in professional education. Otherwise, the vast majority of the South Carolina teachers who seek advanced degrees will continue to gravitate toward the easy methodology courses. Furthermore, if some colleges try to improve their degrees in professional education, the teachers will flock to the weaker institutions.

the 1951 schedule. The Commission then recommended revision of the teacher certification program so as "to reduce emphasis on method courses and to facilitate the employment of persons of superior educational attainment. . . ."[37]

There is also the problem of curriculum. In recent years increased emphasis on extracurricular activities that cut into class time and the addition of many "know-how" subjects have produced thousands of high school students poorly equipped to pursue further study. Of 1685 South Carolina high school graduates that entered the freshman class at Clemson, the University, and the Citadel in 1955-56, only 553 passed all courses taken their first year, and 237 withdrew from college because of failure.[38]

In 1956 the Fiscal Survey Commission recommended that "steps be taken to raise the standards" of the state high schools in both vocational and college preparatory fields. The Commission also recommended that the eighth grade be incorporated with high school, that the number of credits for graduation be increased from 16 to 20, and that students intending to go to college be enabled and encouraged to complete 20 units of work, "largely of college preparatory nature," in four years.[39]

In late 1957 public interest in academic standards was raised further when Russia successfully launched her first

37. *Report No. 1 to the General Assembly . . . by the Fiscal Survey Commission* ([Columbia, S.C.]: House of Representatives, [1956]), pp. 22-23. Of 18,665 teachers in the public school system in 1955-56, 2594 held certificates based on masters' degrees. *Annual Report, Supt. Educ., 1955-1956*, pp. 15, 160. The bulk of these degrees were not held in subject fields but in professional education.

38. *Annual Report, Supt. Educ., 1955-1956, A Supplement*, pp. 31-38. There were 162,694 students enrolled in South Carolina high schools in 1955-56. Of these, 76,400 were currently enrolled in physical education, 27,500 in health, safety, and first aid, 27,000 in home economics, 21,000 in typing, 15,400 in glee club, 13,000 in agriculture, 11,000 in general music, and 10,000 in band. By contrast, 22,900 were enrolled in biology, 10,800 in second-year algebra, 9300 in plane geometry, 8700 in chemistry, 7600 in French, 5600 in Latin, 2800 in physics, and 1700 in trigonometry. *Annual Report, Supt. Educ., 1955-1956*, p. 27.

39. *Report No. 1 by the Fiscal Survey Commission*, pp. 22-23.

"Sputnik." Amid criticism of the public school curriculum, the 1958 legislature decided to increase the mathematics requirements for a high school diploma from one to two units. There was much talk about abandoning the twelfth grade as a useless "stretch-out" of the school program. However, on this point opinions were badly divided among the legislators and no action taken.

The school consolidation program brought a number of problems in administration. Of these, the most important was where the real control of the large school districts would lie.

3. Higher Education in South Carolina

During World War II all the men's colleges curtailed their activities, as the draft act dipped into the eighteen-year-olds. Some schools were aided in keeping their doors open by acquiring special military training programs. In the decade following the war there was an over-all increase in student enrollment in South Carolina colleges, although the contrary was true of some schools—mainly girls' institutions.[40]

Bob Jones University moved from Tennessee to Greenville in 1947. Although still unaccredited in 1959, Bob Jones calls itself the "World's Most Unusual University" and is widely known for its dramatic productions, art collection, religious education, and radio station (WMUU). Elsewhere, the College of Charleston set up a junior college branch at Conway (later taken over by the University); Lander College passed from the hands of the Methodist Episcopal Church to the County of Greenwood; Wesleyan Methodist (junior) College at Central inaugurated a four-year program leading to the A.B. degree; the Southern Methodists established a small college at Aiken; and the University set up branches at Florence, Beaufort, and Aiken.

40. See Table 6 on page 146.

Many of the South Carolina colleges underwent considerable "face-lifting" between 1945 and 1960, bringing them dormitories of modern design, spacious engineering buildings, new libraries, enlarged athletic stadiums, and so on—improvements that ran into the tens of millions of dollars. Furman University moved (1955-58) to an entirely new campus on the outskirts of Greenville. A 1940 graduate of any state-supported college (except Winthrop) would be struck by the physical changes which have occurred since that year if he should now return to his campus for the first time since graduation.

South Carolina colleges also made some significant changes in their curriculums between 1940 and 1960, and nearly all increased the academic requirements for admission.[41] The main curriculum changes were to integrate recent developments and discoveries in the scientific and engineering fields. Clemson College, for instance, added curriculums in chemical, ceramic, and nuclear engineering. Moreover, most institutions improved their library and laboratory facilities and strengthened their teaching staffs with the addition of more members holding the Ph.D. As a result, a student could obtain sound undergraduate education in several South Carolina colleges, both state and private.

Unfortunately, as late as 1951 the Negro colleges, according to one critic, were notoriously weak. Professor Lewis K. McMillan pointed out that, regardless of original purposes, all five Negro senior colleges had become teacher-training institutes, even State A&M.[42] These schools have

41. Academic standards vary somewhat from college to college. A special survey of the academic records of freshmen in South Carolina colleges in 1956 showed that some schools, especially girls' colleges and several private co-educational institutions, had a much lower percentage of failures than the others. *Annual Report, Supt. Educ., 1955-1956, A Supplement,* pp. 30-39.

42. Of 831 graduates from five Negro colleges in 1955-56, 558 qualified for teachers' certificates. *Annual Report, Supt. Educ., 1955-1956,* p. 97.

been hampered by weak staffs, inadequate plants, and opportunistic administrations.[43]   The Negro institutions in their public relations are highly sensitive to white public opinion.[44]   In addition, a Peabody report in 1946 maintained that the "whole program of College education for Negroes is very seriously impaired and conditioned by the unsatisfactory type of elementary and secondary education which South Carolina Negroes have received up to this time."[45]   Yet, State A&M, among the Negro colleges, has made considerable progress under President B. C. Turner since 1950.   It has acquired a number of staff members with Ph.D. degrees and has completed a new building program, including housing for both faculty and students.

In spite of marked improvements in several ways, the higher education system in South Carolina can claim no great university or college.   Church schools are still too numerous and too poor.   And Professor W. H. Hand's statement of 1910 that the state had "blundered badly" in establishing four tax-supported white colleges still seemed to be true in early 1960.   There is considerable duplication of work at Clemson, the University, and the Citadel; some of the recent expensive buildings seem hard to justify; and except for the sake of tradition and to please local

43. Dr. McMillan declared that State College's "entire existence has been characterized by floundering opportunism," that Allen was guilty of "losing her soul," and that Benedict "did not continue growing after having made a substantial start."   For these and other caustic comments about all five Negro colleges, see Lewis K. McMillan, *Negro Higher Education in the State of South Carolina* (Privately printed, 1952), pp. 102, 120, 133-34, 140, 197.

44. In 1957 Governor Timmerman and the State Board of Education pressured Allen and Benedict into firing some staff members reputed to be pro-communist.   The Board temporarily removed Allen from the list of colleges whose graduates are eligible for teacher certification in South Carolina.   This whole action was never explained to the public, and it was widely rumored that Allen's acceptance of a white Hungarian refugee as a student also influenced the Board.

45. *Public Higher Education in South Carolina* (Peabody Survey Report; Nashville, Tenn.: George Peabody College, 1946), p. 347.

interests, there is no real need for the continued operation of the Citadel and Winthrop on their present scale.[46]

There is not a single South Carolina institution of higher learning that offers a broad graduate program leading to the Ph.D. degree. To date, of the accredited institutions only the University has awarded the Ph.D. degree, and this in limited numbers and in three or four disciplines. On the other hand, nearly every college in the state offers masters' degrees of dubious worth in professional education, while several institutions offer creditable masters' in a limited number of fields. Apparently no South Carolina college has the academic atmosphere or resources to inaugurate a first-rate graduate program.[47]

But most South Carolina institutions are ever-ready to hand out honorary degrees. Of the white colleges, Clemson is probably guiltier of bestowing honorary doctorates en masse than any other school. Nevertheless, perhaps no white college has become the "honorary degree mill" that Professor McMillan pictures in Allen University: "Everyone of the older elders [AME Church] and most of the more vain younger ones bear the 'Doctor' title. . . . In the big turnouts like Commencement, these hollow digni-

46. In 1956 "Task Force No. 1" of the legislature's Fiscal Survey Commission took note of Winthrop's empty dormitories, duplication of engineering programs at Clemson and the University, the high cost of educating out-of-state students (over 50 per cent of the student body) at the Citadel, and the haphazard planning for expansion at several colleges. The "Task Force" particularly scored Clemson for exhausting its borrowing capacity by spending almost $4,000,000 on a new agricultural center when agricultural student enrollment had been declining for about ten years previously. It suggested placing Winthrop and the University under the same board of trustees, at least temporarily, and it recommended establishment of an agency with limited power to coordinate the state's program of higher education. *State Institutions of Higher Learning: Report No. 3 to the General Assembly . . . by the Fiscal Survey Commission* ([Columbia, S.C.: House of Representatives, 1956]), pp. 18-23.

47. In 1957 there were 24 institutions of higher learning in the South with endowments of $5,000,000 or more each. Not one was located in South Carolina. *The World Almanac, 1958* (New York: World-Telegram, 1958), p. 480.

taries strut around in their dazzling 'Doctors' Robes' in such a way as to crowd out the few real Doctors, and throw into utter contempt the college's humble but genuine Masters."[48]

Probably the most severe indictment against South Carolina colleges is the absence of an atmosphere conducive to inquiry into and discussion of controversial issues. Generally speaking, academic freedom is altogether absent or greatly restricted in South Carolina institutions of higher learning.[49] For this reason, as well as relatively low salaries, renowned scholars are seldom attracted permanently to South Carolina.

In this one-party state with its omnipresent race problem, no school attempts to formulate public opinion. This is especially true of the state-supported colleges, whose boards of trustees consist mainly of conservative businessmen and politicians. However well-intentioned, these men exhibit little liberal academic leadership. As a consequence, the administrators they place in charge of their respective institutions also tend to "play it safe."[50]

Meanwhile, the South Carolina public, impressed by external appearances, grandiose entertainment spectacles, and a flood of public relations propaganda, is too often unaware of both the truly good features and the weaknesses of its colleges.[51]

48. McMillan, *Negro Higher Education,* pp. 96-97. Several members of the Clemson Board of Trustees hold honorary degrees awarded by the Board itself.

49. Dismissals of faculty members for "objectionable" pronouncements are rare—Professors Chester Travelstead and Joseph Margolis were released from the University for anti-segregation views. More often faculty members are quietly pressured into silence.

50. Frequently in recent years solid academic achievement has counted for little in the selection of college presidents. Of nine presidents who have served Clemson, the Citadel, the University, and Winthrop since 1945, only two have held earned doctors' degrees.

51. In 1959 renowned scholar Jacques Barzun made the following critical comment about the American people: "Indeed, even the best-informed part of the public has no accurate idea of the merits of various colleges. Its opinions are fifteen years behind the times—except as to

4. Recent Religious Currents

Probably the outstanding development in religion in South Carolina since 1940 has been the increase in church membership. For example, the State Baptist Convention claimed a jump in communicants from 159,887 in 1936 to 468,076 in 1957; the Methodist membership rose from 91,514 to 181,651 and the Presbyterian Synod from 37,709 to 60,801.[52]

Accompanying the rise in membership was an increase in church wealth and expansion of church programs. Even in small towns and rural areas, many flimsy wooden church structures have been replaced with spacious brick buildings including fine organs, central heating systems, air conditioning, and rooms for Sunday School classes. A country brick parsonage, almost unknown in 1940, is no longer uncommon. From all appearances the rural church seems to have revived since the 1930's.

In the cities some of the larger white churches are operated on a businesslike basis with pastoral assistants, trained choir directors, young peoples' workers, and secretarial staffs. Quite a few of the larger congregations hold two services each Sunday morning in order to assure the members seats for worship. But most of these churches have dropped the traditional Wednesday evening prayer meeting, and many have ceased to have preaching on Sunday nights. Week-long revivals are also declining among the city churches.

With more funds at their disposal than in the pre-1940 era, the churches are supporting their colleges, orphanages, and foreign missions in much better style. Several of the

social ranking." *The House of Intellect* (New York: Harper and Brothers, 1959), p. 128.

52. *The State,* July 23, 1958; *South Carolina Methodist Advocate,* XII (August 28, 1958), 3; *Annual of the State Convention of the Baptist Denomination in South Carolina* (Charleston, S.C.: privately printed, 1957), p. 246.

denominations have lately established homes for elderly retired members. And a higher proportion of the clergy are now college- and seminary-trained. The younger clergy of the older, better established denominations seem inclined in ever-increasing numbers toward the social gospel rather than fundamentalism. By contrast, the ministers of some of the newer and smaller sects such as the Church of God and the Wesleyan Methodist Church still strongly believe in a strict and literal interpretation of the Bible. Moreover, these churches have increased their membership among the factory workers and farmers in the piedmont.[53]

The South Carolina churches in 1960 are faced with the moral question of racial integration, although there is no pressure from Negroes to join white congregations. Officially, the larger white denominations and some of the smaller ones have declared themselves opposed to segregation of the races as un-Christian in principle. However, many South Carolina clergymen do not support this view, and it is obvious that the majority of the parishioners do not.

53. I do not have statistical information on current membership of these minor sects. I base the statement on general observation of their building activities in northwestern South Carolina and occasional newspaper accounts of their meetings. As for the Negro denominations, there is little published information available about their post-1940 activities.

Chapter Nine

Summary

During the two decades immediately following the ratification of the United States Constitution, South Carolina, under Charleston leadership, developed a one-party, one-crop, slave-holding[1] society. From that time until the Civil War, the state presented more unity of purpose than any of its Southern counterparts.

The crop was cotton. Whitney's gin caused the rapid spread of the fiber staple and plantation slavery which accompanied it to every corner of the state. This agrarian economy, in turn, quickly led to political uniformity under the Democratic party banner. For more than half a century Democratic leaders succeeded in confining most political squabbles within their own ranks, while Federalist, National Republican, and Whig minorities followed one another down to defeat.

Besides its commitment to the plantation system, the institution of slavery, and the Democratic party, South Carolina society leaned on another support—a chivalric cult that nourished oratory, good manners, *noblesse oblige,* horsemanship, military glory, and the *code duello.* According to one recent writer, "the Southern cult of chivalry,

1. In 1928, historian Ulrich B. Phillips wrote that the "central theme" of Southern history is the Negro. He concluded that "until an issue shall arise predominant over the lingering one of race, political solidarity at the price of provincial status is maintained to keep assurance doubly, trebly sure that the South shall remain 'a white man's country.'" "The Central Theme of Southern History," *American Historical Review,* XXXIV (October, 1928), 43.

as it emerged from the Charleston area, was less a withdrawal into the past than a proud badge of nationality to enflame a course of action."[2] In the face of constant attack from the hated abolitionists after the early 1830's, a majority of the South Carolina leaders were ready for this "course of action" in 1850, but chose to wait impatiently another ten years until other black-belt states would rally to their cause.

Secession with its high hopes was closely followed by a brutal conflict which shattered South Carolina society and its institutions. The exhausted state was left with its land worn out, its white manhood dead or physically broken, its white womanhood crushed in spirit, its ex-slaves confused by their new freedom, and all its inhabitants fearful of the uncertain future. Only a thread-bare chivalry seemed to remain.[3]

From the wreckage of the war and the turmoil of Reconstruction there emerged a white-dominated society patterned upon that of ante-bellum years. The Conservatives, who were ex-Confederate planters and lawyers, rejuvenated the Democratic party and wrested control from the scalawag-carpetbag-Republican combination. Aided by textile magnates as new allies, the Conservatives (Bourbons) in time drove most of the Negroes out of politics and reduced the Republican voting strength to a mere token.

2. Rollin G. Osterweis, *Romanticism and Nationalism in the Old South* (New Haven, Conn.: Yale University Press, 1949), p. 131. See especially Chap. IX, "The Romantic Mood in Charleston."

3. On October 8, 1865, Floride Clemson of Pendleton recorded in her diary: "Last Thursday there was a great tournament here. Some fourteen knights rode in various costumes, not at all *knightly* for the most. Two sent their lances to me to trim, & rode for me—Edwin Frost & Ben. Gaillard. My colors were red, white, & black—the Confederate colors, in mourning. The prize was awarded to Ben Crawford, who crowned Miss Sue Lewis, a mere school girl. The crowning was awkwardly managed. Duff Calhoun was leader of the lances, as the 'Great Mogul'; Hall [Calhoun] as an Indian, was judged the best rider. he certainly was the best character. . . . In the evening there was a fancy dress ball." (MS in Clemson College Library, Clemson, S.C.).

With short-lived interruptions, the planter-lawyer-businessman combination controlled the Democratic party and South Carolina politics until 1941. Drawing their chief support from small, rural counties, these conservative-minded leaders consistently outmaneuvered the growing numbers of factory and urban voters. However, after Tillman's reign in the 1890's, the old-line politicians henceforth made concessions to popular demands for educational, social, democratic, and economic changes. These were seldom revolutionary changes, and South Carolina on the eve of World War II was still basically a one-party, one-crop state.[4] Cotton remained the mainstay of the agricultural economy, and farm tenancy, though declining, was still above 50 per cent. The state's industry was likewise concentrated in one "crop"—cotton textiles.

The most important changes in South Carolina society before 1941 resulted not from political forces but rather from technological developments affecting the nation as a whole. Electricity, moving pictures, automobiles, good roads, and radios began to upset the traditional "moonlight and magnolias" social pattern. Chivalry did not immediately succumb. It struggled to hold its own, especially in the lowcountry. Newcomers to the region were courteously, though sometimes patronizingly, received by the indigenous, self-appointed aristocrats. "Proper" ancestry counted for much in the older communities.[5] In the up-

4. Economist William H. Nicholls fervidly believes that Southern tradition has impeded economic progress in a number of ways. He says: "The list is long but can be classified for convenience into five principal categories: (1) the dominance of agrarian values, (2) the rigidity of the social structure, (3) the undemocratic political structure, (4) the weakness of social responsibility, and (5) conformity of thought and behavior." For an analysis of each of these points, see his article, "Southern Tradition and Regional Economic Progress," *The Southern Economic Journal,* XXVI (January, 1960), 187-98; and his book, *Southern Tradition and Regional Progress* (Chapel Hill, N.C.: University of North Carolina Press, 1960).

5. For a lively discussion of this point see William F. Guess, "South Carolina's Incurable Aristocrats," *Harper's Magazine,* CCXIV (Febru-

country's more recently developed industrial areas, class lines were more flexible, and many a newly-arrived Yankee entrepreneur was pleasantly surprised at the hospitality immediately accorded him.

Meanwhile, after Reconstruction the Negroes found their economic lot little improved over slavery times. The vast majority continued to work as field hands, house servants, or unskilled day laborers. Whites violated their civil rights with impunity, frequently resorted to lynch law, and furnished them little opportunity for economic or educational betterment. Most whites considered their Negro neighbors ignorant, uncouth, and immoral, which was oftener true than not. After several decades the Negroes, noting but slight change in their status and witnessing the twentieth-century technological advances about them, became increasingly dissatisfied with their second-class citizenship. A significantly large number annually migrated to the North and West. Between 1910 and 1950, the percentage of non-whites among the South Carolina population dropped from 55.2 to 38.9.[6]

Since 1941 fast-moving events have shaken South Carolina society to its core. During World War II nearly every able-bodied South Carolina male donned a uniform and left home, while thousands of outsiders poured into temporary training centers within the state. The war economy brought unprecedented prosperity, but South Carolina business leaders realized that its continuation after the war depended upon the advent of new industry.

Embarking upon an industrial crusade, the South Carolinians achieved noteworthy, though not spectacular, suc-

---

ary, 1957), 44-48. Guess, in a half-humorous manner, states: "In South Carolina there is no middle class. Either you are somebody or you aren't."

6. Between 1910 and 1950 the non-white population dropped from 836,239 to 823,624. During the same period the white population rose from 679,161 to 1,292,403.

cess. Textiles expanded, but more significantly, new types of manufacturing enterprises moved into South Carolina, giving the state a more diversified and better balanced industrial economy. Simultaneously, changes of an almost revolutionary nature took place in agriculture. "King Cotton" lay on his deathbed; tenants deserted the farms; cotton and corn acreage yielded to trees, cattle, and tobacco; tractors replaced mules; and rural electrification emancipated the farm wives. But for all its economic progress, South Carolina remained a poor state compared with the rest of the nation. In 1957 the per capita personal income for the United States was $2027, for Connecticut (the highest state) $2821, but for South Carolina $1180. Only Arkansas and Mississippi ranked below South Carolina.[7]

Where did the Negroes fit into the post-World-War-II evolutionary pattern? For many decades South Carolina whites had rigorously kept the Negroes "in their place." On the surface, this master-servant relationship had seemed reasonably well-suited to a cotton-growing economy in which the whites owned most of the land. The Negroes, with few alternative opportunities, had accommodated themselves to the system. Now that cotton culture was declining and industry was increasing, however, the traditional white-black relationships were no longer workable. Yet the whites were willing to offer the Negroes only meager opportunities for industrial employment. The state thus continued to waste potentially valuable human resources.

Coincidental to the post-1941 economic changes, the Negroes found an able legal ally—the United States Supreme Court. During the war Negro leaders stridently began to demand the elimination of racial discrimination. The Court, influenced by an equalitarian philosophy, heeded their pleas, and within a decade handed down a number of

7. *Statistical Abstract of the United States, 1959* (Washington: Government Printing Office, 1959), p. 311.

decisions that dealt a death blow to racial inequality by law.

This posed a serious dilemma for South Carolina political leaders. At one moment they vowed to maintain white supremacy, no matter the cost; at the next instant they loudly called for more industry—a natural enemy of racial segregation and much of the state's cultural tradition. Amid much smoke and little fire, white South Carolinians grudgingly accepted most of the Court's decrees. There was one notable exception—desegregated public education. On that score the state's political leaders were adamant. Although decrying violence and pledging allegiance to legality, their bitter denunciation of the federal government in general and the high tribunal in particular gave encouragement to violence.

In early 1960, white determination apparently had kept the NAACP at bay, but how much longer the Negro leaders will withhold an all-out drive on South Carolina's citadel of segregation is a matter of speculation.

A Select Bibliography

Ball, William W. *The State that Forgot: South Carolina's Surrender to Democracy.* Indianapolis, Ind.: Bobbs-Merrill Company, 1932.

Betts, Albert D. *History of South Carolina Methodism.* Columbia, S.C.: Advocate Press, 1952.

Byrnes, James F. *All in One Lifetime.* New York: Harper and Brothers, 1958.

Callcott, Wilfred H. (ed.). *South Carolina: Economic and Social Conditions in 1944.* Columbia, S.C.: University of South Carolina Press, 1945.

Childs, Arney R. (ed.). *The Private Journal of Henry William Ravenel, 1859-1887.* Columbia, S.C.: University of South Carolina Press, 1947.

Coleman, James K. *State Administration in South Carolina.* New York: Columbia University Press, 1935.

Griffin, Charles M. *The Story of the South Carolina Baptists, 1683-1933.* Greenwood, S.C.: Connie Maxwell Orphanage, 1934.

Hallman, S. T. (ed.). *History of the Evangelical Lutheran Synod of South Carolina, 1824-1924.* Columbia, S.C.: Farrell Printing Company, 1925.

Handbook of South Carolina. Columbia, S.C.: State Department of Agriculture, Commerce and Immigration, 1907.

Hennig, Helen K. *Great South Carolinians of a Later Date.* Chapel Hill, N.C.: University of North Carolina Press, 1949.

Heyward, Duncan C. *Seed from Madagascar.* Chapel Hill, N.C.: University of North Carolina Press, 1937.

Hollis, Daniel W. *College to University.* (*University of South Carolina,* Vol. II.) Columbia, S.C.: University of South Carolina Press, 1956.

Holmes, Alester G., and George R. Sherrill. *Thomas Green Clemson, His Life and Work.* Richmond, Va.: Garrett and Massie, 1937.

Jarrell, Hampton M. *Wade Hampton and the Negro: the Road Not Taken.* Columbia, S.C.: University of South Carolina Press, 1949.

Johnson, Guion G. *A Social History of the Sea Islands, with Special Reference to St. Helena Island, South Carolina.* Chapel Hill, N.C.: University of North Carolina Press, 1930.

Jones, F. D., and W. H. Mills (eds.). *History of the Presbyterian Church in South Carolina since 1850.* Columbia, S.C.: R. L. Bryan Company, 1926.

Kohn, August. *The Cotton Mills of South Carolina.* Columbia, S.C.: State Department of Agriculture, Commerce and Immigration, 1907.

McMillan, Lewis K. *Negro Higher Education in the State of South Carolina.* Privately printed, 1952.

Pike, James S. *The Prostrate State: South Carolina under Negro Government.* New York: D. Appleton and Company, 1874.

Potwin, Marjorie. *Cotton Mill People of the Piedmont.* New York: Columbia University Press, 1927.

Quint, Howard H. *Profile in Black and White: a Frank Portrait of South Carolina.* Washington: Public Affairs Press, 1958.

Reynolds, John S. *Reconstruction in South Carolina, 1865-1877.* Columbia, S.C.: State Company, 1905.

Rice, John A. *I Came out of the Eighteenth Century.* New York: Harper and Brothers, 1942.

Robertson, Ben. *Red Hills and Cotton, an Upcountry Memory.* New York: Alfred A. Knopf, 1942.

Sheppard, William A. *Red Shirts Remembered: Southern Brigadiers of the Reconstruction Period.* Atlanta, Ga.: Ruralist Press, 1940.

Simkins, Francis B. *Pitchfork Ben Tillman, South Carolinian.* Baton Rouge, La.: Louisiana State University Press, 1944.
———. *The Tillman Movement in South Carolina.* Durham, N.C.: Duke University Press, 1926.

Simkins, Francis B., and Robert H. Woody. *South Carolina during Reconstruction.* Chapel Hill, N.C.: University of North Carolina Press, 1932.

Simpson, George L., Jr. *The Cokers of South Carolina, a*

Social Biography of a Family. Chapel Hill, N.C.: University of North Carolina Press, 1956.

South Carolina, a Handbook. Columbia, S.C.: State Department of Agriculture, Commerce and Industry, 1927.

South Carolina: a Guide to the Palmetto State. ("WPA Guide Series.") New York: Oxford University Press, 1941.

South Carolina: Resources and Population, Institutions and Industries. (State Board of Agriculture.) Charleston, S.C.: Walker, Evans and Cogswell, 1883.

Taylor, Alrutheus A. *The Negro in South Carolina during the Reconstruction.* Washington: Association for the Study of Negro Life and History, 1924.

Thomas, Albert S. *A Historical Account of the Protestant Episcopal Church in South Carolina, 1820-1957.* Columbia, S.C.: R. L. Bryan Company, 1957.

Tindall, George B. *South Carolina Negroes, 1877-1900.* Columbia, S.C.: University of South Carolina Press, 1952.

Wallace, David Duncan. *South Carolina: a Short History, 1520-1948.* Chapel Hill, N. C.: University of North Carolina Press, 1951.

————. *The History of South Carolina.* 4 vols. New York: American Historical Society, 1934.

Wellman, Manly W. *Giant in Gray: a Biography of Wade Hampton of South Carolina.* New York: Charles Scribner's Sons, 1949.

Williams, Alfred B. *Hampton and His Red Shirts: South Carolina's Deliverance in 1876.* Charleston, S. C.: Walker, Evans and Cogswell, 1935.

Williams, G. Croft. *A Social Interpretation of South Carolina.* Columbia, S.C.: University of South Carolina Press, 1946.

Woodward, William E. *The Gift of Life: an Autobiography.* New York: E. P. Dutton and Company, 1947.

Index

Adams, Doc, Negro Militia Captain, 18
Adult education programs, 135; for Negroes, 137-38
African Methodist Episcopal Church, 164
African Methodist Episcopal Church, Zion, 164-65
Agricultural Adjustment Act, 73, 74
Agriculture, effects of war and reconstruction on, 106-8; depression in, 112-13; returning prosperity, 115-16; during W. W. II, 117; effect of depression of 1930's on, 118-20; reasons for lag in, 120; recent trends in, 222-28; radical changes in, 241 ff. See also Farm life; Farm tenancy; Farm demonstration work.
Aiken, D. Wyatt, and the Grange, 111
Airports, 222
Alcohol, attempts to control, 197-98. See also Barnwell Ring; Dispensary Act.
Allen University, 152, 164, 236
Allwright decision, 169, 170
American Agriculturalist, The, 115
American Federation of Labor, 86
Ansel, Gov. Martin F., 48
Ashley, Josh, 140-41
Ashley Grange No. 1, 111
Athletics, intercollegiate, 149
Atkins, Thomas E., 208

Atlantic Coast Line, 100
Australian ballot, 54

Ball, William Watts, supported Manning for governor, 55
Baptists, 156 ff.
Barnwell Ring, as a political group, 193; attacked by Thurmond, 197-98; mentioned, 185, 198
Baruch, Bernard M., war service of in W. W. I, 59
Baseball, 92
Baskin, W. P., 174
Bates, Lester, 181-82
Benedict College, 152
"Ben Tillman's Baby." See Dispensary Act.
Black Code, 8-9
Blackwood, Gov. Ibra C., and road-building program, 70-71; in depression, 72; and textile strike, 94
Blatt, Speaker Solomon, 193, 198
Blease, Coleman Livingston, as governor, 49; attitude of toward Negro, 50-51; opposed by Tillman in 1912, 52; legislative program of, 51-52; led attack on Manning, 56-57; as senator, 76-77; and University, 141
Blease-Tillman feud, 52-53
Blease, Judge Eugene, 175
Bleaseites in legislature, 1916, blocked reform, 55
Blue, Lt. Victor, 44
Board of Charities and Corrections, established, 54

Bob Jones University, 233
Boll weevil, 117; destroyed Sea Island cotton, 121
Bootlegging, 38, 67
Bratton, John, 33
Brawley, Rev. E. M., 165
Brown, Sen. Edgar A., and Barnwell Ring, 193; mentioned, 182, 183, 195
Bryan, William Jennings, 43
Business leaders, planters align with in 1880's, 30
Butler, Gen. Matthew C., 13, 19, 26, 39, 44
Butler, Thomas, 18
Byrd, Sen. Harry, 176; South's candidate in 1956, 184
Byrnes, Gov. James F., as U. S. senator, 75; distinguished career of, 80ff.; influence of in Washington, 80-81; and the public schools, 230; mentioned, 77, 175, 183, 184, 185

Cain, Richard H., 11, 164
Calhoun, John C., estate of and Clemson College, 32
Campaign of 1876, riots during, 20; election disputed and the outcome, 17-22
Campaign of 1950, 178-80
Campaign of 1956, presidential, 184-85
Campaign of 1958, 185-86
Camp Croft, 209-10
Camp meetings, 166. *See also* Revivals.
Camp Wadsworth, typical training camp, described, 60-63; epidemic in, 62-63
Cardozo, Francis L., 11
Carolina Power and Light Company, 218
Carolinas-Virginia Nuclear Power Association, Inc., 219-20
Carpenter, Judge R. B., 15
Carpetbaggers, in Constitutional Convention of 1868, 11; and state finances, 25
Cash, E. B. C., killed Shannon in duel, 29-30

Celanese's synthetic fiber plant, 213
Chamberlain, Daniel H., elected governor in 1874; as governor, 16-17
Charleston, S. C., destruction in during the war, 4. *See also* Citadel; names of well-known Charlestonians.
Charleston Colored Ministerial Union, 128
Charleston Harbor, importance of to sea-going transportation, 221
Charleston Medical College, 144
Chicora College, 161
Child labor, law against in 1903, 86, 87
Chivalry, attitude toward in S. C., 240-41
Churches, effect of war on, 155; revival and growth of white, 155 ff.; development of Negro, 164-68; increase in membership of since 1940, 238-39; country, 161-63; racial integration and, 239. *See also* names of denominations.
Church of God, 159, 239
Citadel, the, opened after Reconstruction, 138-39, 140; student life in, 151
Civilian Conservation Corps camps, adult schools in, 137
Civil rights, F. D. R.'s program for, 175; Truman supported, 176; issue important in 1952 presidential election, 180-81; in 1956 presidential election, 184; present attitude toward in S. C., 202, 203-4. *See also* Dixiecrat movement.
Claflin College, 152, 153
Clarendon County decision on segregation, nature of, 201; Negroes keep up their fight, 205-6
Clark Hill hydroelectric plant, 218
Clemson, Thomas G., and Clemson College, 140
Clemson College, Tillman pushed construction of, 35; and Farmers' Alliance, 33; as aid to ag-

riculture, 116; agricultural program of, 118; and Opportunity School, 137; financial security of, 140; popularity of, 141-42; has broadened curriculum, 234; and advanced degrees, 236

Cleveland, President Grover, Tillman opposed to, 39, 43

Cleveland, John B., 84

Coastal Nursery, 226

Coker, David R., experimental work of as aid to farming, 118-19; head of State Council of Defense, 58

Coker Pedigreed Seed Company, 118

College of Charleston, 148; and junior branch of at Conway, 233

Colleges, degree-conferring, 146; extracurricular activities of, 147 ff.; Negro, 154-55, 234-35; women's, student life in, 149-50

Colored Alliance, 114

Committee of Industrial Organization (CIO), 199

Conservatives, return of, 1877-1890, 24-35; class alignment of in 1880's, 30; lost 1892 election, 36-37; won control of legislature in 1902, 47

Constitution, of 1868, 11-12; of 1895, 41-42

Constitutional Convention, of 1865, 7; of 1868, 11-12; of 1895, 40-41

Converse, Dexter, 84

Cooper, Gov. Robert A., 66, 67, 69

Cotton, in 1920's, 67; decline of today, 225. See also Cotton mills.

"Cotton Ed," popular name of Smith, Ellison D., which see.

Cotton mills, rise of, 82 ff.; expansion of, 83 ff.; location of, 84; advantages of S. C. for, 84-85; wages in, 90. See also Mill villages.

Crawford, Leon P., 196

Courts of South Carolina: Supreme Court, 191; Circuit Courts, 191-92; Magistrates' Courts, 192; Probate Courts, 192-93

Cuba, revolt of against Spain, 44. See also Spanish-American War.

Currell, President William, Univ. of S.C., 151

Curriculum, as problem today, 232

Dabbs, James, quoted, 24

Daily Register (Columbia), supported Constitutional Convention of 1895, 40

D. A. R. school, Opportunity School at, 137

"Darlington War," 38, 39, 47

Dawson, Francis, of *News and Courier,* 139

Deering-Milliken's three textile mills, 213

De Laine, Joseph, 203

Delany, Martin, 16

Democratic party, in 1876 campaign, 17; splits into two factions, 17-18; in power, 1877-1917, 24 ff.; and white supremacy, 169-173; in S. C. controls state, county, and city government, 195

Democratic primary of 1954, 181 ff.

Democrats (Conservatives), opposed Tillman, 32

Democrats, Southern, opposed Truman in 1948, 176-77

"Democrats-for-Eisenhower," in 1952 election, 181

Dennis, Sen. Rembert, 194, 195

Depression of 1930's, effect of, 72 ff.

Desegregation, 201 ff. See also Segregation.

Dial, Nat B., defeated Blease for Senate, 57, 76

Dispensary Act, background of, 37; described, 38; Tillman attempts to enforce, 38-39; end of, 47-49.

Disputed election of 1876, 20 ff.

Divorce, legalized in 1868, 200; legalized on four grounds in 1948, 200

Dixiecrat movement, 175-78; aftermath of, 178 ff.

Dominick, Fred H., 56

Donaldson, Brig. Gen. T. O., 66

Dorn, Bryan, 178

Dows, David S., 196

Dozier, Lt. James C., 64

Dueling, outlawed in 1868, 12; law passed against in 1881, 29

Duke Power Company, 218, 219

Duncan, D. P., 113

DuPont's orlon establishment, 213

Earle, Joseph H., 33, 43

Edisto State Park, 202

Education, free for all children, advocated by Manning, 54; agricultural, 115-16; from 1865 to 1941, 122-168; growth of in recent years, 228-29. *See also* Schools; Higher education, etc.

"Eight Box" election law, 28, 40

Eisenhower, President Dwight D., 181, 184

Electric power, 218-20. *See also* Hydroelectric power; names of power companies and plants.

"Eleventh hour stab," 52, 53, 76

Ellerbe, Robert, 29

Ellerbe, Gov. William H., and Spanish-American War, 44

Elliott, Robert B., 11, 13

Episcopalians, 160

Epps, Dr. Carl, 198

Erskine College, 138, 147

Evans, Gov. John Gary, 48

Fair Employment Practices Act, 176

Farm children, 109-10;

Farm conditions, attempts to improve, 110-15

Farm demonstration work, 115 ff.

Farm life, described, 108-10

Farmers, rise against Conservative rule, 30-35

Farmers' Alliance, supported Tillman in 1890, 33; program endorsed by Tillman, 36, mentioned 112-14 *passim*

Farmers' Asociation, 32, 112

Farm life, described, 108-10

Farm tenancy, increase in, 1873-1900, 107; in 1920's and 30's, 119

Faubus, Gov. Orval, 204

Featherstone, Judge C. C., 49

Fencing law, 29

Fertilizer, commercial, manufacture of, 95-96

Fifteenth Amendment, 40, 45

Floyd, Mayor John, 63

Football, interest in, 133-34, 147 ff.

Fort Jackson, 209

Foster, Sgt. Gary Evans, 64, 65

Fourteenth Amendment, 9, 10, 22, 45, 201

Freedmen's Bureau, work and character of, 5-6; established schools, 122-23

Free silver, 39, 43, 114-15

Fundamentalists, 159-60

Furman University, 147, 148; moved to Greenville, 234

Fusionists, faction of Democrats in 1876, 17-18

"Gallon-a-Month" law, 49

Gary, Eugene B., 33

Gary, Gen. Martin W., 19, 25, 26, 27-29 *passim*

Geers, the, 84

General Education Board, aided farm demonstration work, 116; and Negro schools, 128

Gerald, J. Bates, in 1953 election, 181

Getzen, Henry, 18

Gonzales, N. G., 44, 86

Gossett, B. B., and coal shortage, 58

Gossett, James P., 84

Grace, John P., 56

Grange, the (Patrons of Husbandry), expansion and work of in S. C., 110-12

Graniteville cotton mill, 83

Grant, President Ulysses S., 16

Grant, Wilbur, 195
Gray, Miss Will Lou, Supervisor of Adult Schools, 136-37
Green, Judge John T., 16
Greenville News, 202
Gregg, William, 82
Grovey v. Townsend, and white primary, 169

Hagood, Brig. Gen. Johnson, backed Hampton for governor, 26; reopened Citadel, 138; mentioned, 28, 29, 30
Hall, Sgt. Thomas Lee, 64
Hamburg Riot, 18-19
Hammetts, the, 84
Hampton, Gen. Wade, defeated for governor in 1865, 8; elected governor in 1876, 19; as governor, 24-39; racial policy of, 25-28; as U. S. Senator, 28
Hand, Prof. William H., 130, 132, 141
Handicapped, in 1954 special program for, 229
Hare, Butler, 186
Hare, James, 186
Hartwell Dam, 218
Harvey, Gov. Wilson G., 66
Haskell, Alexander C., 19, 34
Haskellites ("Straightout" Democrats), 34
Hayes, President Rutherford B., 20, 22
Herbert, R. Beverly, 173
Heriot, Corp. James D., 64
Herty, Dr. Charles, and making newsprint from pine saplings, 226
Heyward, Gov. Duncan Clinch, elected governor in 1902, 47; as governor, 47-49; mentioned, 86
Higher education, at close of Civil War, 138; during Reconstruction, 138; development of in 1920's, 144-45; effect of W. W. II on, 233; still inadequate, 235-36; restriction of academic freedom in institutions of, 237
High schools, 130-35

Highway Act of 1924, and State Highway Department, 104
Highway system today, 220-21
Highways, in 1920's, 67; fight over highway system, 69 ff.; bond issue for, 69-70; early roads described, 102-3; Commission established in 1917, 103; building roads and bridges, 103-4; county roads, 104; improved conditions by 1941, 105
Hilton, Sgt. Richmond H., 64, 65
Hollings, Gov. Ernest F. ("Fritz"), 185, 201, 218
"Holy Rollers," 159
Home front in W. W. II, 209 ff.
Hookworm, 109
Hoover, President Herbert, 73
Horse racing in Charleston, 50
Hydroelectric power, 96; and coming of cotton mills, 84

Independents, in presidential campaign of 1956, 184
Industrial development and growth, 1939-1960, 211-222; new factories in 1955, 214; in fields other than textiles, 213-14; special reasons for, 214-22; encouragement of, 214 ff.
Industrial revolution in S.C., 42 ff.
Insane asylum, reorganized under Tillman, 35
Integration, General Assembly passes legislation to avoid, 201 ff. *See also* Segregation.
Interest rates, reduced during the 1880's, 29
Irby, J. L. M., 33, 35, 41

Jacques, Dr. Daniel Harrison, 111
Jefferies, Sen. Richard M., 171
Jenkins, Maj. Micah, 44
Jillson, Justus K., 11, 122, 123
"Jim Crow," 42, 68
Johnson, President Andrew, program of for Reconstruction, 6-10; supported by Moderate Republicans, 10; issues proclama-

tion of pardons, 6-7; declares rebellion officially ended, 9
Johnson, David Bancroft, 140, 141
Johnson, Sen. Lyndon, quoted on Little Rock incident, 204
Johnston, Alan, 173, 174
Johnston, Gov. Olin D., and State Highway Commission, 71; in senatorial campaign of 1950, 179; loyal to Truman, 180; backed for U. S. Senate by F.D.R., 79; and white primary, 170-71; mentioned, 179 ff. *passim*
Johnston, Mayor William C., 185
Jones, Judge Ira B., 52
Joynes, Prof. Edwin S., 143

Kearse, Sen. J. C., 194
Kelley, Oliver H., 110-11
Kennedy, Col. J. M., 66
Klein, Arthur J., 152
Ku Klux Klan, in campaign of 1870, 15-16; in 1920's, 68-69; acts of violence against suspected integrationists, 203
Knapp, Seaman, and demonstration farms, 116

Labor, favorable legislation for secured in 1916 by Gov. Manning, 54; legislative attitude toward is more favorable to management, 216-18; organized, fight of business against, 199; unions, 199-200
Lander College, 233
Law School at U. of S.C., 144
"Lay by" time, 110
Legge, Associate Justice Lionel K., 191
Lever, A. Frank, and Smith-Lever Act, 116
Liberty Loans, 58
Ligon, Robert E., 84
Limestone College, 150
Little Rock incident, impact of, 204-5
Livestock and poultry, increase in, 228
Long, Sen. John D., 195, 227

Lowcountry-upcountry antagonism, 7, 12; lessening, 200-1
Lutherans, 160

Mabry, George L. Jr., 208-9
McBee, Vardry, 82
McBees, the, 84
McBrayer, D. P., 84
McCully, Col. Peter K., 63
McFall, Dr. T. C., Negro physician, 180
McGowan, Gen. Samuel, 26
Mackay, Dr. Albert G., 11
Mackay, Judge T. J., 18
"Mackay House," in disputed election, 21
McKinley, President William, and Spanish-American War, 44
McLaurin, Sen. John L., fight of with Tillman in Senate, 45-46
McLeod, Dr. James, "businessman's candidate" for governor in 1946, 198-99
McLeod, Gov. Thomas G., 66, 67, 69
McMaster, Capt. G. H., 44
McMillan, Claude R., 221
McMillan, Lewis K., 234
McWhorter, William A., 208
Maine, the battleship, sinking of in Havana Harbor, 44
Malaria, 109
Manning, Gov. Richard I., progressive administration of, 53 ff.; his program of reform, 53-55; war service of, 57 ff. and child labor, 87, 88
Maybank, Gov. Burnet R., 79, 81, 200-1; as senator, 170, 174; death of, 182; mentioned, 200
Medical College of Charleston, 51
Melton, President William D., of University of S.C., 144
Methodists, 156 ff.
Miller, Thomas E., president of State A&M, 154
Mill villages, life in, 88 ff.; schools in, 91, 134-35; compared with farm life, 91-92; recreation in, 92; effect of depression of

1930's upon, 93; passing of factory-owned, 221

Mill workers, during W. W. I, 59; during depression of 1930's, 72

Mitchell, Samuel C., 141

Montgomery, John S., 84

Montgomery, Victor, 84

Montgomery, Walter, 84

Moore, Jerry, 115

Morris College, 167

Moses, Gov. Franklin J., Jr., 15, 17

Moss, Associate Justice Joseph R., 191

Mozingo, Sen. J. P., 194, 195

National Association for the Advancement of Colored People, and white primary, 171, 182

Negroes, in Constitutional Convention of 1868, 11; voting rights of assured by Radical Republicans in 1868, 10-11; effects of Reconstruction on, 22-23; segregated by Constitution of 1895, 42; and labor problem after the Civil War, 106-7; and adult education projects, 137-38; of Clarendon County, applied for admission to white schools, 205; migration of to South and West, 243. *See also* Negro suffrage; Schools, Colleges, Churches, etc.

Negro suffrage, and the Fourteenth Amendment, 9-10; and Wade Hampton, 25 ff.; Tillman hoped to eliminate in 1895, 40, 41; and Constitution of 1895, 41; Clarendon County Negroes sued for right to vote, 172; some have voted in every primary since 1948, 174; and Republican party, 196

Negro troops, in W. W. II, 206

Newberry College, 142-43

New Deal, 73-75, 78, 118

News and Courier, Charleston, quoted on corruption of Radical government, 17; backed Hampton for governor, 26-27; Tillman writes to, 32; mentioned, 202 and *passim*

O'Dowd, Jack, threatened by Ku Klux Klan, 203

Old Hickory Division, 60-64

O'Neal, Del, 197

One-teacher schools, described, 125-26

"Operation Dixie," of CIO, 217-18

Opportunity School, 137

O'Byan, Maj. Gen. John F., at Camp Wadsworth, 61

Orr, Gov. James L., 8, 9

Orr, James L., II, 36, 84

Owens, Robert A., 208

Oxner, Assoc. Justice George D., 191

Paper manufacturing, 95, 226 ff.

Pardoning power, and Blease, 51-52

"Pardon racket," 200

Parker, Brig. Gen. Frank, 66

Parker, Lewis W., 84

Parler, Sen. J. D., 194, 195

Parris Island, Marine Corps base, 210

Patrons of Husbandry, 110, 111. *See also* Grange.

Patterson, "Honest John," 13, 27

Payne, Bishop Daniel A., and AMEC, 164

Peabody Fund, and Negro Schools, 128

Pearl Harbor, 81

Pentecostal Holiness Church, 159-60

Perry, Benjamin F., 7

Piedmont Nursery, 226

Pike, James S., quoted on S. C. House of Representatives in 1873, 13

Plantation system, effect of, 240

Planters, life of, 119

Plant Hagood, 219

Plant Urquhart, 219

Polk, Col. L. L., and Farmers' Alliance, 113

Populist party, 114
Presbyterians, 158, 160, 161
Press and Banner (Abbeville), and taxes for schools, 124
Primary system introduced, 37
Private schools and academies, established during Reconstruction, 122-23
Prohibition, problem of 20's, 67-68; state-wide referendum on, 197. *See also* Alcohol, control of.
Public schools, "6-0-1" school law, 92, 129; beginning of, 122; financing of, 122-24; Radical program for, 122-23; reorganized by Constitution of 1895, 126; white, improved by 1923; black, inferior, 126-27; revolution in, 1940-1958, 228 ff.; problems of today, 230-33. *See also* Schools.

Radical Reconstruction, and the Hamburg Riot, 18-19
Radical Republican government, under Scott and Moses, 12 ff.; nature of, 10, 13, 14; early opposition to, 13, 15 ff.; party split in, 16
Railroads, under Radical government, 14, 25; regulation of under Tillman, 37
Railway system, 99, 101; effect of competition on, 101; today, 220. *See also* names of railroads.
Rainbow Division, 63
Randolph, President Harrison, College of Charleston, 143
Reconstruction, presidential, 6-10; Radical, 10-15; end of, 22; results of, 22-23
Red Cross, 58, 61
Red Shirt campaign, 1876, 19-20
Reformers (Tillman Democrats), 33; reform victory, 34; end of, 44
Religion, recent trends in, 238-39
Religious denominations, as founders of schools and colleges, 155 ff. *See also* names of denominations.

Republican party, divided into Radicals and Moderates in 1865, 10 ff.; in S. C., too weak locally to oppose Democrats successfully, 195; state convention of 1958, 196; damaged by Little Rock crisis, 186, 196
Revivals, 157-58
Rice industry, ruined, 120-21
Richards, Gov. John G., 53, 66, 69
Richards, James P., on Little Rock incident, 204
Richardson, Gov. John P., 29, 30
Richardson, Col. R. C., 66
Riley, John, 186
"Ringism," 197-98
Rivers, Prince, Negro Justice, 18
Robertson, Thomas J., 11
Rogers, F. M., introduced bright-leaf tobacco, 118
Roosevelt, President Franklin D., election of, 72, 73; and U. S. Supreme Court, 74-75; and Conservative Democrats, 75; and "Cotton Ed" Smith, 79; and civil rights, 175
Roosevelt, Mrs. Franklin D., 75
Roosevelt, President Theodore, 46
Roper, Sec. Daniel A., in Roosevelt's cabinet, 73
Rosenwald Fund, and Negro schools, 128
"Rough Riders," 44
Rural Electric Cooperative Act, 220
Rural electrification, aid to farming, 119
Rural South Carolinian, The, 111, 112
Russell, Donald, 185, 198
Russell, Sen. Richard, 176

Saluda Dam, 219
Santee-Cooper project, 218
Sawmilling, 94-95
Sawyer, Ben, and Highway Commission, 71-72
Saxon mill village, in 1926, 92
Scalawags, in Constitutional Convention, 1868, 11

School bus, operations expanded for Negro children, 229

Schools, compulsory attendance law, 1917, 86-87; in mill villages, 91; curriculum broadened, 229; administration streamlined, 230; problems facing in 1960, 230-33. *See also* Education; Public schools.

Scott, Gov. Robert K., 15

Seaboard Air Line, 100-1

Sea Islanders, and the "shout," 166

Sea Islands, "two day" labor system, 108

Segregation, as political issue, 185; problem of tackled by legislature in 1956, acts passed to abolish public schools if necessary, 202-3; and possible closing of schools, 230-31; in 1960 a matter of speculation, 245

Selective Service Act, denounced by Blease, 57

Self, James C., 93

Senate, alignment of power in (1958), 195

Senators, key men in state legislature, 194-95

Seneca Junior College, and Opportunity School, 137-38

Shannon, W. M., killed in duel, 29-30

"Shell Manifesto," 32

Sheppard, John C., 36

Sherrill, Prof. George R., quoted on power of legislature, 194

Shorey, Gregory D., Jr., 196

Sickles, Gen. Dan, Union commander in S. C., and the Black Code, 8-9; and the "stay law," 8-9

Simkins, Prof. Francis B., on Blease, 50

Sims, Hugo, 186

Slater Fund, and Negro schools, 128

Smith, Alfred E., 72

Smith, Augustus W., 84

Smith, Sen. Ellison D. ("Cotton Ed"), senatorial career of, 52, 77-80, 193; and race issue, 171-72

Smith, Furman L., 208, 209

Smith, Sen. Hoke, of Ga., 116

Smith-Lever Act, 116

Smith v. Allwright, and white primary, 169-70

Smyth, Capt. Ellison, 84

Social Security System, 229

Soil Bank program, 226

South Carolina, at end of Civil War, 3-6; social and economic upheaval in, 5; Presidential Reconstruction in, 6-9; Radical Reconstruction in, 10-15; in W. W. I, 56 ff., 60 ff.; in W. W. II, 207-11; problems of 1920's and depression, 66 ff.; in national affairs, 72 ff.; location of political power in, 193 ff.; recent political problems in, 196-206; interpretive summary of, 249-45

South Carolina College, 142. *See also* University of South Carolina.

South Carolina Electric and Gas Co., 213

South Carolina government, organization and operation of, 186-93; constitutional framework of, 186 ff.; legislative, 187-89; executive, 189-91; judicial, 191-93; in battle action W. W. I, 63-66; battle honors received in both wars, 64-65, 208-9

South Carolina High School League, 132, 133

Southern Association of Colleges and Secondary Schools, 142-44

Southern Democrats, opposed civil rights program, 176

Southern Railway System, 99

Spanish-American War, South Carolina in, 44 ff.

Springs, Col. Leroy, 84

Sputnik, and present curriculum content, 232

Stackhouse, Eli T., 113

Starks, Dr. J. J., 167-68

State, The, opposed child labor, 86; cited, 171-72

State A&M, 154, 239
State Board of Education, 121
State Commission of Forestry, 226
State debt, during Reconstruction, 25 ff., 29; refundment of, 37. *See also* Highways.
State exchange, 113-14
State Hospital, pathetic conditions in, 54
"Statehouse Ring," 28
State Ports Authority, work of, 221-22
State Tree Farm Committee, 226-27
"Stay law," passed in 1865, 9
Steam plants: Plant Hagood, 219; Plant Urquhart, 219; Duke steam plant near Williamston, 219; steam plant for Charlotte area, 219
Stevenson, Adlai, in 1952 election, 181; carried state in 1956, 184
Straightouts, defeated Fusionists because of Hamburg Riot, 18-19, 34
Stukes, Chief Justice Taylor H., 101
Sullivan, Ens. Daniel, 64

Talbert, W. J., 33
Tax Commission, established by Manning, 54
Taxes, reduced, under Tillman, 35, 37; for education, 124-25; made attractive to new industries, 215
Taylor, Assoc. Justice Claude A., 101
Teachers, certification provided for in Constitution of 1895, 126; new certification program for, 1945, 229; shortage of today, 231-32
Terrell, Ben, 114
Textile industry, working hours limited, 37; growth of, 1860-1880, 83 ff.; growth of, 1880-1920, 83-84; importance of to nation, 83; raising the capital for, 87-88; growth of, 1939-1960, 212 ff.; slump and recovery of in 1950's, 213
Textile mills, in W. W. II, 209. *See also* Cotton mills.
Textile workers, UTW strike, 93-94
Thirteenth Amendment, 7, 201
Thompson, Gov. Hugh S., 29, 30, 124
Thornwell Orphanage, 161
Thurmond, Gov. J. Strom, 172; as leader of Dixiecrats, 177-78; wins U. S. senatorship, 183-84; and the Barnwell Ring, 197-98; opposed to federal power projects, 218
Tilghman Nursery, 226
Tillman, Gov. Benjamin Ryan ("Pitchfork Ben"), and the Hamburg Riot, 19; in Red Shirt campaign of 1876, 31; sketch of as agrarian leader, 31-32; wins governorship 1890, 32-34; leader of Reformers, 33-34; Tillman in control of State Democratic Convention, 1890, 34; reasons for victory of, 34; as governor, 35 ff.; earned sobriquet, "Pitchfork Ben," 39; quoted in 1892 campaign, 36-37; in senatorial campaign of 1894, 39-40; as senator, 40 ff. *passim;* popularity of, 43; program of reform deteriorates, 44-45; and the Negro, 45; fight of in Senate with Sen. Mc-Laurin, 45-46; and the Farmers' Alliance, 112 ff. *passim;* and the Citadel, 139; and Clemson College, 139-40; and the University, 140-41
Tillman, George, brother of Ben, 31; Tillman's feud with, 36
Tillman, James H. (nephew of Ben), on trial for murder, Tillman defends, 46
Timber resources, 226-28
Timmerman, Gov. George Bell, Jr., in Democratic primary, 1954, 179, 181-82 *passim;*

quoted on President Eisenhower and Little Rock, 204-5

Tindal, A. J., 115

Tobacco crop, increasing, 225

Tomkins, Daniel A., of Charlotte, N. C., 84

Tournament, in Pendleton in 1865, described, 241, n. 3

Transportation, S. C.'s, good system of attracts new industries, 220. *See also* Railroads; Highways, etc.

Trowbridge, John T., quoted, 4

Turner, President B. C., State A&M, 235

Turpentine and rosin industry, 95

"Two day" labor system, 108

Union Reform party, organized by former Democrats, 15-16

U. S. courts, and white primary, 169-70

U. S. Department of Agriculture, 116, 120

U. S. Study Commission on Southeast River Basins, 218

U. S. Navy Yard, Charleston, 209

U. S. Supreme Court, and civil rights decision, 245

United Textile Workers in S. C., 74; organized in 1930's, 93; strike, 93-94

University of North Carolina, state's support of compared with that of S. C., 144

University of South Carolina, during Reconstruction, 138; closed, 138; reopened with inadequate funds, 139; antagonism toward, 139-140; reorganized in Tillman's administration, 35; difficulties of under Tillman and Blease, 140 ff.; development of in 1920's, 144; early football contests of, 147-49; rivalry of with Clemson, 148; women students admitted in 1895, 150; student life in 30's, 150-51; and advanced degrees, 236

University of Virginia, 142

Vanderbilt, Cornelius, at Camp Wadsworth, 61

Veterans' pensions, increased, 37

Villepigue, Corp. John C., 64, 65

Virginia Electric and Power Co., 219-20

Vocational training schools, 136

Wallace, Dr. D. D., quoted on Darlington War, 39; on Constitution of 1895, 42; on Blease, 50; on churches and education, 157

Wallace, Gen. William A., 21

"Wallace House," 21

Waring, Judge J. Waties, and Negro right to vote, 172-74 *passim*

Weinges, Conrad, 29-30

Wesleyan Methodist Church, 239

Whipper, W. J., 17

White primary, and U. S. courts, 169-75; Blease fought for, 50-51; influence of on Democratic party in S. C., 72; threatened by civil rights program, 175; and Negro suffrage, 175-86. *See also* Dixiecrat movement.

Whittemore, B. F., 11

Wildcat (or Stonewall) Division, 63

Willard, Assoc. Justice A. J., 26

Williams, Dr. C. Fred, head of reorganization of State Hospital, 54

Williams, Ransome, and state control of liquor, 107

Williams, W. B., 195

Wilson, President Woodrow, 56

Winthrop College for girls, 35, 140; popularity of, 141-42; mentioned, 234

Wofford College, 71, 147, 148

Woodrow, Prof. James, and evolution, 158

Woodsides, the, 84

Woodward, William E., on life in Citadel, 151

Works Progress Administration, 73, 74

World War I, overshadowed domestic issues, 55. *See also sub*
South Carolina.

World War II, 207-11. *See also
sub* South Carolina.
Wright, Jonathan J., 11